# THE PHENOMENOLOGICAL PROBLEM

# THE
# PHENOMENOLOGICAL
# PROBLEM

### EDITED BY
### ALFRED E. KUENZLI

HARPER & BROTHERS, PUBLISHERS
NEW YORK

Library of Congress catalog card number: 59-9475

# CONTENTS

▪▪▪▪▪▪▪▪▪▪▪▪▪▪▪▪▪▪▪▪▪▪▪▪▪▪▪▪▪▪▪▪▪▪▪▪▪▪▪▪▪▪▪▪▪▪▪▪▪▪▪▪▪▪▪▪▪▪▪▪▪▪▪▪▪▪▪▪▪▪▪

## IV.  Discussion

# PREFACE

Creative work in the sciences, as in the arts, does not, of course, take place *de novo*. Each new generation builds upon the old although its "view from the bridge" can be counted on to be not quite the same.

In psychology, as in other disciplines, development is something other than a simple process of addition or accretion. The history of this field shows that we have arrived at our present point as a result of a series of theses and antitheses, insights and reorganizations. Within our ongoing science and profession, we shall both expect and want to encourage more of this dialectical development in the future. In our present state of emergence, it would be foolish to believe that things could be otherwise in the next years ahead.

Recognizing that new theory and research must have its roots in existing resources and sources of stimulation, my purpose in compiling this volume has been to bring together a set of papers that will be maximally useful and provocative, especially to the younger men in the field, both professionals and students. I have deliberately tried to choose papers that open up new paths to the future rather than papers that make dogmatic pronouncements about the present or the past. While the authors who speak here do, quite clearly, have their convictions, the prevailing spirit is that of active seeking, of vigorous inquiry. It is in this sense that I hope this collection will be regarded as truly a set of "working papers," not just a book of readings.

Recognizing that development in any field is not linear, i.e., that there are theses and antitheses which stimulate progress, I am not apologetic about bringing together a set of papers that converge around a point of view. While this outlook or "frame of reference" may not be completely correct in every respect, and no one here claims that it *is*, it provides, at the least, a *position* from which to view and formulate problems. To be "open-minded" and engaged in vigorous inquiry does not mean that one has to proceed without any postulates.

What these papers have in common, although differing in points of detail, is their acknowledgment that it is necessary to postulate, for the individual, a "phenomenal field," "life space," "reality world," "universe of events," or "behavioral environment." Why this postulate is necessary is abundantly illustrated, I believe, between these covers. Anyone who fails to be convinced herein needs to be reminded of Klüver's classic demonstration (1936).

The phenomenological problem begins then, as I see it, with acceptance of Professor Snygg's postulate (1941) that "behavior is completely determined by and pertinent to the phenomenological field of the behaving organism." This granted, the problem becomes primarily a methodological and investigative one. The primary focus of these papers is, therefore: How can we study the nature of the "personal world" and the influences which shape it? Ultimately the question is: What findings do our studies yield which make it possible to understand and predict more adequately the behavior of the individual?

Probably Gordon Allport (1937) and Kurt Lewin (1935) have been more adamant than anyone in insisting that psychologists should study individuality. While Professor Allport has always been a little too "eclectic" to be labeled a phenomenological psychologist, I believe that his basic insights and emphases have found their greatest fulfillment within the recent phenomenological movement. Certainly Kurt Lewin would have enjoyed these papers.

This volume will, I hope, help to clarify what is meant by a phenomenological emphasis in modern psychology. Rather than going back to Husserl, who does not seem to be especially pertinent to the concerns of contemporary psychologists, perhaps students can come to turn increasingly to the papers presented here, together with the items listed in the bibliography. Certainly phenomenology, as it has been developed within the framework of Gestalt psychology, is not to be equated with "introspection"—a common confusion. Probably Köhler's third chapter (1947) is as devastating a critique of introspection as one finds in the literature!

A modern phenomenological psychologist uses any and all methods—such as clinical interviews, projective techniques, observation of behavior, and laboratory experimentation—that will help him to gain understanding of the individual's view of reality. Thus psychological phenomenology, as MacLeod (1947) defines it, is but one of the methods of phenomenological psychology.

The division of the content into two main sections is, it will be seen, rather arbitrary since there is a considerable amount of "group" psychology in the section on "the self" and since there is no dearth of "personality" psychology in the section on "the self and others." It is mainly a matter of what kinds of problems and methods clinical psychologists have emphasized as compared with the kinds of problems and methods that have interested social psychologists. Clearly the clinical and social areas are drawing ever more closely together today and one of the aims of this volume is, in fact, to achieve a greater degree of integration of our knowledge within these fields. The two papers by Rogers, one in each section, are a testimony to the editor's desire in this respect.

How is this book to be used? Probably it will serve best in an upper-level seminar, particularly for majors in clinical and social psychology, where its very challenging points can be considered in vigorous discussion. The index of subjects at the end of the volume suggests various term-paper and thesis topics which follow out of the articles. The selected bibliography represents, in the editor's view, the most provocative materials, relevant to the phenomenological problem, existing in the English language. Additional references are to be found at the conclusions of the various selections.

These articles have appeared in 10 different journals over the past 20 years. L. K. Frank's classic discussion of projective methods is the earliest (1939). The papers by Jessor (1956), Combs and Soper (1957), Cantril (1957), and Luchins (1957) are the most recent. The editor wishes to express his appreciation to the authors and publishers who granted permission to reprint these articles. The original source is cited at the bottom of the first page of each selection.

I am grateful to the contributors for their many encouraging comments and stimulating suggestions, several of which I was able to follow.

A. E. K.

*Alton, Illinois*
*March, 1959*

# Part I

---

**PERSPECTIVE**

# CHAPTER 1

........................................................................................................

# The Need for a Phenomenological System of Psychology

## BY DONALD SNYGG

No visitor to a meeting of any psychological society in the last few years can fail to be impressed by the wide diversity of opinion there expressed. After fifty years of apparent progress American psychology has reached a point where two psychologists wishing to carry on a professional discussion must spend most of the time defining the terms they are using. As Hull has said, "One of the most striking things about the theory of learning and of psychological theory in general is the wide disagreement among individual psychologists" (8).[1] The confusion is so great that already leading psychologists have predicted the impending dismemberment of psychology.

Controversy over clear-cut and well-defined points of view is a necessary prelude to progress in the development of any

[1] Boldface numbers refer to bibliographical entries at the end of this chapter.

From *Psychological Review,* 1941, **48**, 404–424. Reprinted by permission of the author and the publisher.

science. It does not appear, however, that the "wide disagreement" cited by Hull above holds the promise of an impending step forward in the history of psychology. It is more likely that the confusion is a symptom of defeat and of the present inability of the science to live up to its early promise, a failure that is implicit in Pratt's statement that "For a long time to come psychology should remain in the laboratory and the library" (13).

Some writers have sought to gloss over this chaotic situation by insisting that the disagreements concern theory only and that there is little difference over questions of fact. This evasion can be of little consolation to the vast number of parents, teachers, physicians, and other workers in the applied fields who must depend upon theory for guidance in their attempts to predict and control human behavior.

Prediction of new phenomena is necessarily based upon theory, not directly upon the results of previous observations. Knowledge of the results of a large number of discrete experiments, without theoretical interpretation, offers no way of predicting results when the experimental situation is different in the least degree. It may be anticipated that the differing conditions may lead to different behavior, but the kind and degree of differences are unpredictable without some theory of causation. Such circumstances are universal in any field of applied psychology where the teacher, the clinician, or the psychiatrist is always endeavoring to predict and control behavior in situations which are in some degree new and unique. Applied psychology is in vital need of principles of prediction that are simple, accurate, and unambiguous, that can function as principles for prediction rather than as myths for explanation, and that can be applied with precision in situations never before investigated.

It is precisely at these points that the current body of psychological theory is defective. It is complex, cumbersome and contradictory, and each of the conflicting systems is itself a welter of contradictory principles of causation and description. Catching phenomena coming and going, these systems serve nicely as explanatory concepts after the event but, because of their antagonistic character, are relatively useless for prediction. Ego-id, primacy-recency, similarity-contrast, differentiation-integration, facilitation-inhibition, learning-forgetting, self-preservation–death wish are only a few examples. In the effort to explain all known facts every current system has been forced into the use of conflicting principles such as these. Each system has a large number of principles because it must account for a large number of facts; and in each system some of the principles are conflicting because the facts which they attempt to explain are conflicting. It is the thesis of this paper that this apparent conflict is an artifact. The facts are conflicting because they are derived from two mutually exclusive frames of reference.

## TWO FRAMES OF REFERENCE FOR THE OBSERVATION OF BEHAVIOR

It has become a common-place in physics that the obtained figures for the mass, velocity, and path of any object are dependent upon the point from which they are observed. It is less widely recognized that the same principles apply to the collection of psychological data. For whatever purpose behavior is to be studied it must be observed from one of two distinct points of view. It may be studied objectively, as by an outside observer; or it may be studied phenomenologically, from the point of view of the behaving organism itself (17). The facts derived from these two points of view are non-identical and are often completely contradictory. As seen by an outside observer, for instance, learning is a process of progressive change in the learner's response to a static situation. During this process the situation or task remains unchanged while the behavior becomes more relevant and efficient. Since the situation remains unchanged, improvement is ascribed to hypothetical changes within the learner. Thus the objective approach inevitably includes among its derived facts random molar behavior and improvement with repetition, usually by association or integration. Educational procedures based upon objective facts customarily stress frequency, drill, reward and punishment.

From the phenomenological point of view, that is to say, from the point of view of the learner, the facts are quite different. The learner remains unchanged. It is his experience of the situation or task which changes. From his point of view his behavior is always insightful, that is to say, it is always relevant to the situation as he interprets it at the moment. Improvement is concurrent with changes in the observed nature of the task, usually described as differentiation, individuation, or increase in detail. These data are in direct contradiction to the data derived from the objective approach; the observed facts of one frame of reference completely contradict the observed facts of the other. Educational procedures based upon phenomenological facts also differ from those based upon objective facts since they stress understanding of the individual child, pacing, and clear presentation of material.

Twenty years ago the point of view in American psychology was predominantly objective. An attempt was being made by one school, the behaviorists, to construct a methodologically pure theory of learning from that point of view. Since then, largely due to the influence of the Gestalt movement, the trend has been toward increasing acceptance of facts derived from the phenomenological point of view. Unfortunately the trend has, in most cases, manifested itself in the attempted assimilation of phenomenological facts into a basically objective theory.

An analogous situation might have arisen during the shift of astronomers from the Ptolemaic to the Copernican frame of reference. If we take our place of residence as the fixed unmoving point of observation, it follows as a necessary and undeniable fact that the sun revolves around the earth. It is a fact that can be verified by independent observation on any clear day. On the other hand, if the sun is taken as the fixed point of reference it is an equally observable fact that the earth revolves around the sun. Both facts are not only verifiable by observation but can be used in the prediction of phenomena, for example eclipses. They are not, however, co-existent facts since they are derived from two mutually exclusive points of view. It is not likely that during the long controversy over the "truth" of the two systems any eclectic ever had the hardihood to predict an eclipse from a synthesis of Ptolemaic and Copernican facts, with the earth going around the sun while the sun went around the earth and both stood still.

Precisely such a synthesis, however, is continually attempted in psychological discussions of learning. A glance at any current text will show how *error, reflexes, stimuli, frequency,* and other data derived from the objective point of view are complemented with such phenomenological concepts as *trial, insight,* and *belonging.* The statement found in a widely used outline for students, that we learn usually by trial and error but sometimes by insight, is only an extreme example of this generous and uncritical point of view. Nor should it be supposed that the indiscriminant amalgamation of objective and phenomenological data is confined to the works of avowed eclectics. "Effect" and "consequences" have long done duty in both camps, referring on the same page to changes in the structure of the organism and to changes in the way the learner experiences the task. Even Gestalt psychologists have failed to recognize the non-simultaneity of the derived data. Koffka's invocation of the "geographic" environment (9), necessitated by his desire to assimilate data derived from an objective approach, is a case in point. By its introduction into an essentially phenomenological system it is possible for him to take cognizance of items which exist in the phenomenal field of the experimenter but not in that of the behaving organism.

Given a theory of learning based upon one of the two points of view, an assimilation of facts derived from the other can be achieved only by introducing additional and necessarily conflicting laws and principles. This was done by Thorndike (effect-belonging, 21) and, more recently, by Maier (learning-reasoning, 11) in adding phenomenological data to objective systems. Koffka and Freud, in adding objective data to phenomenological systems, attempted to avoid the uncertainty involved in a multiplicity of independent processes but found it necessary to postulate new loci of action (geographic environment, unconscious) not open to direct observation by either the observer or the participant. Uncertainty in prediction arises, on the one hand, from the multiplicity of independent laws and, on the other, from the circumstance that the postulated law is held to be operating in a field inaccessible to observation. In either case the increased possibility of a plausible explanation for any specific act is more than counter-balanced by the decrease of certainty in prediction. Mixed systems are therefore better suited for explanation in retrospect than as principles for prediction in advance. Data derived from the two frames of reference are not co-existent and a genuinely predictive psychology will be impossible of attainment until we stop treating them as if they were. Such a psychology must be either completely objective or completely phenomenological. It is the purpose of this paper to examine the value of data derived from each type of approach for their comparative value in prediction.

## INADEQUACY OF THE OBJECTIVE APPROACH FOR PREDICTION OF HUMAN BEHAVIOR

Of the two possible points of view it is probable that most psychologists would prefer to use the objective approach because of its record of success in the physical sciences. It does not appear, however, that any observational approach is adequate at the present time to furnish the required principles for prediction. Whatever their possibilities for the future, attempted objective systems have up to now shared the defects of mixed systems by leaning heavily upon hypothetical loci of action or by requiring an unwieldy number of independent causal principles.

As viewed by outside observers, the behavior of living organisms varies even when the environment remains unchanged. This variability has been explained in the past by postulating mind as an unseen determiner of behavior. It is more frequently explained at present by assigning the same determining function to hypothetical changes in the organism, usually in the nervous system. If instruments can be invented which will make organic states more accessible to observation, the latter concept may prove to be a very fruitful one; but up to the present time both concepts have functioned almost exclusively as explanatory concepts, being relatively useless for prediction. Accurate prediction is possible only when the causal entities are open to inspection.

A tempting alternative to the use of unexplored causal fields is that adopted by the early behaviorists who attempted to refrain completely from causal inferences and to restrict themselves to data which could be objectively observed. Because of the notorious variability of animal behavior under objectively identical conditions such attempts to discover purely descriptive laws have not, however, been very successful. A common and necessary assumption of the objective way of search has been that the apparent irresponsibility of living organisms to physical causation is due to the gross character of the units studied. Further analysis, it is hoped, will show the parts of the organism functioning in ways predictable by an adequate physics. By withdrawing from the study of organismic behavior into the study of part behavior, of reflexes, or of S-R bonds, it is possible to maintain the concept of lawful causation of events and at the same time maintain the objective approach. This procedure, however, involves an indefinite multiplication of causal processes, with attendant confusion in prediction. Since it is possible to investigate the relation between an animal's behavior and any feature of a situation which can be experienced by the experimenter, present-day objectivists are embarrassed by a plethora of causal factors. Buel (4) has reviewed eighty-three factors which have been found to affect the pathway chosen by a white rat approaching a point of bifurcation in a maze. He points out that the list is not exhaustive and the eighty-third factor is "chance." The hopelessness of using such a large number of independent principles as bases for accurate prediction is obvious.

The situation, then, is this: From the objective point of view, behavior which is not pertinent to the situation as viewed by the experimenter is random, indeterminate, fortuitous. To accept this indeterminism, however, as final would involve the abandonment of all hope for accurate prediction. Any science which hopes to predict must postulate lawfulness. Lawfulness in an objective system, however, can be maintained only by postulating additional causal agents unseen by the experimenter, as mind, past experience, instincts, or organic change. As long as these entities remain inaccessible to the experimenter they can be endowed with any necessary characteristics and are ideally suited to function as explanatory concepts. But, conversely, as long as these agents remain inaccessible the systems of which they are parts will have vital gaps in their causal fields with consequent inaccuracy in prediction. Since the unseen agents are usually invoked to explain individual variations in behavior, objective systems are apt to restrict themselves in practice to the prediction of normative behavior, concerning themselves chiefly with the establishment of norms and coefficients of correlation. This knowledge of what "most people," "the average individual," or "the typical three-year-old" is most likely to do in a given situation "other things being equal" is of little value, however, to the applied worker, the clinical psychologist, or the classroom teacher who must predict and control the specific behavior of particular individuals. If the analysis of this paper is correct, the accurate prediction of such specific individual behavior, from an objective point of view, will have to wait until one of the explanatory agents, most probably the physical organism, is laid open to observation by methods and instruments not yet devised.

Pending the perfection of these devices, it appears desirable that an attempt be made to explore the possibilities of the alternative point of view, that of the behaving organism. The remainder of this paper is devoted to a discussion of a phenomenological system that has been used with some success in predicting previously unobserved behavior (18, 19, 20). The discussion is restricted roughly to the field of learning, which is the most crucial to the problem of prediction.

The reader will bear in mind that the "facts" of such a system will necessarily conflict with those derived from the objective point of view and that the validity of any frame of reference must be judged, not by the degree to which its facts correspond to the facts derived from other approaches, but by its usefulness in prediction.

## THE CHARACTERISTICS OF A PHENOMENOLOGICAL SYSTEM

### I. The basic postulates

Assuming that the task of psychology is the prediction and control of behavior, a phenomenological system must rest upon three basic assumptions[2] and three principles.

[2] The first assumption is common to all scientific systems, the second and third are matters of direct observation but impossible of proof.

*A.* All behavior is lawful. This is a necessary assumption of any system, since chance behavior would be unpredictable.

*B.* Behavior is completely determined by and pertinent to the phenomenological field of the behaving organism. By phenomenological field, hereafter abbreviated to p.f., is meant the universe, including himself, as experienced by the behaver at the moment.

*C.* There is some relationship between the phenomenological fields of different individuals. This is a necessary assumption, since control is impossible if one individual is unable to affect another's field. The locus of the relationship, usually presumed to be an underlying reality, is not open to observation.

*D.* Greater precision of behavior (learning) is concomitant with greater differentiation of the phenomenological field. Another characteristic of p.fs. is that they are fluid and shifting; their phenomena are continually reshaped and given new meanings by the character of the total configuration. Memories, for example, are strongly affected in this way (1). Maier (11) found that the crucial act of solutions was forgotten as soon as the solution was made; and Wees and Line (23) found that school children, in the act of reading a story, distorted its details in ways that made it more meaningful and pertinent to their own experiences. Since behavior is part of the field, taking part in the field's interaction, principle *E* is in some ways a restatement of the second postulate *B*.

*E.* The characteristics of the parts of the phenomenological field are determined by the character of the field itself. More specifically, the direction and degree of differentiation are determined by the phenomenological needs of the behaver.[3] The reader may find, for example, that in reading this paper he has

---

[3] Both *D* and *E* invalidate introspection by the learner as a means of reconstructing his own field. Much of the field is too vague and undifferentiated (*D*) to be verbalized; and the need to observe and report may considerably alter the character of the field (*E*) and the nature of the problem.

been particularly aware of the points which substantiate his own views. The fundamental need in a phenomenological system appears to be the preservation of the organization and integrity of the p.f. and especially of that part of the field which is the phenomenal self, whence our tendency to remain unaware of, or to reject with emotion, data inconsistent with our own beliefs.[4]

F. Differentiation takes time. It follows from this principle that the way to accelerate learning is to arrange the situation so that the required differentiations are either more obvious or are unnecessary. For instance, in a black Warden multiple-U maze of the LRRRLLRLLR pattern which had been learned by a group of white rats in a median of 29 trials, the application of white paint to the critical 2, 5, 7, 8, and 10 sections, where changes in procedure were necessary, enabled an experimental group to learn the maze in a median of 12 trials (19).When the differentiation of individual sections from one another was made completely unnecessary by painting the blind alleys white and the correct pathway black, or vice-versa, the median number of trials required for learning was lowered to 7 (18).

## 2. The problem of prediction

By postulate B the determining locus of action is the be-haver's p.f. This is not open to direct observation by any outside observer. The process of prediction therefore involves two steps: (1) the securing of an understanding of the subject's

----

[4] This recognition that the self we are trying to preserve is the phenomenal self, that is to say, is our own picture of ourselves, explains the need which various schools have described as drives for self-esteem, self-respect, security, status, superiority, power, or complacency. When self-preservation is thus referred to the phenomenal self, it is adequate for the explanation of suicide and martyrdom. These two forms of behavior have always been a source of difficulty from a systematic point of view. Objective systems have been forced to ignore them, along with other un-normal behavior, and mixed systems can include them only by postulation of independent motives conflicting with self-preservation, such as Menninger's death wish (12).

field by inference or reconstruction, (2) the projection of the future field.

The first operation is of the common "Now why did he do that?" or "Under what circumstances would I have done that?" character. Much of the topological work of Lewin is of this type and essentially the same procedure was used by Shepard (15) when from the behavior of his rats he inferred the existence of floor cues which he himself was unable to experience. The teacher who hears his pupil report that 3 x 0 is 3 and infers that his reasoning is "Zero is nothing so it does nothing to the three" has taken this step. The operation acquires its validity in this system by the postulate (B) that behavior is completely determined by the p.f., whence it follows that variations in behavior are always indicative of concurrent variations in the field. The complete operation of prediction imposes two important conditions. To reconstruct an individual's field from his behavior it is necessary to have some idea what fields are like, and to project the future field it is necessary to understand how fields change.

### 3. The nature of the field

The p.f. is simply the world of naive, immediate experience in which each individual lives, the everyday situation of self and surroundings which the unsophisticated person takes to be real. Studies on the nature of this field indicate that all parts of the field are not equally distinct. The field consists of figure and ground, or focus and margin; there are not two definite, static levels, but one level may shade the other so that the figure may be large and relatively indistinct or small and highly differentiated. Experience in any sense field can be figure. Pain, fatigue, or the disturbed organic states involved in emotion may emerge so sharply as the focus of the field, with all the rest of the field fading into the homogeneity of ground, that the individual will lose touch with his surroundings and become unconscious. Since by postulate $B$ behavior is completely determined by the p.f., a highly detailed and differentiated field will include definite and precise behavior, while, as anyone who has tried to find a snap switch in a strange room in the dark will agree, behavior in a vague and undifferentiated field is vague and confused. This leads to principle $D$.

## 4. How fields change

Principle $D$ of our system identified differentiation with learning; principle $E$ made the determinants of differentiation somewhat explicit. Differentiation may be defined as knowing a difference, the basic act of knowledge. It is the manifestation of the continuous process by which the integrity and organization of the field are maintained. "When an individual, rat or human, is confronted with a task . . . the general procedure is determined by his initial perception of the nature of the problem; it is a gross response to a relatively undifferentiated situation. Should the first procedure, the response to the gross situation, prove inadequate the task is differentiated perceptually into segments each of which is solved by simple procedures" (19).

Although he is aware that his own field may be affected ($E$) by his desire to maintain the predictive advantages of having only one process in the system, the writer feels that differentiation may be safely assumed to be the only process of change in the p.f. The emergence of a new entity or character into figure implies the lapse of other characters into ground. Both are necessary for the existence of a difference and are not two independent processes, but complementary aspects of the same process, which might be called "change." Since, however, it is the newly emerged figure, the focus of the behaver's field, which is the most directly potent in determining behavior, it seems more practical to emphasize the more effective aspect of the process and call it "differentiation" or "individuation" rather than the non-valuative "change."

The basic assumptions and principles are now complete. There remains to be discussed principle $F$, which is subsidiary and based on experimental evidence (3, 16).

### 5. Use of the system in prediction

Several examples of the use of this system for the prediction of previously unreported animal behavior have been published (2, 18, 19, 20), the last of which may serve as an example. The purpose of the study was to test the comparative usefulness of phenomenological and objective principles in the prediction of maze behavior. Since DeCamp's experiment (5), reported in 1920, it had been almost axiomatic that rats tend to adopt the shorter of two alternative paths to food. Now suppose that the structure of a rat's field is such that a path which is objectively the longer of two alternative paths to food appears to the rat to be the shorter. If, as we have postulated $(B)$, the animal's behavior is completely determined by his p.f. he will choose this phenomenologically shorter path in spite of the fact that it appears to the experimenter to be the longer. According to objective principles, on the other hand, the effective determinant would be the physical lengths of the two paths "other things being equal," irrespective of how the situation was experienced by the rat.

Such a situation was arranged in a ten section Warden U LLLLLLLLL maze, in which an alternative food-box was attached to the right hand alley of the third section. Thus it was possible for the rats to take either a short three section LLR path or a long ten section LLLLLLLLLL path to the food. If the behavior were governed by the objective situation it would be predicted that they would choose the shorter LLR path. However, previous experiments from a phenomenological point of view had led to the inference that "maze learning is a process of increasing differentiation in the total situation, during which the maze is first perceived as a general path to the food-box and is then differentiated into sub-mazes. . . ." (19). It was therefore predicted that in this maze the animals would at the end of the first trial experience the path to either food-box as a general leftward path. As a consequence they would take the longer LLLLLLLLLL path on later trials. The experiment was made by running a group of rats in this maze once a day for 100 days. During the first 75 days the animals verified the prediction by taking the longer path on 74 per cent of the runs. During the last 10 days the longer path was taken on 89 per cent of the runs. This behavior conformed to the inferred p.fs. of the rats, thus demonstrating the usefulness of the postulates used in prediction.

In the same way, it was predicted that animals in a similar maze where the alternative food-box was on the right hand alley of the second section, which is directly in front of the maze entrance, would experience this LR path as something like "ahead" or "around the corner." This would not lead them to take the long leftward path. This prediction, also, was verified. The rats in this maze took the shorter path on 64 per cent of the runs during the first 75 days, and on 66 per cent of the runs during the last ten days.

## 6. The conditioned response

The only real and valid test of any system in science is its effectiveness in predicting previously undiscovered phenomena, as in the case just cited. Ability to explain phenomena already known is, of course, no criterion of usefulness in prediction. It is true, nevertheless, that inability to explain known phenomena is presumptive evidence of inadequacy in prediction as well.

For this reason it is interesting to test the adequacy of the proposed system to explain some of the phenomena of the conditioned response, upon which objective systems commonly base their description of learning. A phenomenological explanation would be something like the following, the capital letters referring to the principles involved:

(1) CONDITIONING

*a.* Objective description: Given an animal with a need (e.g., for food) and a means of affecting that need (e.g., food). Present a signal (e.g., a tone) of a kind that in sufficient volume and under favorable circumstances is capable of eliciting a response from the animal, then, in fairly close temporal and spatial contiguity, present the means of affecting the need (the "unconditioned stimulus"). After one or more presentations the signal will elicit the same response as the unconditioned stimulus or a response similar to it.

*b.* Explanation: Given time $(F)$ and a need to be satisfied $(E)$, the signal and the unconditioned stimulus will be differentiated as a unit from a relatively homogeneous field. Since the degree of differentiation required is determined by the precision of response required $(D)$ signals for diffuse bodily and postural activity may be effective at a very low level of awareness. The closer the signal and unconditioned stimulus in the experimenter's time and space, the more apt they are to be differentiated as a unit from the rest of the learner's field $(C)$. It would not be expected $(B)$ that the response to the signal-stimulus unit would be exactly the same as to the stimulus alone. In a class demonstration with a human subject, using a strong buzzer tone one second before a strong shock to the right fore-finger from a curved finger rest, the unconditioned response was an extension of the finger. The conditioned response, however, was flexion together with a lifting of the finger, the whole action taking it off the grill. Phenomenologically the subject was bracing himself for the expected shock.

(2) IRRADIATION

*a.* Objective description: If the signal is altered within a varying range the established response will still be made.

*b.* Explanation: If the signal is incompletely differentiated it may be confused with other signals. If it is experienced as a vague feeling of discomfort or expectancy a large number of signals in different sense fields might elicit the response. If it is more clearly individuated there will be less opportunity for confusion with other signals.

On the basis of this inference that "irradiation" and "generalization" are incomplete differentiation, it would be predicted that continued presentations of the signal-stimulus unit will, by giving more opportunity for precise differentiation ($F$) of the signal, lessen the number of signals with which it might be confused and diminish the probability of "irradiation" responses. This prediction corresponds to the results reported by Razran (**14**, see pages 7 and 8), although it does not agree with his interpretation.

(3) DIFFERENTIATION

*a.* Objective description: Both signal A and sign A′ elicit the response. If signal A is given with the unconditioned stimulus and signal A′ without it, the latter signal will cease to elicit the response.

*b.* Explanation: Presentation of signal A′ without food makes it necessary ($E$) and possible ($F$) for the subject to differentiate it from signal A.

(4) UNCONDITIONING

*a.* Objective description: If the signal is given without the unconditioned stimulus or some time after it, it will, after a varying number of presentations, cease to elicit the unit response.

*b.* Explanation: Separate presentation provides the subject with an opportunity for differentiating them from one another (*C*) (*F*). The signal from a signal-food unit should have no effect even the first time it is given food if the need for food has been completely satisfied (*E*). The signal from signal-punishment units, however, would be effective for several presentations when given after the punishment, since the need to escape punishment is not satiable. Repeated presentations, however, will give an opportunity for differentiation and the signal will eventually emerge as a cue that punishment has ceased and will then evoke a different response.

(5)  PSEUDO-CONDITIONING

*a.* Objective description: "In some cases a response is elicited by a formerly inadequate stimulus (signal) which has been preceded by an unconditioned stimulus" (7).

*b.* Explanation: In cases where the unconditioned stimulus is one, like punishment, that leads to a continuing state of need and tension, the animal will differentiate out and respond to features of the field previously ignored. The signal is effective because it is unfamiliar, that is to say, it is incompletely differentiated from the shock situation. "The animals gave the impression of responding *as if* a shock were expected and *as if* they knew no appropriate response to make" (7, p. 372). In cases where the unconditioned stimulus satisfies the subject's need pseudo-conditioning will not occur.

## 7. Other concepts of learning

One of the greatest advantages of the phenomenological method is that it is able to bring the experimenter within the scope of its system and to apply its laws to the observer himself. When examined in this manner, most of the conventional concepts of learning prove to be products of the relationship between the p.fs. of the observer and the learner. For example: If the observer's field is more highly differentiated than the learner's, the latter's less precise behavior (D), since it does not conform to the situation as experienced by the observer, is said to be *error*. Phenomenologically errors are recognized only in retrospect, that is to say, when an individual compares his past behavior with his present more highly differentiated field.

If the learner's field closely approximates the field of the observer, so that the learner does what the observer would do, the behavior is said to be *correct* or *insightful*.

If the observer's field is less differentiated than the learner's there are two possibilities: (1) The learners' more precise and efficient behavior may lead the observer to discover features of the situation of which he had previously been unaware; in which case a third party might infer the observer had learned by *imitation*. (2) The learner's mysteriously precise behavior in what to the observer is a relatively undifferentiated field may lead to the assumption that the behavior is determined by *instinct*. The farther removed an animal is from the human in sensory and behavioral possibilities, and the more difficult the reconstruction of its field, the greater the chances that instinct will be invoked as an explanation for its behavior.

## 8. Association or differentiation?

If an observer in a highly differentiated field, which he naively takes to be real, watches the behavior of a learner he is certain to interpret the process as one in which the highly individuated items in his own field are *combined, organized, associated,* or *integrated* by the learner. Because he believes his own field to be real, he postulates that the learner's field is made up of the same items, but in an inferior state of organization. Objective theories of learning, therefore, begin with an unorganized field and attempt to show how it becomes organized.

Cross section studies of the learner's p.f. at different stages of learning, however, show that the field is always organized. The change lies in increasing detail rather than organization. Entities are thus "associated" when they are incompletely differentiated, having emerged together out of a common ground to satisfy a need. They are experienced as contiguous when they are incompletely differentiated in space or time and as like or opposite when they emerge in some mutual relationship. The so-called laws of association: *contiguity, similarity,* and *contrast* thus become descriptive of incomplete differentiation in the phenomenological field.

## 9. Frequency

Frequency is the basic but unreliable causal factor of most objective systems. From the phenomenological point of view it may afford an opportunity for learning $(F)$ but cannot cause or guarantee it. What is learned depends upon the phenomenological needs of the learner $(E)$. This accounts for the success of Dunlap's method of breaking habits by practicing them (6, 22).

## 10. Relationship to the physical sciences

One of the most interesting implications of the phenomenological approach is the status it assigns to the physical sciences. Physicists secure regularity and lawfulness by restricting themselves to a common and rigorously limited phenomenological field. They share this common p.f. (sometimes called the physical universe) by the process of taking all measurements from a standard position in front of their instruments and confining their observations to the pointer-readings thus derived. This process gives to physical scientists the unique advantage of a common field; but it is a field where all the characteristics of phenomena are eliminated except those reducible to length; where light, color, temperature, taste, and odor exist, if at all, only as readings on a scale; and where song, oratory, poetry, and propaganda are alternating areas of condensation and rarefaction. As long as the physicists can remain in this common field their behavior is identical. They make the same calculations and predictions because they are living in identical fields.

This use of mediate observation in the physical sciences has led to spectacular agreement in some fields. It is, however, essentially a search for agreement by elimination of phenomena and is therefore limited in its possibilities. Since the phenomena that must be excluded are essentially those necessary for the prediction and control of human behavior, it is becoming apparent that the methods of the physical sciences cannot be taken over bodily by the psychologists.

## 11. Advantages of the phenomenological approach

Philosophically a phenomenological system has a number of advantages, several of which have been enumerated or implied. From the point of view of practical use for the prediction and control of behavior, however, four are outstanding:

1. A phenomenological system is anthropomorphic. Its data are stated in terms of immediate experience and require no translation to make them meaningful.

2. It is concerned with the prediction and control of individual behavior, a field closed to objective systems because of their necessary assumption of variability in individual behavior. For this reason, psychiatrists, applied psychologists, and teachers when dealing with individuals commonly adopt a phenomenological view. This accounts for the great use by these groups of

psychoanalysis, Gestalt, and private non-academic systems which have large phenomenological components. The use of a general field can result in the prediction of general, normative behavior only.

3. As compared with the objective approach, the phenomenological approach is more inclusive. Individual behavior cannot be predicted from normative behavior. On the other hand, accuracy in predicting individual behavior makes possible the prediction of normative behavior as well.

4. The particular system outlined in this paper has the predictive advantage of postulating only one process, which is descriptive rather than causal or explanatory.

## 12. Relation to other systems

It is impossible to say whether this system is the only possible phenomenological system. The first three principles are certainly basic and the next three appear to follow. Gestalt psychologists and their pupils have made the major recent contributions in this field and have failed to achieve a purely phenomenological system only because of their failure to appreciate its necessity. As soon as non-phenomenological data are eliminated from Gestalt psychology, it becomes the system that has been described.

Psychoanalysis, the other semi-phenomenological system, differs basically in its interpretation of the nature of the field. Freud recognized the figure-ground character of the field and the importance of the ground in behavior but, lacking experimental evidence, distorted the figure-ground relations into an antagonistic dichotomy in which the ground (unconscious) had all the characteristics of figure (conscious) including a self (id). Since these characteristics are not experienced by the individual the system ceased to be purely phenomenological. The methods of analysis are directed toward securing an understanding of the patient's field and have resulted in the accumulation of important data, especially in the area of motivation. Since the conscious-unconscious dichotomy is the cornerstone of the system it is impossible to see, however, how psychoanalysis can evolve into the purely phenomenological system that is needed.

## SUMMARY

The current confusion in psychology is largely due to the uncritical combination of data from two different frames of reference. Facts derived from a phenomenological point of view are non-identical with and often completely contradictory to facts derived from an objective point of view. Systems attempting to combine facts derived from both frames of reference are forced into a multiplicity of conflicting laws and concepts or into the postulation of loci of action inaccessible to observation. In either case accurate prediction of behavior is impossible. Objective systems, although philosophically more satisfactory than mixed systems, have been forced in practice to confine themselves to the prediction of normative behavior. For this reason psychiatrists, applied psychologists, and teachers when dealing with individuals commonly adopt a phenomenological view. This accounts for the great use by these groups of psychoanalysis, Gestalt, and private non-academic systems having large phenomenological components. The best immediate prospects for a psychology able to accurately predict individual behavior lie in the development of Gestalt psychology along purely phenomenological lines.

## REFERENCES

1.   Bartlett, F. C. *Remembering.* New York: Macmillan, 1932.
2.   Bernhardt, K., & Snygg, D. The effect of cues upon the choice of the shorter path. *J. comp. Psychol.,* 1937, **24,** 269–276.

3.  Brigden, R. L. A tachistoscopic study of the differentiation of perception. *Psychol. Monogr.*, 1933, **44**, 153–166.

4.  Buel, J. Differential errors in animal mazes. *Psychol. Bull.*, 1935, **32**, 67–99.

5.  DeCamp, J. E. Relative distance as a factor in the white rat's selection of a path. *Psycho-biol.*, 1920, **2**, 245–253.

6.  Dunlap, K. *Habits: their making and unmaking.* New York: Liveright, 1932.

7.  Harlow, H. F., & Toltzien, F. Formation of pseudo-conditioned responses in the cat. *J. gen. Psychol.*, 1940, **23**, 367–375.

8.  Hull, C. L. The conflicting psychologies of learning—a way out. *Psychol. Rev.*, 1935, **42**, 491–516.

9.  Koffka, K. *The principles of Gestalt psychology.* New York: Harcourt, Brace, 1935.

10. Maier, N. R. F. Reasoning in humans. II. *J. comp. Psychol.*, 1931, **12**, 181–194.

11. Maier, N. R. F. The behavior mechanisms concerned with problem solving. *Psychol. Rev.*, 1940, **47**, 43–58.

12. Menninger, K. *Man against himself.* New York: Harcourt, Brace, 1938.

13. Pratt, C. C. *The logic of modern psychology.* New York: Macmillan, 1939.

14. Razran, G. H. S. Studies in configural conditioning: V. Generalization and transposition. *J. genet. Psychol.*, 1940, **56**, 3–11.

15. Shepard, J. F. More about the floor cue. *Psychol. Bull.*, 1935, **32**, 696.

16. Snygg, D. Configurational aspects of tachistoscopic observation. Unpublished thesis, State Univ. Iowa, 1931.

17. Snygg, D. The relative difficulty of mechanically equivalent tasks: I. Human learning. *J. genet. Psychol.*, 1935, **47**, 299–320.

18. Snygg, D. The relative difficulty of mechanically equivalent tasks: II. Animal learning. *J. genet. Psychol.*, 1935, **47**, 321–336.

19. Snygg, D. Maze learning as perception. *J. genet. Psychol.*, 1936, **49**, 231–239.

20. Snygg, D. Mazes in which rats take the longer path to food. *J. Psychol.*, 1936, **1**, 153–166.

21. Thorndike, E. L. *Human learning*. New York: Appleton-Century, 1931.

22. Wakeham, G. A. A quantitative experiment on Dunlap's revision of the law of habit formation. *J. comp. Psychol.*, 1930, **10**, 235–236.

23. Wees, W. R., & Line, W. The influence of the form of a presentation upon reproduction: the principle of determination. *Brit. J. Psychol.* (Gen. Section), 1937, **28**, 167–189.

# Part II

---

## THE SELF

# CHAPTER 2

••••••••••••••••••••••••••••••••••••••••••••••••••••••••••••••••••••••••••••••••••••••

# The Self, Its Derivative Terms, and Research

## BY ARTHUR W. COMBS AND DANIEL W. SOPER

With the increasing tendency of social scientists to be "self-oriented" in their study of human behavior, a large number of terms has been developed for use in describing and studying the phenomenon of self. Some of these terms are: "self," "concepts of self," "self concept," "self-ideal," "self-adequacy," "self-acceptance," etc. As these terms have become adopted and used by an increasing number of people from a wide variety of theoretical frames of reference, the literature dealing with them has become more and more confused. This paper attempts to re-examine conceptual bases, to point up ambiguities and problems which exist, and to arrive at definitions of these terms consistent with a "self" frame of reference and capable of providing a

From the *Journal of Individual Psychology,* 1957, **13**, 134–145. Reprinted by permission of the authors and the publisher.

more adequate base for the planning of research, and thus to facilitate communication among workers in this area.

Although we have, in the following, occasionally pointed to some published research as illustration of what we believe to be errors in conceptualization, we hasten to add that we have done this without malice. Indeed, had we not ourselves fallen so resoundingly into the same pitfalls, we would not have embarked upon this paper.

### SELF AND REAL SELF

The word "self" is a generic term referring to a specific human personality and has been indispensable in the historical development of man as a conscious and thinking entity. The assertion that a "self" exists may involve only the assumption that for a given human being, there exist identity (uniqueness) and consciousness of self and environment. If, however, we wish to go beyond this point and describe the characteristics and attributes of a given self, the job becomes a more complex and difficult one, for the self can be observed from many different frames of reference. It may be described from the point of view of innumerable observers, including the individual himself.

No one can ever observe a "real" self—his own or someone else's—directly. It can only be approached through the perceptions of someone. An individual attempting to describe *his own self,* can provide only an approximation of his "real" self; at any given time, only a part of the "real" self is "visible" to the individual. Another person attempting to describe *someone else's self,* can only approximate the "real" self, for its very existence is a philosophical question. It is sufficient that the ways in which the self is *perceived* can be studied. This, we think, *is* necessary; for these perceptions are among the most important determinants of behavior.

## CONCEPTS OF SELF

The number of ways in which the self may be perceived are practically limitless. Individuals may see themselves as men or women, children or adults, Republicans or Democrats. More specifically, a particular individual may see himself as John Smith, owner of a 1956 Dodge, who lives at 627 Edgemere Street, St. Albans, Utah. Descriptions like these serve to distinguish the self as unique from all other selves. But self-description does not stop with this. We are seldom content with description alone. Thus, even more important are the values the individual places upon his various qualities of self. People do not regard themselves as fathers or mothers only but as "good" fathers and mothers or "bad" ones. They see themselves, not simply as people, but as attractive or ugly, pleasant or unpleasant, fat or thin, happy or sad, adequate or inadequate people.

Each individual, within a comparatively short time after birth, has developed a large number of perceptions about himself. These more or less separate perceptions of self might be termed "concepts of self." They are more or less discrete perceptions of self which the individual regards as part or characteristic of himself. They include all the self-perceptions which the individual has differentiated as descriptive of the self he calls "I" or "me" (32). These concepts are not of equal importance in the peculiar economy of a human being. They vary in at least two important respects.

1. Some are more central, such as conceiving of self as man or woman, and are more resistant to change. Other concepts of self are less strongly defended because they do not seem quite so important in a particular organization, such as being the driver of a 1956 Dodge.

2. Concepts of self will also vary in sharpness or clarity. At any moment we observe a human being, we will find the con-

cepts of self which he holds to vary from those in clear, sharp figure to those so vague and fuzzy as to be inexpressible even by the person himself (15). The mother in the psychological clinic, for example, may be quite certain that she is Jimmy's mother. Whether she is a "good" mother is a perception far less clear to her. Indeed, it may be this very confusion that causes her difficulty.

## THE SELF CONCEPT

Whereas the "concepts of self" about which we have just been speaking describe isolated aspects of the person, the "self concept" is the organization of all that the individual refers to as "I" or "me" (32). It is himself from his own point of view. The self concept is not a mere conglomeration or addition of isolated concepts of self, but a patterned interrelationship or "gestalt" of all these (6, 27, 28). Like many of the concepts of which it is composed, the self concept has a degree of stability and consistency which gives predictability to the individual and his behavior (37, 38).

The perceptual field of an individual includes much more than his perceptions of self. It includes, for example, perceptions of the objects and events in the world about him, perceptions of his physical being, the goals and values he has differentiated as means of achieving need satisfaction, the techniques which have come to seem appropriate ways of reaching his goals, and perceptions of abstract ideas and concepts. These perceptions, in the same fashion as perceptions of self, will also vary in importance and clarity.

The perceptual field which includes all of an individual's perceptions may be represented by a large circle, A. Within this perceptual field we may think of a second and smaller circle, B, which includes all those perceptions which the person holds about himself, irrespective of their importance or clarity to him at any particular moment. Snygg and Combs (32) have called this the "phenomenal self." Within the phenomenal field we may think of a third, still smaller circle, C, which includes only those aspects which are important or vital to the self. This is the self concept. It is a stable, important and characteristic organization composed of those perceptions which seem to the individual preeminently himself (15, 32).

## INFERENTIAL NATURE OF THE SELF

Both the self concept and concepts of self are inferences about the self. They are sheer abstractions, or interpretations useful in helping us understand ourselves and to make communication possible. The self as a discrete entity does not exist. Allport warns against reifying the self, making it into a homunculus to solve all problems without in reality solving any (1, p. 54). Like the concept of the atom or of electricity, the self concept is an inference which enables us to deal with a complex function not directly observable. The fact that it is a product of inference does, however, not make it invalid. To the individual, his perceptions of self, like all his other perceptions, have the feeling of reality. His self concept seems to him to be truly what he is.

The self concept is created by the individual's inferences from his unique experiences. It is derived from observations about his own behavior and the behavior of other people toward him. The child who perceives adults push him away, may come to perceive himself as unliked or unwanted. The adult observing himself to be badly winded while playing with his young son, may revise his self concept with the perception that he no longer has the old pep. Whatever self concept the individual holds, has been acquired from the data of his own observations of behavior.

The outsider hoping to understand the self concept of another individual also attempts to assess it through inference. If each individual behaves in terms of his self concept, then it should be possible for an outsider, by observing the behavior of an individual, to infer the nature of the self concept. This is what each of us does quite automatically in dealing with other people. We infer, from the behavior we see, what other people are thinking and feeling, and adjust our own behavior accordingly. What the layman does as a matter of "common sense," the behavioral scientist seeks to do more exactly and precisely. The data used by the psychologists in studying the self concept are exactly the same as those used in studying any other human characteristic, namely, the observed behavior of the subject.

## THE SELF REPORT

The self report is the individual's self-description; it represents what the individual *says* he is. Like any other act, the self report is a *behavior* revealing in larger or smaller degree what is going on within the organism. The self report and the self concept, although often confused, are by no means synonymous. One is a behavior, the other, a perception or inference made from behavior. To treat the two as synonymous is to introduce into our research a large and unknown degree of error.

The self report is valuable as a means of exploring the self concept. Like any other behavior, the self report is a product of the individual's *total* perceptual field. It is a product of *both* the subject's perceptions of self and not-self, without having a one-to-one relationship to the self concept. Confusion of the self report with the self concept in research has led to similar confusion in thinking and research results, making communication extremely difficult. Confusion of the two terms represents a return to introspection, a technique of observation no more acceptable to phenomenological psychology than to more traditional approaches (2, 10).

For research purposes we must know the degree to which the self report can be relied upon as an indication of the self concept. This will depend on at least the following factors:

### 1. Clarity of the subject's awareness

We have already seen that the self concept varies in degrees of clarity, and that some concepts of self at any moment are in clear figure while others may be immersed in ground. Whether or not they may be reported to others will depend in some measure on whether they can truly be called into clear figure at the moment they are asked for. Lack of clarity may also be of a more permanent character; some concepts of self may exist at very low levels of awareness for most of our lives. These correspond to the so-called "unconscious," and attempts to report them to others may be impossible.

### 2. Lack of adequate symbols for expression

Closely related to the problem of clarity is the question of the possession of the necessary symbols in which self concepts may be adequately expressed. Self descriptions can only be reported in words. But words are notoriously inadequate, and may not mean the same things to others as they mean to us. The degree to which the self report approaches the self concept is thus open to all the errors of any human communication.

### 3. Social expectancy

In our society it is customary, indeed practically necessary, for the individual to hide his true concepts of self even if he is able to report them accurately. Though a person may think of himself as very charming or as very stupid, he certainly would be most unlikely to express such feelings even under the most favorable circumstances. We can never quite escape the effects of our society, no matter how hard we may try. We are always aware of the expectancies of others toward us, and the things we say about ourselves are always more or less affected by this fact. Perhaps in psychotherapy, when a strong relationship with an accepting counselor has developed, the client may be able to report his feelings and attitudes toward himself with a lower degree of distortion. This seldom occurs elsewhere in life, however.

### 4. Cooperation of the subject

The accuracy of the self report depends greatly on the motivation of the subject. If he wishes to hide an aspect of self, he can well do so. He does not even have to reveal his lack of cooperation, if indeed he is aware of a decision not to cooperate. But even with the best of intentions to cooperate, a subject may be quite unable to give the desired information accurately for reasons of which he himself is not clearly aware.

### 5. Freedom from threat and personal adequacy

In general, the more adequate the individual feels, the more likely his self report will approach an accurate description of the self concept, other factors being equal. The more threatened, inadequate, or maladjusted the individual, the more vulnerable will be his concepts of self and the greater the necessity for him to defend the self.

Some experimenters have attempted to circumvent the difficulties of the self report by various methods of forcing choices or of requiring subjects to categorize statements about themselves. Most notable of these is the Stephenson Q technique which has been used for a number of researches on the self concept (13, 19, 29, 30, 34, 35, 37). This technique requires the subject to sort a large number of statements about self into a series of "more or less so" piles. While such techniques force the subject to consider a number of self descriptions he might otherwise avoid, most of the variables described above continue to operate, for the most part uncontrolled. Sophisticated statistical manipulation cannot overcome inadequacies of basic conceptualization.

Although the self report is quite different from the self concept, a surprising number of researches purporting to deal with the self concept have turned out, on closer examination, to be experiments on the self report (3, 4, 7, 8, 9, 11, 12, 17, 19, 21). Thus some, very valuable studies run the risk of being rejected because they are mislabeled rather than being accepted for the valuable contributions they make.

## THE SELF IDEAL

It has become generally accepted that an individual's perception of himself as an adequate or inadequate person—his confidence in his own ability to satisfy his basic needs—is extremely important in determining his reaction to people and situations. At first glance the fact that an individual may see himself as inadequate would seem to require that he have differentiated certain goals for himsef which he defines as "adequate" and "satisfactory." The aggregate of these characteristics of self which the person feels are necessary to attain adequacy (sometimes, perhaps unfortunately, perfection) has been termed the "self ideal" (9, 14, 20, 22, 25), and it has been assumed that the discrepancy between a person's "self concept" and his "self ideal" would provide a relatively objective measure of "adequacy" or "inadequacy" (8, 20, 22).

Estimates of the self ideal have usually been based on responses by the subject to questions of the same general type as are used in paper and pencil personality inventories. Sometimes the individual has been asked to describe or rank personal characteristics and goals which are representative of his ideal self, or to describe as satisfactory or unsatisfactory certain words and phrases (9, 14, 20, 22).

Description of the self ideal runs into much the same difficulties as the self report. It cannot be accepted at face value. We must try to find out not only *what* the individual says, but *why* he says it under the conditions of the specific observation. Acceptance of a person's responses at face value can quickly lead to misinformation, ambiguous research findings, and further confusion. Yet a number of studies have accepted the subject's description of the "person I would like to be" as the self ideal (9, 14, 20, 22, 27).

Another difficulty is that the individual may never have formulated a clear self ideal. When we ask him to report his self ideal, we may thus be forcing him to invent for us a concept which does not normally exist in his economy in a meaningful way. A person may learn to see himself as very inadequate without ever developing a clear picture of what constitutes adequacy. Indeed, this would seem to be true of most persons who suffer from strong feelings of basic inadequacy. Their inability to differentiate clear and realistic goals is familiar to clinicians and counselors everywhere. Much of the distress of the client in psychotherapy seems to occur precisely because of this inability. He feels that what he *is,* is unsatisfactory; his attempts to define criteria of satisfaction for himself reveal less a self ideal than confusion and lack of clear differentiation.

Finally, an individual's perception of himself as adequate or inadequate, and his differentiation of the qualities which would be ideal for him, involves a great deal more than static or cross-sectional descriptions of self and ideal. Adequacy is a dynamic function. The apparent difference between an individual's self concept and his self ideal, statically described, may be less important than his satisfaction with his current movement toward improvement and his confidence in being able to bridge the gap between "what is" and "what should be." It is quite possible, for example, that two individuals might describe their selves and ideals in very similar terms, yet would differ greatly in their feelings of adequacy to progress toward their goals. Both may see themselves as lacking in a particular area; one may consider this an exciting problem to be solved; the other, a forbidding and insurmountable obstacle. These differences are *perceived* distances between self and ideal. They are distances as the behaver, rather than the observer, sees them; they are "psychological" distances. The observer can only make inferences about these "perceived distances" from the behavior which he observes. He cannot subtract the one set of statements from the other!

The use of the term self ideal, then, and attempts to arrive at objective measurement of this concept, are subject to a number of limitations which have not always been observed. The self ideal involves important dynamic as well as static elements, and can only be studied under the conditions which are common to all phenomenological observations. The term must be recognized as referring to a highly abstract construct, which may or may not have its counterpart in the perceptual field of the individual.

## THE SELF AND ADJUSTMENT

A large number of terms have been developed to indicate good adjustment from various points of view. "Self-acceptance," "self-adequacy," and "the non-threatened personality" are perhaps the most representative (**12, 15, 29, 32**).

Unfortunately, these terms are sometimes used to refer to an individual as *totally* self-acceptant, or *totally* adequate, or *completely* non-threatened, conditions which represent ultimate desirable goals along various dimensions of self-perception. These ultimate goals, like most ultimates, represent static conditions which can *never be achieved*. Life is a dynamic process, and individuals continue to strive for growth and self-enhancement. Allport has expressed this function as follows:

Here seems to be the central characteristic of propriate striving: its goals are, strictly speaking, unattainable. Propriate striving confers unity upon personality, but it is never the unity of fulfillment, or repose, or of reduced tension. The devoted parent never loses concern for his child; the devotee of democracy adopts a lifelong assignment in his human relationships. The scientist, by the very nature of his commitment, creates more and more questions, never fewer. Indeed the measure of our intellectual maturity, one philosopher suggests, is our capacity to feel less and less satisfied with our answers to better and better problems (1, p. 67).

Furthermore, the terms self-acceptant, adequate, and nontheatened, are used in so many ways as to be more confusing than helpful. Actually each describes the same state, yet stresses a different aspect of the field. Let us look at each term briefly.

### Self-acceptance

This term, as used by Rogers (29), Maslow (23), Snygg and Combs (32), Murphy (25), and others (5, 18, 24, 25, 31, 36), refers to the ability of the individual to accept into awareness facts about himself with a minimum of defense or distortion. It is related to the *accuracy* of observation and self-awareness, and does not imply approval or disapproval of self. Thus, a well-adjusted, self-accepting individual may be able to say of himself, "Yes, indeed, I have a very bad habit of interrupting people sometimes," and this unflattering judgment can be made without the necessity for defending himself or denying the existence of the perception.

Some experimenters, however, have equated self-acceptance with self-approval or liking (9, 18, 31). To do this would lead to the ridiculous conclusion that a person who says of himself accurately, "I am a very cruel person most of the time, and I like myself this way very much," is a well-adjusted person! The truly well-adjusted person may confess to an overall feeling of satisfaction, but probably has no great feeling of like or dislike of self.

## Self-adequacy

This is another characteristic of the individual self concept. It is an overall evaluation of self, at all levels of awareness. It is the individual's judgment of his present and future ability to achieve basic need-satisfaction. An individual always has as a goal a greater degree of adequacy—this is part of the dynamic process of living. To the degree that he sees himself as adequate, however, he can select among the goals he perceives, or reject them, or try and fail, without disorganization and self-defeating reactions. He feels adequate to achieve enhancement through goals which are realistically available in terms of immediate or predicted situations. His feeling of adequacy, then, does not depend on the restrictions of his immediate environment.

Objective appraisal of an individual's success as culturally defined, of his brilliance in contributing to art, science, or literature, does not provide in itself satisfactory evidence of an individual's self-adequacy. Adequacy is an attribute of his own perception of himself. Two people may be equally convinced that they are unable to deal with mathematical problems; for one, this is a realistic and matter-of-fact situation which he can use effectively in decision-making, and has relatively little relevance to his feeling of worth-whileness; for the other, it may be further evidence of personal inadequacy, a weakness which is not acceptable to him. Adequacy or inadequacy are *personal* perceptions of events.

## Non-threatened personality

Generally speaking, the "adequate" person is also "non-threatened." There is a reciprocal relationship between self-adequacy and perceived threat on the part of an individual. Threat occurs when a person sees himself as basically inadequate to satisfy need. The result is a narrowing and distortion of perception so that he is not able to admit into clear awareness those aspects of self and environment which contribute to the threat, nor to relate these meaningfully and realistically to other perceptions of self and environment. Threat produces defense. The self concept, as it exists at the time, is defended more vigorously and is less capable of change and growth. To speak of a nonthreatened person, then, is another way of referring to one who is self-acceptant and who perceives himself as a basically adequate person.

One of the problems involved here is that the term "threat" has been used differently in different frames of reference. Traditionally, we have spoken of one person as threatening another; here the emphasis is on the purpose of the threatener. In self-theory, however, threat exists only as it is perceived by the individual. Thus, when an experiment is set up to provide a threatening situation, some subjects may respond with effective and well-organized behavior. Instead of the threat they may have perceived a potentially rewarding situation and felt relatively adequate to deal with it. The ambiguous results achieved in some research on "stress" and "threat" may well stem from the differences in the ways individuals perceived the experimental situation (13, 16).

## PHENOMENOLOGICAL RESEARCH

Phenomenological research, like any other research, begins with careful observation. From such observations it develops inferences as to the perceptions of the subject, which inferences are checked against further observations of behavior. By such a repeated process of observation, inference, prediction, observation, inference, etc., the psychologist using a perceptual frame of reference is able to explore the dynamics of the subject's behavior. Phenomenological research, however, involves the observer in a much more active role than traditional approaches. In perceptual research, he is not a passive but an active instrument of observation (33). This more active role affords vast opportunities to explore the private world of the behaver, on the one hand, but calls for far greater control and discipline of the observer himself, on the other hand.

The first essential to moving forward in this type of research, it seems to us, is to achieve clarity and precision of our fundamental concepts. Confusion in our concepts can only lead to similar confusion in our research endeavors. Without clear understanding of the problems we seek to explore, we run the risk of becoming the victims of our own perceptions.

## SUMMARY

With the ever-increasing use of perceptual approaches to personality study there is need for rigorous examination of basic premises and conceptualizations. The authors discuss a number of self-oriented terms commonly employed in the literature, point out some common pitfalls in their use, and suggest some steps toward clearer, more precise use of these terms. Among the terms described are: self, self concept, self report, self-ideal, self-acceptance, self-adequacy, and non-threatened self.

## REFERENCES

1. Allport, G. W. *Becoming*. New Haven: Yale Univ. Press, 1955.
2. Bakan, D. A reconsideration of the problem of introspection. *Psychol. Bull.*, 1954, **51**, 105–118.
3. Balester, R. The self concept and juvenile delinquency. Unpublished doctor's dissertation, Vanderbilt Univ., 1956.

4. Benjamins, J. Changes in performance in relation to influences upon self-conceptualization. *J. abnorm. soc. Psychol.*, 1952, **45**, 473–480.

5. Berger, E. M. The relation between expressed acceptance of self and expressed acceptance of others. *J. abnorm. soc. Psychol.*, 1952, **47**, 778–782.

6. Bertocci, P. A. The psychological self, the ego, and personality. *Psychol. Rev.*, 1945, **52**, 91–99.

7. Bice, H. Factors in self concept of child with cerebral palsy. *Ment. Hyg.*, 1954, **38**, 120–131.

8. Bills, R. E. Self concepts and Rorschach signs of depression. *J. consult. Psychol.*, 1954, **18**, 135–137.

9. Bills, R. E., Vance, E. L., & McLean, O. S. An index of adjustment and values. *J. consult. Psychol.*, 1951, **15**, 257–261.

10. Boring, E. G. A history of introspection. *Psychol. Bull.*, 1953, **50**, 169–186.

11. Brownfain, J. J. Stability of the self-concept as a dimension of personality. *J. abnorm. soc. Psychol.*, 1952, **47**, 597–606.

12. Calvin, A. D., & Holtzman, W. H. Adjustment and the discrepancy between self concept and inferred self. *J. consult. Psychol.*, 1953, **17**, 39–44.

13. Chodorkoff, B. Adjustment and the discrepancy between the perceived and the ideal self. *J. clin. Psychol.*, 1954, **10**, 266–268.

14. Chodorkoff, B. Self perception, perceptual defense, and adjustment. *J. abnorm. soc. Psychol.*, 1954, **49**, 508–513.

15. Combs, A. W. A phenomenological approach to adjustment theory. *J. abnorm. soc. Psychol.*, 1949, **44**, 29–35.

16. Cowen, E. L. The negative self concept as a personality measure. *J. consult. Psychol.*, 1954, **18**, 138–142.

17. Epstein, S. Unconscious self-evaluation in a normal and schizophrenic group. *J. abnorm. soc. Psychol.*, 1955, **50**, 65–70.

18. Fey, W. Acceptance by others and its relation to acceptance of self and others; a revaluation. *J. abnorm. soc. Psychol.*, 1955, **50**, 274–276.

19. Fitts, H. The role of the self-concept in social perception. Unpublished doctor's dissertation, Vanderbilt Univ., 1954.

20. Hanlon, T. E., Hofstaetter, P., & O'Conner, J. P. Congruence of self and ideal self in relation to personality adjustment. *J. consult. Psychol.*, 1954, **18,** 215–218.

21. Hartley, M. Changes in the self-concept during psychotherapy. Unpublished doctor's dissertation, Univ. Chicago, 1951.

22. Havighurst, R. J., *et al.* Development of the ideal self in childhood and adolescence. *J. educ. Res.*, 1946, **40,** 41–57.

23. Maslow, A. H. *Motivation and personality.* New York: Harper, 1954.

24. McIntyre, C. J. Acceptance by others and its relation to acceptance of self and others. *J. abnorm. soc. Psychol.*, 1952, **47,** 624–625.

25. Murphy, G. *Personality: a biosocial approach to origins and structure.* New York: Harper, 1947.

26. Omwake, K. T. The relation between acceptance of self and acceptance of others shown by three personality inventories. Paper read at South. Soc. Phil. Psychol., Atlanta, Ga., April 17, 1954.

27. Raimy, V. C. Self-reference in counseling interviews. *J. consult. Psychol.*, 1948, **12,** 153–163.

28. Raimy, V. C. The self concept as a factor in counseling and personality organization. Unpublished doctor's dissertation, Ohio State Univ., 1943.

29. Rogers, C. R. *Client-centered therapy.* Boston: Houghton Mifflin, 1951.

30. Rogers, C. R., & Dymond, R. F. (Eds.). *Psychotherapy and personality change.* Chicago: Univ. Chicago Press, 1954.

31. Sheerer, E. T. An analysis of the relationship between acceptance of and respect for self and acceptance of and respect for others in ten counseling cases. *J. consult. Psychol.*, 1949, **13,** 169–175.

32. Snygg, D., & Combs, A. W. *Individual behavior.* New York: Harper, 1949.

33. Soper, D. W., & Combs, A. W. Planning future research in education. *Educ. Leadership,* 1957, **14,** 315–318.

34. Stephenson, W. A. A statistical approach to typology; the study of trait universes. *J. clin. Psychol.*, 1950, **6,** 26–37.

35.  Stock, D. An investigation into the interrelations between the self concept and feelings directed toward other persons and groups. *J. consult. Psychol.*, 1949, **13**, 176–180.

36.  Taylor, C., & Combs, A. W. Self-acceptance and adjustment. *J. consult. Psychol.*, 1952, **16**, 89–91.

37.  Taylor, D. H. Consistency of the self concept. Unpublished doctor's dissertation, Vanderbilt Univ., 1953.

38.  Walsh, A. M. *Self concepts of bright boys with learning difficulties.* New York: Bureau Publ., Teachers Coll., Columbia Univ., 1956.

## CHAPTER 3

•••••••••••••••••••••••••••••••••••••••••••••••••••••••••••••••••••••••••••••••••

# Some Observations on the
# Organization of Personality

## BY CARL R. ROGERS

In various fields of science rapid strides have been made when direct observation of significant processes has become possible. In medicine, when circumstances have permitted the physician to peer directly into the stomach of his patient, understanding of digestive processes has increased and the influence of emotional tension upon all aspects of that process has been more accurately observed and understood. In our work with nondirective therapy we often feel that we are having a psychological opportunity comparable to this medical experience—an opportunity to observe directly a number of the effective processes of personality. Quite aside from any question regarding nondirective therapy as therapy, here is a precious vein of ob-

From *The American Psychologist*, 1947, **2**, 358–368. Reprinted by permission of the author and the publisher. Presented as the retiring President's address at the annual convention of the American Psychological Association in 1947.

servational material of unusual value for the study of personality.

## CHARACTERISTICS OF THE OBSERVATIONAL MATERIAL

There are several ways in which the raw clinical data to which we have had access is unique in its value for understanding personality. The fact that these verbal expressions of inner dynamics are preserved by electrical recording makes possible a detailed analysis of a sort not heretofore possible. Recording has given us a microscope by which we may examine at leisure, and in minute detail, almost every aspect of what was, in its occurrence, a fleeting moment impossible of accurate observation.

Another scientifically fortunate characteristic of this material is the fact that the verbal productions of the client are biased to a minimal degree by the therapist. Material from client-centered interviews probably comes closer to being a "pure" expression of attitudes than has yet been achieved through other means. One can read through a complete recorded case or listen to it, without finding more than a half-dozen instances in which the therapist's views on any point are evident. One would find it impossible to form an estimate as to the therapist's views about personality dynamics. One could not determine his diagnostic views, his standards of behavior, his social class. The one value or standard held by the therapist which would exhibit itself in his tone of voice, responses, and activity, is a deep respect for the personality and attitudes of the client as a separate person. It is difficult to see how this would bias the content of the interview, except to permit deeper expression than the client would ordinarily allow himself. This almost complete lack of any distorting attitude is felt, and sometimes expressed by the client. One woman says:

"It's almost impersonal. I like you—of course I don't know why I should like you or why I shouldn't like you. It's a peculiar thing. I've never had that relationship with anybody before and I've often thought about it. . . . A lot of times I walk out with a feeling of elation that you think highly of me, and of course at the same time I have the feeling that 'Gee, he must think I'm an awful Jerk' or something like that. But it doesn't really—those feelings aren't so deep that I can form an opinion one way or the other about you."

Here it would seem that even though she would like to discover some type of evaluational attitude, she is unable to do so. Published studies and research as yet unpublished bear out this point that counselor responses which are in any way evaluational or distorting as to content are at a minimum, thus enhancing the worth of such interviews for personality study.

The counselor attitude of warmth and understanding, well described by Snyder (9) and Rogers (8), also helps to maximize the freedom of expression by the individual. The client experiences sufficient interest in him as a person, and sufficient acceptance, to enable him to talk openly, not only about surface attitudes, but increasingly about intimate attitudes and feelings hidden even from himself. Hence in these recorded interviews we have material of very considerable depth so far as personality dynamics is concerned, along with a freedom from distortion.

Finally the very nature of the interviews and the techniques by which they are handled give us a rare opportunity to see to some extent through the eyes of another person—to perceive the world as it appears to him, to achieve at least partially, the internal frame of reference of another person. We see his behavior through his eyes, and also the psychological meaning which it had for him. We see also changes in personality and behavior, and the meanings which those changes have for the individual. We are admitted freely into the backstage of the person's living where we can observe from within some of the dramas of internal change, which are often far more compelling and moving than the drama which is presented on the stage viewed by the public. Only a novelist or a poet could do justice to the deep struggles which we are permitted to observe from within the client's own world of reality.

This rare opportunity to observe so directly and so clearly the inner dynamics of personality is a learning experience of the deepest sort of the clinician. Most of clinical psychology and psychiatry involves judgments *about* the individual, judgments which must, of necessity, be based on some framework brought to the situation by the clinician. To try continually to see and think *with* the individual, as in client-centered therapy, is a mindstretching experience in which learning goes on apace because the clinician brings to the interview no pre-determined yardstick by which to judge the material.

I wish in this paper to try to bring you some of the clinical observations which we have made as we have repeatedly peered through these psychological windows into personality, and to raise with you some of the questions about the organization of personality which these observations have forced upon us. I shall not attempt to present these observations in logical order, but rather in the order in which they impressed themselves upon our notice. What I shall offer is not a series of research findings, but only the first step in that process of gradual approximation which we call science, a description of some observed phenomena which appear to be significant, and some highly tentative explanations of these phenomena.

## THE RELATION OF THE
## ORGANIZED PERCEPTUAL FIELD TO BEHAVIOR

One simple observation, which is repeated over and over again in each successful therapeutic case, seems to have rather deep theoretical implications. It is that as changes occur in the perception of self and in the perception of reality, changes occur in behavior. In therapy, these perceptual changes are more often concerned with the self than with the external world. Hence we find in therapy that as the perception of self alters, behavior alters. Perhaps an illustration will indicate the type of observation upon which this statement is based.

A young woman, a graduate student whom we shall call Miss Vib, came in for nine interviews. If we compare the first interview with the last, striking changes are evident. Perhaps some features of this change may be conveyed by taking from the first and last interviews all the major statements regarding self, and all the major statements regarding current behavior. In the first interview, for example, her perception of herself may be crudely indicated by taking all her own statements about herself, grouping those which seem similar, but otherwise doing a minimum of editing, and retaining so far as possible, her own words. We then come out with this as the conscious perception of self which was hers at the outset of the counseling.

"I feel disorganized, muddled; I've lost all direction; my personal life has disintegrated.

"I sorta experience things from the forefront of my consciousness, but nothing sinks in very deep; things don't seem real to me; I feel nothing matters; I don't have any emotional response to situations; I'm worried about myself.

"I haven't been acting like myself; it doesn't seem like me; I'm a different person altogether from what I used to be in the past.

"I don't understand myself; I haven't known what was happening to me.

"I have withdrawn from everything, and feel all right only when I'm all alone and no one can expect me to do things.

"I don't care about my personal appearance.

"I don't know *anything* any more.

"I feel guilty about the things I have left undone.

"I don't think I could ever assume responsibility for anything."

If we attempt to evaluate this picture of self from an external frame of reference various diagnostic labels may come to mind. Trying to perceive it solely from the client's frame of reference we observe that to the young woman herself she appears disorganized, and not herself. She is perplexed and almost unacquainted with what is going on in herself. She feels unable and unwilling to function in any responsible or social way. This is at least a sampling of the way she experiences or perceives her self.

Her behavior is entirely consistent with this picture of self. If we abstract all her statements describing her behavior, in the same fashion as we abstracted her statements about self, the following pattern emerges—a pattern which in this case was corroborated by outside observation.

"I couldn't get up nerve to come in before; I haven't availed myself of help.

"Everything I should do or want to do, I don't do.

"I haven't kept in touch with friends; I avoid making the effort to go with them; I stopped writing letters home; I don't answer letters or telephone calls; I avoid contacts that would be professionally helpful; I didn't go home though I said I would.

"I failed to hand in my work in a course though I had it all done; I didn't even buy clothing that I needed; I haven't even kept my nails manicured.

"I didn't listen to material we were studying; I waste hours reading the funny papers; I can spend the whole afternoon doing absolutely nothing."

The picture of behavior is very much in keeping with the picture of self, and is summed up in the statement that "Everything I should do or want to do, I don't do." The behavior goes on, in ways that seem to the individual beyond understanding and beyond control.

If we contrast this picture of self and behavior with the picture as it exists in the ninth interview, thirty-eight days later, we find both the perception of self and the ways of behaving deeply altered. Her statements about self are as follows:

"I'm feeling much better; I'm taking more interest in myself.

"I do have some individuality, some interests.

"I seem to be getting a newer understanding of myself. I can look at myself a little better.

"I realize I'm just one person, with so much ability, but I'm not worried about it; I can accept the fact that I'm not always right.

"I feel more motivation, have more of a desire to go ahead.

"I still occasionally regret the past, though I feel less unhappy about it; I still have a long ways to go; I don't know whether I can keep the picture of myself I'm beginning to evolve.

"I can go on learning—in school or out.

"I do feel more like a normal person now; I feel more I can handle my life myself; I think I'm at the point where I can go along on my own."

Outstanding in this perception of herself are three things— that she knows herself, that she can view with comfort her assets and liabilities, and finally that she has drive and control of that drive.

In this ninth interview the behavioral picture is again consistent with the perception of self. It may be abstracted in these terms.

"I've been making plans about school and about a job; I've been working hard on a term paper; I've been going to the library to trace down a topic of special interest and finding it exciting.

"I've cleaned out my closets; washed my clothes.

"I finally wrote my parents; I'm going home for the holidays.

"I'm getting out and mixing with people; I am reacting sensibly to a fellow who is interested in me—seeing both his good and bad points.

"I will work toward my degree; I'll start looking for a job this week."

Her behavior, in contrast to the first interview, is now organized, forward-moving, effective, realistic and planful. It is in accord with the realistic and organized view she has achieved of her self.

It is this type of observation, in case after case, that leads us to say with some assurance that as perceptions of self and reality change, behavior changes. Likewise, in cases we might term failures, there appears to be no appreciable change in perceptual organization or in behavior.

What type of explanation might account for these concomitant changes in the perceptual field and the behavior pattern? Let us examine some of the logical possibilities.

In the first place, it is possible that factors unrelated to therapy may have brought about the altered perception and behavior. There may have been physiological processes occurring which produced the change. There may have been alterations in the family relationships, or in the social forces, or in the educational picture or in some other area of cultural influence, which might account for the rather drastic shift in the concept of self and in the behavior.

There are difficulties in this type of explanation. Not only were there no known gross changes in the physical or cultural situation as far as Miss Vib was concerned, but the explanation gradually becomes inadequate when one tries to apply it to the many cases in which such change occurs. To postulate that some external factor brings the change and that only by chance does this period of change coincide with the period of therapy, becomes an untenable hypothesis.

Let us then look at another explanation, namely that the therapist exerted, during the nine hours of contact, a peculiarly potent cultural influence which brought about the change. Here again we are faced with several problems. It seems that nine hours scattered over five and one-half weeks is a very minute portion of time in which to bring about alteration of patterns which have been building for thirty years. We would have to postulate an influence so potent as to be classed as traumatic. This theory is particularly difficult to maintain when we find, on examining the recorded interviews, that not once in the nine hours did the therapist express any evaluation, positive or negative, of the client's initial or final perception of self, or her initial or final mode of behavior. There was not only no evaluation, but no standards expressed by which evaluation might be inferred.

There was, on the part of the therapist, evidence of warm interest in the individual, and thorough-going acceptance of the self and of the behavior as they existed initially, in the intermediate stages, and at the conclusion of therapy. It appears reasonable to say that the therapist established certain definite conditions of interpersonal relations, but since the very essence of this relationship is respect for the person as he is at that moment, the therapist can hardly be regarded as a cultural force making for change.

We find ourselves forced to a third type of explanation, a type of explanation which is not new to psychology, but which has had only partial acceptance. Briefly it may be put that the observed phenomena of change seem most adequately explained by the hypothesis that *given certain psychological conditions, the individual has the capacity to reorganize his field of perception, including the way he perceives himself, and that a concomitant or a resultant of this perceptual reorganization is an appropriate alteration of behavior.* This puts into formal and objective terminology a clinical hypothesis which experience forces upon the therapist using a client-centered approach. One is compelled through clinical observation to develop a high degree of respect for the ego-integrative forces residing within each individual. One comes to recognize that under proper conditions the self is a basic factor in the formation of personality and in the determination of behavior. Clinical experience would strongly suggest that the self is, to some extent, an architect of self, and the above hypothesis simply puts this observation into psychological terms.

In support of this hypothesis it is noted in some cases that one of the concomitants of success in therapy is the realization on the part of the client that the self has the capacity for reorganization. Thus a student says:

"You know I spoke of the fact that a person's background retards one. Like the fact that my family life wasn't good for me, and my mother certainly didn't give me any of the kind of bringing up that I should have had. Well, I've been thinking that over. It's true up to a point. But when you get so that you can see the situation, then it's really up to you."

Following this statement of the relation of the self to experience many changes occurred in this young man's behavior. In this, as in other cases, it appears that when the person comes to see himself as the perceiving, organizing agent, then reorganization of perception and consequent change in patterns of reaction take place.

On the other side of the picture we have frequently observed that when the individual has been authoritatively told that he is governed by certain factors or conditions beyond his control, it makes therapy more difficult, and it is only when the individual discovers for himself that he can organize his perceptions that change is possible. In veterans who have been given their own psychiatric diagnosis, the effect is often that of making the individual feel that he is under an unalterable doom, that he is unable to control the organization of his life. When however the self sees itself as capable of reorganizing its own perceptual field, a marked change in basic confidence occurs. Miss Nam, a student, illustrates this phenomenon when she says, after having made progress in therapy:

"I think I do feel better about the future, too, because it's as if I won't be acting in darkness. It's sort of, well, knowing somewhat why I act the way I do . . . and at least it isn't the feeling that you're simply out of your own control and the fates are driving you to act that way. If you realize it, I think you can do something about it."

A veteran at the conclusion of counseling puts it more briefly and more positively: "My attitude toward myself is changed now to where I feel I *can* do something with my self and life." He has come to view himself as the instrument by which some reorganization can take place.

There is another clinical observation which may be cited in support of the general hypothesis that there is a close relationship between behavior and the way in which reality is viewed by the individual. It has been noted in many cases that behavior changes come about for the most part imperceptibly and almost automatically, once the perceptual reorganization has taken place. A young wife who has been reacting violently to her maid, and has been quite disorganized in her behavior as a result of this antipathy, says "After I . . . discovered it was nothing more than that she resembled my mother, she didn't bother me any more. Isn't that interesting? She's still the same." Here is a clear statement indicating that though the basic perceptions have not changed, they have been differently organized, have acquired a new meaning, and that behavior changes then occur. Similar evidence is given by a client, a trained psychologist, who after completing a brief series of client-centered interviews, writes:

"Another interesting aspect of the situation was in connection with the changes in some of my attitudes. When the change occurred, it was as if earlier attitudes were wiped out as completely as if erased from a blackboard. . . . When a situation which would formerly have provoked a given type of response occurred, it was not as if I was tempted to act in the way I formerly had but in some way found it easier to control my behavior. Rather the new type of behavior came quite spontaneously, and it was only through a deliberate analysis that I became aware that I was acting in a new and different way."

Here again it is of interest that the imagery is put in terms of visual perception and that as attitudes are "erased from the blackboard" behavioral changes take place automatically and without conscious effort.

Thus we have observed that appropriate changes in behavior occur when the individual acquires a different view of his world of experience, including himself; that this changed perception does not need to be dependent upon a change in the "reality," but may be a product of internal reorganization; that in some instances the awareness of the capacity for reperceiving experience accompanies this process of reorganization; that the altered behavioral responses occur automatically and without conscious effort as soon as the perceptual reorganization has taken place, apparently as a result of this.

In view of these observations a second hypothesis may be stated, which is closely related to the first. It is that *behavior is not directly influenced or determined by organic or cultural factors, but primarily,* (and perhaps only) *by the perception of these elements.* In other words the crucial element in the determination of behavior is the perceptual field of the individual. While this perceptual field is, to be sure, deeply influenced and largely shaped by cultural and physiological forces, it is nevertheless important that it appears to be only the field as it is *perceived,* which exercises a specific determining influence upon behavior. This is not a new idea in psychology, but its implications have not always been fully recognized.

It might mean, first of all, that if it is the perceptual field which determines behavior, then the primary object of study for psychologists would be the person and his world *as viewed by the person himself.* It could mean that the internal frame of reference of the person might well constitute the field of psychology, an idea set forth persuasively in a significant manuscript by Snygg and Combs (11). It might mean that the laws which govern behavior would be discovered more deeply by turning our attention to the laws which govern perception.

Now if our speculations contain a measure of truth, if the *specific* determinant of behavior is the perceptual field, and if the self can reorganize that perceptual field, then what are the limits of this process? Is the reorganization of perception capricious, or does it follow certain laws? Are there limits to the degree of reorganization? If so, what are they? In this connection we have observed with some care the perception of one portion of the field of experience, the portion we call the self.

## THE RELATION OF THE
## PERCEPTION OF THE SELF TO ADJUSTMENT

Initially we were oriented by the background of both lay and psychological thinking to regard the outcome of successful therapy as the solution of problems. If a person had a marital problem, a vocational problem, a problem of educational adjustment, the obvious purpose of counseling or therapy was to solve that problem. But as we observe and study the recorded accounts of the conclusion of therapy, it is clear that the most characteristic outcome is not necessarily solution of problems, but a freedom from tension, a different feeling about, and perception of, self. Perhaps something of this outcome may be conveyed by some illustrations.

Several statements taken from the final interview with a twenty-year-old young woman, Miss Mir, give indications of the characteristic attitude toward self, and the sense of freedom which appears to accompany it.

"I've always tried to be what the others thought I should be, but now I am wondering whether I shouldn't just see that I am what I am.

"Well, I've just noticed such a difference. I find that when I feel things, even when I feel hate, I don't care. I don't mind. I feel more free somehow. I don't feel guilty about things.

"You know it's suddenly as though a big cloud has been lifted off. I feel so much more content."

Note in these statements the willingness to perceive herself as she is, to accept herself "realistically," to perceive and accept her "bad" attitudes as well as "good" ones. This realism seems to be accompanied by a sense of freedom and contentment.

Miss Vib, whose attitudes were quoted earlier, wrote out her own feelings about counseling some six weeks after the interviews were over, and gave the statement to her counselor. She begins:

"The happiest outcome of therapy has been a new feeling about myself. As I think of it, it might be the only outcome. Certainly it is basic to all the changes in my behavior that have resulted." In discussing her experience in therapy she states, "I was coming to see myself as a whole. I began to realize that I am *one* person. This was an important insight to me. I saw that the former good academic achievement, job success, ease in social situations, and the present withdrawal, dejection, apathy and failure were all adaptive behavior, performed by *me*. This meant that I had to reorganize my feelings about myself, no longer holding to the unrealistic notion that the very good adjustment was the expression of the real "me" and this neurotic behavior was not. I came to feel that I am the same person, sometimes functioning maturely, and sometimes assuming a neurotic role in the face of what I had conceived as insurmountable problems. The acceptance of myself as one person gave me strength in the process of reorganization. Now I had a substratum, a core of unity on which to work." As she continues her discussion there are such statements as "I am getting more happiness in being myself." "I approve of myself more, and I have so much less anxiety."

As in the previous example, the outstanding aspects appear to be the realization that all of her behavior "belonged" to her, that she could accept both the good and bad features about herself and that doing so gave her a release from anxiety and a feeling of solid happiness. In both instances there is only incidental reference to the serious "problems" which had been initially discussed.

Since Miss Mir is undoubtedly above average intelligence and Miss Vib is a person with some psychological training, it may appear that such results are found only with the sophisticated individual. To counteract this opinion a quotation may be given from a statement written by a veteran of limited ability and education who had just completed counseling, and was asked to write whatever reactions he had to the experience. He says:

"As for the consoleing I have had I can say this, It really makes a man strip his own mind bare, and when he does he knows then what he realy is and what he can do. Or at least thinks he knows himself party well. As for myself, I know that my ideas were a little too big for what I realy am, but now I realize one must try start out at his own level.

"Now after four visits, I have a much clearer picture of myself and my future. It makes me feel a little depressed and disappointed, but on the other hand, it has taken me out of the dark, the load seems a lot lighter now, that is I can see my way now, I know what I want to do, I know about what I can do, so now that I can see my goal, I will be able to work a whole lot easyer, at my own level."

Although the expression is much simpler, one notes again the same two elements—the acceptance of self as it is, and the feeling of easiness, of lightened burden, which accompanies it.

As we examine many individual case records and case recordings, it appears to be possible to bring together the findings in regard to successful therapy by stating another hypothesis in regard to that portion of the perceptual field which we call the self. It would appear that *when all of the ways in which the individual perceives himself—all perceptions of the qualities,*

*abilities, impulses, and attitudes of the person, and all percep-*
*tions of himself in relation to others—are accepted into the*
*organized conscious concept of the self, then this achievement is*
*accompanied by feelings of comfort and freedom from tension*
*which are experienced as psychological adjustment.*

This hypothesis would seem to account for the observed fact
that the comfortable perception of self which is achieved is
sometimes more positive than before, sometimes more negative.
When the individual permits all his perceptions of himself to
be organized into one pattern, the picture is sometimes more
flattering than he has held in the past, sometimes less flattering.
It is always more comfortable.

It may be pointed out also that this tentative hypothesis sup-
plies an operational type of definition, based on the client's
internal frame of reference, for such hitherto vague terms as
"adjustment," "integration," and "acceptance of self." They
are defined in terms of perception, in a way which it should be
possible to prove or disprove. When all of the organic perceptual experiences—the experiencing of attitudes, impulses,
abilities and disabilities, the experiencing of others and of
"reality"—when all of these perceptions are freely assimilated
into an organized and consistent system, available to consciousness, then psychological adjustment or integration might be said
to exist. The definition of adjustment is thus made an internal
affair, rather than dependent upon an external "reality."

Something of what is meant by this acceptance and assimilation of perceptions about the self may be illustrated from the
case of Miss Nam, a student. Like many other clients she gives
evidence of having experienced attitudes and feelings which
are defensively denied because they are not consistent with the
concept or picture she holds of herself. The way in which they
are first fully admitted into consciousness, and then organized
into a unified system may be shown by excerpts from the re-

corded interviews. She has spoken of the difficulty she has had in bringing herself to write papers for her university courses.

"I just thought of something else which perhaps hinders me, and that is that again it's two different feelings. When I have to sit down and do (a paper), though I have a lot of ideas, underneath I think I always have the feeling that I just can't do it. . . . I have this feeling of being terrifically confident that I can do something, without being willing to put the work into it. At other times I'm practically afraid of what I have to do. . . ."

Note that the conscious self has been organized as "having a lot of ideas," being "terrifically confident," but that "underneath," in other words not freely admitted into consciousness, has been the experience of feeling "I just can't do it." She continues:

"I'm trying to work through this funny relationship between this terrific confidence and then this almost fear of doing anything . . . and I think the kind of feeling that I can really do things is part of an illusion I have about myself of being, in my imagination, sure that it will be something good and very good and all that, but whenever I get down to the actual task of getting started, it's a terrible feeling of—well, incapacity, that I won't get it done either the way I want to do it, or even not being sure how I want to do it."

Again the picture of herself which is present in consciousness is that of a person who is "very good," but this picture is entirely out of line with actual organic experience in the situation.

Later in the same interview she expresses very well the fact that her perceptions are not all organized into one consistent conscious self.

"I'm not sure about what kind of a person I am—well, I realize that all of these are a part of me, but I'm not quite sure of how to make all of these things fall in line."

In the next interview we have an excellent opportunity to observe the organization of both of these conflicting perceptions into one pattern, with the resultant sense of freedom from tension which has been described above.

"It's very funny, even as I sit here I realize that I have more confidence in myself, in the sense that when I used to approach new situations I would have two very funny things operating at the same time. I had a fantasy that I could do anything, which was a fantasy which covered over all these other feelings that I really couldn't do it, or couldn't do it as well as I wanted to, and it's as if now those two things have merged together, and it is more real, that a situation isn't either testing myself or proving something to myself or anyone else. It's just in terms of doing it. And I think I have done away both with that fantasy and that fear. . . . So I think I can go ahead and approach things—well, just sensibly."

No longer is it necessary for this client to "cover over" her real experiences. Instead the picture of herself as very able, and the experienced feeling of complete inability, have now been brought together into one integrated pattern of self as a person with real, but imperfect abilities. Once the self is thus accepted the inner energies making for self-actualization are released and she attacks her life problems more efficiently.

Observing this type of material frequently in counseling experience would lead to a tentative hypothesis of maladjustment, which like the other hypothesis suggested, focuses on the perception of self. It might be proposed that the tensions called psychological maladjustment exist when the organized concept of self (conscious or available to conscious awareness) is not in accord with the perceptions actually experienced.

This discrepancy between the concept of self and the actual perceptions seems to be explicable only in terms of the fact that the self concept resists assimilating into itself any percept which is inconsistent with its present organization. The feeling that she may not have the ability to do a paper is inconsistent with Miss Nam's conscious picture of herself as a very able and confident person, and hence, though fleetingly perceived, is denied organization as a part of her self, until this comes about in therapy.

## THE CONDITIONS OF CHANGE OF SELF PERCEPTION

If the way in which the self is perceived has as close and significant a relationship to behavior as has been suggested, then the manner in which this perception may be altered becomes a question of importance. If a reorganization of self perceptions brings a change in behavior; if adjustment and maladjustment depend on the congruence between perceptions as experienced and the self as perceived, then the factors which permit a reorganization of the perception of self are significant.

Our observations of psychotherapeutic experience would seem to indicate that absence of any threat to the self concept is an important item in the problem. Normally the self resists incorporating into itself those experiences which are inconsistent with the functioning of self. But a point overlooked by Lecky and others is that when the self is free from any threat of attack or likelihood of attack, then it is possible for the self to consider these hitherto rejected perceptions, to make new differentiations, and to reintegrate the self in such a way as to include them.

An illustration from the case of Miss Vib may serve to clarify this point. In her statement written six weeks after the conclusion of counseling Miss Vib thus describes the way in which unacceptable percepts become incorporated into the self. She writes:

"In the earlier interviews I kept saying such things as, 'I am not acting like myself', 'I never acted this way before.' What I meant was that this withdrawn, untidy, and apathetic person was not myself. Then I began to realize that I was the same person, seriously withdrawn, etc. now, as I had been before. That did not happen until after I had talked out my self-rejection, shame, despair, and doubt, in the accepting situation of the interview. The counselor was not startled or shocked. I was telling him all these things about myself which did not fit into my picture of a graduate student, a teacher, a sound person. He responded with complete acceptance and warm interest without heavy emotional overtones. Here was a sane, intelligent person wholeheartedly accepting this behavior that seemed so shameful to me. I can remember an organic feeling of relaxation. I did not have to keep up the struggle to cover up and hide this shameful person."

Note how clearly one can see here the whole range of denied perceptions of self, and the fact that they could be considered as a part of self only in a social situation which involved no threat to the self, in which another person, the counselor, becomes almost an alternate self and looks with understanding and acceptance upon these same perceptions. She continues:

"Retrospectively, it seems to me that what I felt as 'warm acceptance without emotional overtones' was what I needed to work through my difficulties. . . . The counselor's impersonality with interest allowed me to talk out my feelings. The clarification in the interview situation presented the attitude to me as a 'ding an sich' which I could look at, manipulate, and put in place. In organizing my attitudes, I was beginning to organize me."

Here the nature of the exploration of experience, of seeing it as experience and not as threat to self, enables the client to reorganize her perceptions of self, which she says was also "reorganizing me."

If we attempt to describe in more conventional psychological terms the nature of the process which culminates in an altered organization and integration of self in the process of therapy it might run as follows. The individual is continually endeavoring to meet his needs by reacting to the field of experience as he perceives it, and to do that more efficiently by differentiating elements of the field and reintegrating them into new patterns. Reorganization of the field may involve the reorganization of the self as well as of other parts of the field. The self, however, resists reorganization and change. In everyday life individual adjustment by means of reorganization of the field exclusive of the self is more common and is less threatening to the individual. Consequently, the individual's first mode of adjustment is the reorganization of that part of the field which does not include the self.

Client-centered therapy is different from other life situations inasmuch as the therapist tends to remove from the individual's immediate world all those aspects of the field which the individual can reorganize except the self. The therapist, by reacting to the client's feelings and attitudes rather than to the objects of his feelings and attitudes, assists the client in bringing from background into focus his own self, making it easier than ever before for the client to perceive and react to the self. By offering only understanding and no trace of evaluation, the therapist removes himself as an object of attitudes, becoming only an alternate expression of the client's self. The therapist by providing a consistent atmosphere of permissiveness and understanding removes whatever threat existed to prevent all perceptions of the self from emerging into figure. Hence in this situation all the ways in which the self has been experienced can be viewed openly, and organized into a complex unity.

It is then this complete absence of any factor which would attack the concept of self, and second, the assistance in focusing upon the perception of self, which seems to permit a more differentiated view of self and finally the reorganization of self.

## RELATIONSHIP TO CURRENT PSYCHOLOGICAL THINKING

Up to this point, these remarks have been presented as clinical observations and tentative hypotheses, quite apart from any relationship to past or present thinking in the field of psychology. This has been intentional. It is felt that it is the function of the clinician to try to observe, with an open-minded attitude, the complexity of material which comes to him, to report his observations, and in the light of this to formulate hypotheses and problems which both the clinic and the laboratory may utilize as a basis for study and research.

Yet, though these are clinical observations and hypotheses, they have, as has doubtless been recognized, a relationship to some of the currents of theoretical and laboratory thinking in psychology. Some of the observations about the self bear a relationship to the thinking of G. H. Mead (7) about the "I" and the "me." The outcome of therapy might be described in Mead's terms as the increasing awareness of the "I," and the organization of the "me's" by the "I." The importance which has been given in this paper to the self as an organizer of experience and to some extent as an architect of self, bears a relationship to the thinking of Allport (1) and others concerning the increased place which we must give to the integrative function of the ego.

In the stress which has been given to the present field of experience as the determinant of behavior, the relationship to Gestalt psychology, and to the work of Lewin (6) and his students is obvious. The theories of Angyal, (2) find some parallel in our observations. His view that the self represents only a small part of the biological organism which has reached symbolic elaboration, and that it often attempts the direction of the organism on the basis of unreliable and insufficient information, seems to be particularly related to the observations we have made.

Lecky's posthumous book (4), small in size but large in the significance of its contribution, has brought a new light on the way in which the self operates, and the principle of consistency by which new experience is included in or excluded from the self. Much of his thinking runs parallel to our observations. Snygg and Combs (11) have recently attempted a more radical and more complete emphasis upon the internal world of perception as the basis for all psychology, a statement which has helped to formulate a theory in which our observations fit.

It is not only from the realm of theory but also from the experimental laboratory that one finds confirmation of the line of thinking which has been proposed. Tolman (12) has stressed the need of thinking as a rat if fruitful experimental work is to be done. The work of Snygg (10) indicates that rat behavior may be better predicted by inferring the rat's field of perception than by viewing him as an object. Krech (Krechevsky, 3) showed in a brilliant study some years ago that rat learning can only be understood if we realize that the rat is consistently acting upon one hypothesis after another. Leeper (5) has summarized the evidence from a number of experimental investigations, showing that animal behavior cannot be explained by simple S-R mechanisms, but only by recognizing that complex internal processes of perceptual organization intervene between the stimulus and the behavioral response.

Thus there are parallel streams of clinical observation, theoretical thinking, and laboratory experiment, which all point up the fact that for an effective psychology we need a much more complete understanding of the private world of the individual, and need to learn ways of entering and studying that world from within.

## IMPLICATIONS

It would be misleading however if I left you with the impression that the hypotheses I have formulated in this paper, or those springing from the parallel psychological studies I have mentioned, are simply extensions of the main stream of psychological thinking, additional bricks in the edifice of psychological thought. We have discovered with some surprise that our clinical observations, and the tentative hypotheses which seem to grow out of them, raise disturbing questions which appear to cast doubt on the very foundations of many of our psychological endeavors, particularly in the fields of clinical psychology and personality study. To clarify what is meant, I should like to restate in more logical order the formulations I have given, and to leave with you certain questions and problems which each one seems to raise.

If we take first the tentative proposition that the specific determinant of behavior is the perceptual field of the individual, would this not lead, if regarded as a working hypothesis, to a radically different approach in clinical psychology and personality research? It would seem to mean that instead of elaborate case histories full of information about the person as an object, we would endeavor to develop ways of seeing his situation, his past, and himself, as these objects appear to him. We would try to see with him, rather than to evaluate him. It might mean the minimizing of the elaborate psychometric procedures by which we have endeavored to measure or value the individual from our own frame of reference. It might mean the minimizing or discarding of all the vast series of labels which we have painstakingly built up over the years. Paranoid, preschizophrenic, compulsive, constricted—terms such as these might become irrelevant because they are all based in thinking which takes an external frame of reference. They are not the ways in which the individual experiences himself. If we consistently studied each individual from the internal frame of reference of that individual, from within his own perceptual field, it seems probable that we should find generalizations which could be made, and principles which were operative, but we may be very sure that they would be of a different order from these externally based judgments *about* individuals.

Let us look at another of the suggested propositions. If we took seriously the hypothesis that integration and adjustment are internal conditions related to the degree of acceptance or nonacceptance of all perceptions, and the degree of organization of these perceptions into one consistent system, this would decidedly affect our clinical procedures. It would seem to imply the abandonment of the notion that adjustment is dependent upon the pleasantness or unpleasantness of the environment, and would demand concentration upon those processes which bring about self-integration within the person. It would mean a minimizing or an abandoning of those clinical procedures which utilize the alteration of environmental forces as a method of treatment. It would rely instead upon the fact that the person who is internally unified has the greatest likelihood of meeting environmental problems constructively, either as an individual or in cooperation with others.

If we take the remaining proposition that the self, under proper conditions, is capable of reorganizing, to some extent, its own perceptual field, and of thus altering behavior, this too seems to raise disturbing questions. Following the path of this hypothesis would appear to mean a shift in emphasis in psychology from focusing upon the fixity of personality attributes and psychological abilities, to the alterability of these same characteristics. It would concentrate attention upon process rather than upon fixed status. Whereas psychology has, in personality study, been concerned primarily with the measurement of the fixed qualities of the individual, and with his past in order to explain his present, the hypothesis here suggested would seem to concern itself much more with the personal world of the present in order to understand the future, and in predicting that future would be concerned with the principles by which personality and behavior are altered, as well as the extent to which they remain fixed.

Thus we find that a clinical approach, client-centered therapy, has led us to try to adopt the client's perceptual field as the basis for genuine understanding. In trying to enter this internal world of perception, not by introspection, but by observation and direct inference, we find ourselves in a new vantage point for understanding personality dynamics, a vantage point which opens up some disturbing vistas. We find that behavior seems to be better understood as a reaction to this reality-as-perceived. We discover that the way in which the person sees himself, and the perceptions he dares not take as belonging to himself, seem to have an important relationship to the inner peace which constitutes adjustment. We discover within the person, under certain conditions, a capacity for the restructuring and the reorganization of self, and consequently the reorganization of behavior, which has profound social implications. We see these observations, and the theoretical formulations which they inspire, as a fruitful new approach for study and research in various fields of psychology.

## REFERENCES

1. Allport, G. W. The ego in contemporary psychology. *Psychol. Rev.*, 1943, **50**, 451–478.
2. Angyal, A. *Foundations for a science of personality.* New York: Commonwealth Fund, 1941.
3. Krechevsky, I. Hypotheses in rats. *Psychol. Rev.*, 1932, **39**, 516–532.
4. Lecky, P. *Self-consistency: a theory of personality.* New York: Island Press, 1945.
5. Leeper, R. The experimental psychologists as reluctant dragons. Paper presented at APA meeting, September 1946.
6. Lewin, K. *A dynamic theory of personality.* New York: McGraw-Hill, 1935.
7. Mead, G. H. *Mind, self, and society.* Chicago: Univ. Chicago Press, 1934.
8. Rogers, C. R. Significant aspects of client-centered therapy. *Amer. Psychologist*, 1946, **1**, 415–422.
9. Snyder, W. U. "Warmth" in nondirective counseling. *J. abnorm. soc. Psychol.*, 1946, **41**, 491–495.

10. Snygg, D. Mazes in which rats take the longer path to food. *J. Psychol.*, 1936, **1**, 153–166.

11. Snygg, D., & Combs, A. W. *Individual behavior.* New York: Harper, 1949.

12. Tolman, E. C. The determiners of behavior at a choice point. *Psychol. Rev.*, 1938, **45**, 1–41.

........................................................................................

# CHAPTER 4

# Self-Reference in Counseling Interviews

## BY VICTOR RAIMY

Successful counseling or psychotherapy implies that changes take place in the personality of the client or patient. The problem of the psychologist who seeks to analyze conscious, deliberate attempts to alter behavior in a clinical situation, lies essentially in determining specifically what changes take place during treatment and what conditions are necessary to produce them. Many things have been suggested as "essential changes" but so far there is almost a complete dearth of reliable evidence, aside from clinical interpretations, to bolster the constructs which have been advanced. Among the terms in common use which supposedly define such changes are release of feelings or tensions, emotional re-education, making the unconscious conscious, modifying responses, reorganization or reintegration of personality, modification of goals or pathways to goals, etc.

Such terms are so schematic, so indefinite or so circular that

From the *Journal of Consulting Psychology,* 1948, **12,** 153–163. Reprinted by permission of the author and the publisher. A condensation of a Ph.D. thesis at the Ohio State University in 1943.

the very existence of the psychological events to which they refer cannot be determined by objective measures or else *every event considered fits the theory*. Changes in "needs" or in "attitudes" or in "traits" have also been suggested as occurring in therapeutic situations as well as in normal personality development. So far there has been little systematic application of these concepts to the artificially induced changes occurring during treatment. As for trait constructs, in clinical work these have usually been applied to manifestations of ability or capacity which the counselor is more interested in unmasking than in modifying.

It becomes imperative to search for constructs which can be investigated with the usual safeguards of objectivity and reliability. When and where to apply available and plausible measures is at present a matter of feasibility rather than desirability. The methods of measurement are crude and time consuming. Clinicians are usually unwilling to disturb both their own delicate methods of treatment as well as the precarious balance achieved by the individuals treated. The application of measuring methods has been a matter of catch-as-catch-can, although recent developments in the use of recording equipment open a new field for the analysis of hitherto unobtainable data within which may be found some of the essential clues. Unfortunately, techniques for analyzing verbatim interview material are in their infancy.

Most certainly, the events taking place in the counseling interview are the events which furnish a very logical focus and locus of investigation. It is equally certain that even verbatim recordings furnish only selected portions of the interview events. Such recordings contain only the remarks of the counselor and the client's verbalizations, most of which are concerned with himself and his relations to other people. How can one abstract from such material clues which are relevant to the basic problem of how personality undergoes change?

## THE SELF CONCEPT AND PERSONALITY ORGANIZATION

Perhaps in the search for dominant factors in personality the obvious has been too long neglected because it is obvious and therefore deemed unworthy of attention. In our sophisticated intercourse with personality dimensions which require for their comprehension a neologism, a factor analysis or a re-redefinition, it is only too easy to neglect in the laboratory much of the wisdom we use in the parlor or office.

What a person *believes about himself* is a generally accepted factor in the social comprehension of others. Peculiar or just different behavior in our associates can frequently be understood by clichés such as "He has an inferiority complex" or "She is conceited." In such thumb-nail analyses we are referring to a description of himself which the person referred to has apparently accepted and acts upon. The analysis, if accurate, is useful in understanding others even when we are ignorant of the historical development of the self-belief, as is usually the case.

In the present study, the Self Concept theory postulates that a person's notion of himself is an involved, complex and *significant* factor in his behavior. One can build a systematic theory of personality organization which neglects neither historical nor physiological events yet depends essentially on the data of immediate experience. Briefly, the Self Concept theory (or the Body-Schema of Schilder or the Ego of Koffka) predicates that each individual's perception of himself is of ultimate psychological significance in organized behavior. The person in his biological, social, and historical setting is the concrete object of self-perception. The Self Concept is the more or less organized perceptual object resulting from present and past self-observation. Self-perception is a process which is more than activation of internal or distance receptors. In agreement with text-book definitions, there is in self-perception an organization which involves memorial and situational factors as well as the sense data themselves.

To oversimplify the theoretical position, one can say that we perceive ourselves just as we perceive a chair or another person. *What* we perceive in ourselves (the Self Concept) may have only partial correspondence with what other people perceive in us or the so-called objective personality. Yet, as always, we behave in accordance with our own perceptions even though the opinions of others or the urgencies of our biological make-up interact to influence our perceptions of ourselves. Our general behavior, then, is to a large extent regulated and organized by what we perceive ourselves to be just as behavior toward a chair is regulated by our perception of a given chair. When tired we observe what appears to be a rickety antique and walk away in search of something more substantial quite unaware that the wary hostess has introduced reinforcements at the joints. In the same way, we may perceive ourselves to be fatigued and spend hours resting when the physiological facts may or may not be in agreement with our self-perception.

How can Self Concept theory be applied to those changes which take place in personality during counseling and psychotherapy? It is exceedingly difficult to obtain objective and meaningful data from the verbalizations which are the raw material of immediate experience. Some studies of content changes before and after counseling have been made by the writer but these are fragmentary approaches. The method chosen in the present study postulates that self-approval and self-disapproval represent two ends of a continuum which may be viewed as one of the major dimensions of the Self Concept. McDougall's "sentiment of self-regard" obviously refers to this fact: that persons make self-evaluations. He says (4, p. 428) concerning the ubiquity of this sentiment:

And the conative dispositions of the system, being brought into play so frequently, by every social contact whether actual or imagined, become delicately responsive in an extraordinary degree, as well as very strong through much exercise.

This study was therefore directed toward simple quantitative analysis of changes in self-approval displayed by college student clients. Fourteen complete series of counseling interviews were analyzed.

The basic postulations of the study were as follows. The Self Concept is the map which each person consults in order to understand himself, especially during moments of crisis or choice. The approval, disapproval, or ambivalence he "feels" for the Self Concept or some of its sub-systems is related to his personal adjustment. A heavy weighting of disapproval or ambivalence suggests a maladjusted individual since maladjustment in a psychological sense inevitably implies distress or disturbance in connection with oneself. When successful personality reorganization takes place in a maladjusted individual we may also expect a shift from self-disapproval to a positive or self-approving balance. The adjusted individual may dislike or disapprove of certain aspects of the Self Concept but in general he finds himself to be attractive and desirable. The studies of self-ratings, presumably carried out on unselected populations, corroborate the final postulation. Allport summarizes (1, p. 444), "In self-ratings there is a tendency to overestimate those qualities considered desirable and to underestimate those considered undesirable."

The present study was limited by the small number of completely recorded counseling cases available. Despite this limitation, other investigators have used similar methods and emerged with fruitful hypotheses if not completely defensible conclusions. These studies, beginning with Porter's (5) highly original exploitation of the checklist method with interviews, are carefully reviewed in Curran's recent book (3).

## THE METHOD OF CLASSIFYING SELF-REFERENCES

In order to quantify the verbalized changes in self-approval taking place during counseling, a six-category checklist was devised to permit classification of all client utterances. Reproduced below is a summary of the method used to classify verbatim transcripts of 14 completely recorded counseling cases. The summary is an abridged form of a six-page set of instructions given to four judges who participated in determination of reliability.

### Summary of Directions for Classifying Self-References

*Purpose:* To classify the responses of clients in counseling interviews into categories based on the client's attitude toward himself. It is hoped that this procedure will be useful as a means of showing changes in the client during the course of counseling.

*Definition of Self-References:* A Self-Reference (SR) is a group of words spoken by the client which directly or indirectly describes him as he appears in his own eyes. In a counseling interview the client is usually discussing himself and his reactions. Responses of the client which are not self-references are called External References or "Other" and are symbolized as "O."

*The Unit is the Client's Complete Response:* A complete response consists of all words spoken by the client between two responses of the counselor. Each numbered response of the client in the typescript is to be classified for its self-reference evaluation or lack of self-reference. For purposes of brevity, the self-evaluating aspect of the response is referred to as its "value," which is simply the positive or negative attitude toward self manifest in the response.

*The Task of the Judge:* 1. Read through the complete interview or portion of an interview to familiarize yourself with the general content of the material and the manner of speaking of the client and counselor. 2. Starting with the first numbered client response, decide whether it is a self-reference or external reference. 3. If it is an SR, classify it in one of the categories described below. 4. The decision as to the meaning intended by the client in a particular response should rest upon a commonsense deduction and should not be a tenuous theoretical deduction based upon a series of inferences.

*The Six Categories:*

P . . . . Positive SR indicating a positive or favoring attitude toward self.

N . . . . Negative SR indicating a negative or disapproving attitude toward self.

Av. . . . Ambivalent SR in which there is a clear conflict between the positive and negative attitudes toward self in the same response.

A . . . . Ambiguous SR in which some self-reference is manifest but either the value is too vague to be classified or the response lacks value altogether.

O . . . . Other or External Reference in which the client himself is not implicated.

Q . . . . A nonrhetorical question in which the client is actually asking for information. If a question is only part of a complete response, the question is ignored in the classification.

## SOME PROBLEMS INVOLVED IN THE METHOD

Finding units in oral material is no less difficult than finding the units of any psychological event. The arbitrary definition of the unit in this study as all words spoken by the client between two utterances of the counselor provides objectivity and avoids the fractionation which so often obscures meaning. It is possible that some of the client responses treated as units may be fragments of units or may be multiple units. While the unit of self-reference may be patently nonunitary in some instances, it is defined objectively and repetition of the procedure becomes possible.

A further problem is found in the assumptions underlying the use of a method which simply summates the responses in each category for a complete interview. Why should one expect to obtain an accurate indication of a client's attitude toward himself by such a procedure? Logic would predict that certain factors in the interview situation such as reactions to the counselor, defensiveness, etc. would result in distortions of the true attitudes. It is believed that distorting factors are present and do operate particularly during early stages of contact. It needs little imagination to envisage the clumsy or ardent interview forcing a client into defensive or angry self-description. When, however, the counselor aims skillfully at obtaining free expression by the client, there is reason to suspect that the resulting responses will bear a considerable resemblance to the picture which the client perceives.

The use of simple summation as a method of analysis is crude and liable to a variety of distorting factors. The problem thus becomes one of validity. One can theorize that an individual will reveal himself by the quantity of his self-references as well as in the quality of any selected individual response. Perhaps the frequency with which a person returns to a given topic indicates the concern or importance that topic has for him. Concretely, if a person thoroughly approves of himself we should expect to find very few if any statements of self-depreciation in free conversation. (Stylistic phrases intended to insure modesty are not difficult to identify.) Present-day measures of personality, projective or nonprojective, utilize such a frequency principle in one form or another.

## THE RELIABILITY AND OBJECTIVITY OF THE METHOD

Two determinations of reliability were made. The writer classified two complete cases totalling 874 client responses in 13 verbatim interviews.[1] Six months later he reclassified the same material without referring to the earlier classification. A frequency count of the number of times that the same response was

[1] Both cases have been published in toto and can be found in references (6) and (7).

reclassified in the same category revealed 80.8% identical classification for the 874 client responses. The results of similar
analysis by particular categories are shown in Table I. Thus of

TABLE I.   Percent of Agreement When 874 Responses Were Reclassified
After a 6-Month Interval by One Judge

|  | Category | | | | | |
| --- | --- | --- | --- | --- | --- | --- |
|  | P | N | Av | A | O | Q |
| % Agreement | 72.9 | 76.8 | 47.5 | 61.9 | 64.5 | 87.2 |

the three significant categories, positive and negative self-
references were identified with much more certainty than were
ambivalent responses.

An interview-by-interview chi-square analysis of the differences between the two classifications by the writer indicated
that probably all such differences in category totals could be attributed to chance factors. Chi-square values for the differences
were all less than those required at the .05 level.

The same methods of studying reliability were used with the
data obtained from four judges all of whom classified the same
four selected interviews. All judges were graduate students in
clinical psychology who were given detailed written instructions
plus a one-hour conference period before they independently
classified all client responses in the four interviews. The four
interviews were selected as follows: two were believed easy and
two were believed hard to classify; two were from successful
cases, two from unsuccessful; three were from cases counseled
somewhat nondirectively, one from a case of very directive counseling; two were first interviews, one was a second contact, one
was a fourth and penultimate interview; two of the interviews
were conducted by the same counselor. A total of 356 client
responses were classified by the four judges.

Analysis of the classification by the four judges revealed

results very similar to those obtained by the writer with a six-month interval between classifications. With agreement between three of the four judges as a criterion, 81.8% of all client responses were classified "correctly" by three of the four judges. As in the analysis of particular categories by the writer, the judges found P and N responses fairly easy to detect while Av was more difficult to detect with certainty. Table II presents the percentage results for each category. Chi-square analysis of the

TABLE II.  Percent of Agreement (3 of 4 Judges) When 356 Client
Responses Were Classified by Four Judges

|  | Category | | | | | |
|---|---|---|---|---|---|---|
|  | P | N | Av | A | O | Q |
| % Agreement | 62.6 | 82.0 | 50.5 | 75.0 | 63.7 | 81.0 |

differences between judges for each of the four interviews revealed that for one of the interviews chi-square had a value greater than that required at the .05 level indicating that there is much probability that for one of the four interviews the difference between judges is no accident.

While complete agreement on classification of responses was neither expected nor obtained, the reliability studies indicate that the method can be applied to verbatim responses of clients with considerable hope of gaining an objective picture of changes taking place in verbalized self-references.

## VALIDITY OF THE METHOD

The results of two long cases were compared with the independent analyses of the same cases by their respective counselors. In his published account of the case of "Herbert Bryan," Rogers (6) lists at the end of each verbatim interview "the outstanding attitudes which have been spontaneously expressed" by the client. He also gives brief subjective descriptions of what happened during the interview. The "outstanding attitudes expressed" apparently were selected without reference to such a notion as the Self Concept or self-approving attitudes as defined in this study. His list of attitudes were classified according to the present method and the results compared with the results obtained by classifying the verbatim material for the eight interviews of the case. Some differences were found, but in general a high degree of correspondence was noted. Table III illustrates

TABLE III.   Comparison of Results of Applying the Method to Rogers'
"Outstanding Attitudes" of Interview 2 (Bryan) with
the Method Applied to Verbatim Interview

|              | Total Items | %P | %N | %Av | Total % |
|--------------|-------------|------|------|------|---------|
| Rogers' list | 15 | 20.0 | 73.5 | 6.5 | 100.0 |
| Verbatim     | 43 | 16.2 | 69.8 | 14.0 | 100.0 |

the correspondence found in a typical interview. Chi-square was applied to the differences obtained by the two methods for each interview. The Probability (from Fisher's Table of P) was found to lie between .80 and .90 indicating that the differences were primarily due to chance.

The second attempt to ascertain validity was a comparison of results for seven interviews of the case of "Alfred" with the results of a different method of interview analysis made by the counselor, Father Charles Curran, and reported completely in his book (3). The results of this comparison revealed that in the seven interviews analyzed by both methods, where marked changes in an interview were revealed by one method, similar marked shifts in results were obtained by the other method.

When such attempts to *seek* validity for a method of analysis are attempted, one cannot expect to emerge with hard and fast conclusions. Nonetheless, the results of the comparisons are sufficiently encouraging to indicate that a quantitative analysis of client statements contains distinct possibilities for unraveling the complexities of basic personality dimensions. Curran's (3) intensive analysis of a single counseling case and Baldwin's (2) approach to the same problem using personal documents reveal the tedious but fruitful possibilities of the quantitative approach to verbatim verbal output.

## APPLICATION OF THE METHOD TO 14 CASES

In order to explore the possibilities of the method, all responses in all interviews of 14 selected and completed counseling cases were classified by the writer. The clients were primarily referrals to a psychological clinic conducted for college students. The number of interviews ranged between two and 21 per case, the median being seven interviews. The criteria of selection were as follows:

1. All should involve primarily the counseling of students with personal problems rather than cases originating in vocational or educational problems.

2. Different counselors should be represented. (There were 11 different counselors.)

3. Some should represent nondirective, others should represent directive counseling. (This criterion was met as only three were nondirective, one was clearly directive, and the remainder represented blends of the two methods.)

4. Unsuccessful as well as successful cases should be included. (See below.)

5. Verbatim recordings should be available for all interviews of all cases. (This criterion was approached closely although 24 of the 111 interviews were recorded by counselor notes, some of which were condensations with an unknown number of client words omitted.)

6. Each case should contain all interviews held between first and last contact. (Only one interview in a case of eight contacts was unobtainable. One half of another interview was lacking because of recording difficulties.)

The judgment of "success of the counseling" was made prior to the development of the method of analysis and was based upon clinical appraisal by the counselor involved, the professor of clinical psychology under whose direction most of the cases had been counseled, and the writer. Some follow-up data was available for four of the group judged successful and for three of the group judged unsuccessful. The criteria of success included reports of actually changed behavior and social relationships where follow-up was available as well as client expressions of satisfaction with the counseling at the conclusion of contact. Included in the successful group were several clients who referred friends or relatives to the same counselor although this was not used as a criterion of successful counseling. For the unsuccessful group, judgment was based upon follow-up data showing presence of the same problem, failure to return for another interview, and obvious dissatisfaction with the progress of counseling during the final interview. Two cases represented questionable successes, leaving five unsuccessful cases and seven judged successful.

## RESULTS OF THE METHOD APPLIED TO 14 CASES

In view of the small number of cases available for analysis, conclusions resulting from the application of the method must be regarded as tentative. Elaborate statistics were avoided since there were only five unsuccessful cases and seven clearly successful cases. Nonetheless, all results obtained seemed to fit the original hypothesis that in successful counseling cases there is a shift in self-evaluation from an original preponderance of disapproval to a preponderance of self-approval at the end of counseling. In unsuccessful cases such a shift was not found.

One of the most striking indications of this finding is obtained by examining the graphs constructed for each case based upon the interview-by-interview plotting of the relative frequency of the responses classified in the P, N, and Av categories. Percentages rather than raw scores were used in order to eliminate fluctuations due to the total number of responses varying from interview to interview. Only two illustrative graphs are presented here:

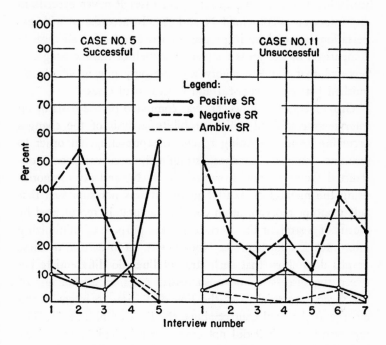

The principal characteristics of successful and unsuccessful cases are exemplified above. The progression of percent P shows a decline from the first to the second interview in both successful and unsuccessful cases, while percent N tends to rise in both groups. This inverse relationship can probably be explained in terms of the dropping away of some of the client's initial defensiveness. As contacts continue, there are wide fluctuations in both percent P and percent N with P tending to rise and N to decline. Percent of ambivalence rises for both groups (probably indicating increased uncertainty) but disappears, in the successful cases only, near the end of the counseling.

Concluding contacts show P rising to almost 100 percent in the final interview in the success group, while N declines to the vanishing point. In the unsuccessful cases P never exceeds in any interview a combined N and Av. In accordance with expectations aroused by inspection of the graphs for all cases, a comparison of the gross frequency of each of the six categories revealed that the P category was the only one which distinguished between successful and unsuccessful cases.

Gross frequency, however, was computed on the basis of all interviews combined which prohibits analysis of the changes occurring from beginning to end of counseling. In order to examine temporal changes, straight line curves were constructed from the raw scores of the P, N, and Av categories using the method of Least Squares. It was not supposed that Self Concept reorganization could be accurately represented by means of a straight line derived for the purpose of minimizing inter-interview fluctuations. Nonetheless, an inspection of these graphs does show that such straight lines do differentiate between the successful and unsuccessful cases. In all but one of the seven successful cases the line of P rises to intersect and emerge at the final contact above the lines of N and Av. The one case in which P did not cross above N had 21 interviews in which the personal problems seemed to be solved at the 11th interview and the counseling from then on resembled a student-faculty member relationship. In *none* of the five unsuccessful cases did the straight line of P cross above or even rise to meet the N and Av lines.

Despite the apparent differences between the two groups, no statistical reliability for the slopes of any curve in either group was found when Fisher's "t" was applied as a test of significance and .05 was made the fiducial limit. A trend toward reliability was found in the successful cases which was not approached by the unsuccessful group. Thus we are dealing with trends and since there are few grounds for believing that the change in self-approval can be represented by a straight line function, the statistical measures used may obscure rather than clarify the facts.

A further study was made of longitudinal changes in each case by cumulating raw scores of P and dividing by cumulated N at the end of each interview. Inspection of these quotients after graphing them revealed that the .50 level was reached by all of the successful cases by the end of counseling. (One case in this group had a final ratio of .49). Of the unsuccessful groups, one case showed an initial ratio starting *above* the .50 level, never dropping to that level in four interviews. This client, interestingly enough, was the only one in the group of 14 who expressed any resentment against initiating counseling and was the only one who would be considered a nonvoluntary referral. Of the other four unsuccessful cases, only one had a ratio as high as .33 at any time.

The finding that in successful cases cumulative P divided by cumulative N reaches the .50 level by the end of counseling (which is not approached by any of the unsuccessful cases) seems to be artifactual insofar as its usefulness for prediction is concerned. There is no plausible reason to believe that before a case is successfully concluded the client must express at least half as many positive self-references as negative self-references. Nonetheless, the technique of the cumulative ratio opens interesting possibilities for further analysis of data obtained by this method.

Another index, called the "Av ratio," was computed by finding the percentage which the Ambivalent category forms of the total of the three significant categories, P, N, and Av. Analysis of this ratio for each case indicates that it may differentiate between clients who are seriously concerned about themselves and enter counseling under considerable tension from clients manifesting less personal disturbance. The hypothesis was generally upheld when the cases were ranked subjectively but there were inconsistencies in the middle range.

## DISCUSSION

The principal findings can be summarized very simply. At the beginning of counseling the clients disapproved of and had ambivalent attitudes toward themselves. As counseling progressed fluctuations in approval occurred with mounting ambivalence. At the conclusion of counseling the *successful* cases showed a vast predominance of self-approval; the *unsuccessful* cases showed a vast predominance of self-disapproval and ambivalence. There is nothing startling about such conclusions and it is doubtful if anyone experienced in counseling would seriously deny that considerably increased "self-respect" is observed in the client who has been successfully "treated." The significance of the finding that changes in "self-respect" can be objectively followed during counseling becomes a crucial matter. A devotee of "dynamic tensions" might be justified in regarding the present findings as superfluous if not amusing. Interpretation thus becomes a matter of relating the findings to one's frame of reference where personality organization is concerned. The crucial question becomes: *When dealing with self-evaluations as defined in this study are we dealing with epiphenomena or with indicators of more fundamental changes?*

Psychological events are rarely considered to be epiphenomenal. Even the strict behaviorist of twenty years ago rejected the data of immediate experience because of its unreliability rather than because of its nonexistence. The issue is one of the ultimate significance which can legitimately be inferred from subjective report for the understanding of the behavior in question. The findings of the present study can be regarded as contributing only fragmentary or biased insight into personality changes but the findings cannot be dismissed as "mere superficial description of feeling." It would indeed be a sorry system of psychodynamics which dismissed "feelings" (which are probably self-judgments, for the most part) from the realm of psychological significance.

The conclusion which can be drawn from the present findings, and the interpretation which would be in line with Self Concept theory, is essentially the hypothesis that changes in self-approval are indicative of changes taking place in personality although the observed changes may not be direct measures of the fundamental changes themselves. Violent fluctuations in self-approval such as those occurring at the onset of a frank psychotic episode have not been studied quantitatively and need not contradict the present hypothesis in view of their bizarre setting. In some instances they probably corroborate the general hypothesis.

It is believed that intimate knowledge of self-perceptions or their organized totality, the Self Concept, may well be one of the major pathways to detecting changes in personality if objective methods of study can be developed. The self-perceptions may not reveal the fundamental nature of the changes taking place nor the exact means by which the changes occur. An analogy might be drawn to the use of the thermometer for observing changes in temperature. The change in elevation of the column of mercury gives no direct knowledge to the observer of the altered velocities of the molecules surrounding the thermometer nor of the conditions which produce the altered velocities. Yet the thermometer can be used as a stable probe body for studying the conditions under which changes in molecular velocity can be brought about.

The fact that the present method of following changes in self-approval is relatively reliable and objective lends further hope for its usefulness as a probe body. Much work remains to be done before its ultimate usefulness can be determined. Yet it is suspected by the writer and to some degree confirmed by the present study that counselors or psychotherapists may well have been using a similar technique on an intuitive level in diagnosing and judging the progress of their clients and patients.

A final question. Cannot the present research be viewed simply as indicating changes occurring in attitudes toward oneself without dragging in the Self Concept? Perhaps. The answer depends upon how one views attitudes. As atomistically conceived, attitudes may be tabulated as entities in themselves. Present theory seems to demand, however, a more complex and higher order construct to account for the functional interrelationships of attitudes. This demand accounts, in part, for the inclusion of the Self Concept as an explanatory principle in personality organization.

## SUMMARY

In the analysis of personality changes occurring in counseling and psychotherapy it is necessary to find constructs which can be investigated with the usual safeguards of objectivity and reliability. The events occurring in the interview provide a logical focus for such research. The verbal aspects of the interview are mainly concerned with the client's discussion of himself. It is postulated that a person's Self Concept is a significant factor in his behavior and personality organization. By measuring changes which occur in clients' attitudes toward themselves, it is believed that changes in Self Concept and therefore in personality organization can be detected.

The present study used a six-category checklist to classify all client statements in terms of self-reference with three significant categories relating to approval, disapproval, and ambivalence. Objectivity and reliability of the categories were determined statistically. Validity was investigated by comparing results of the method with independent analyses of two counseling cases by two different methods of analysis.

When the present method was applied to 14 counseling cases for which there were almost verbatim recordings of the 111 interviews, consistent differences were discovered between cases judged to have been counseled successfully and those resulting unsuccessfully. In the successful cases there was a marked shift from a preponderance of self-disapproval and ambivalence at the beginning of counseling to a strong emphasis on self-approval at the conclusion of contact. This shift in self-evaluation was not found in unsuccessfully counseled clients. The results are interpreted as being in accord with the hypothesis that successful counseling involves essentially a change in the client's Self Concept.

## REFERENCES

1. Allport, G. W. *Personality.* New York: Holt, 1937.
2. Baldwin, A. L. Personal structure analysis: a statistical method for investigating the single personality. *J. abnorm. soc. Psychol.,* 1942, **37,** 163–183.
3. Curran, C. A. *Personality factors in counseling.* New York: Grune and Stratton, 1945.
4. McDougall, W. *An introduction to social psychology* (14th ed.). Boston: Luce, 1921.
5. Porter, E. H., Jr. The development and evaluation of a measure of counseling interview procedures. *Educ. psychol. Measmt,* 1943, **3,** 105–126, 215–238.
6. Rogers, C. R. *Counseling and psychotherapy.* Boston: Houghton Mifflin, 1942.
7. Snyder, W. U. A short-term non-directive treatment of an adult. *J. abnorm. soc. Psychol., Clin. Suppl.,* 1943, **38,** 87–137.

# CHAPTER 5

# Projective Methods for the Study of Personality

## BY LAWRENCE K. FRANK

An initial difficulty in the study of personality is the lack of any clear-cut, adequate conception of what is to be studied. The recent volumes by Allport and by Stagner and the monograph by Burks and Jones[1] may be cited as indicators of the confusion in this field where, as they show, there are so many conflicting ideas and concepts, each used to justify a wide variety of methods, none of which are wholly adequate.

A situation of this kind evokes different responses from each person according to his professional predilections and allegiances. Obviously pronouncements will be resisted, if not derided, while polemics and apologetics will only increase the

[1] *Cf.*, Allport, G. W. *Personality: a psychological interpretation.* New York: Holt, 1937; Stagner, R. *Psychology of personality.* New York: McGraw-Hill, 1937; Burks, B. S., & Jones, M. C. Personality development in childhood: a survey of problems, methods, and experimental findings. *Mong. Soc. Res. Child Devel.*, 1936, **1**, 1–205.

From *The Journal of Psychology*, 1939, **8**, 389–413. Reprinted by permission of the author and the publisher.

confusion. The question may be raised whether any light upon this situation can be obtained by examining the *process* of personality development for leads to more fruitful conceptions and more satisfactory methods and procedures.

## THE PROCESS OF PERSONALITY DEVELOPMENT

Specifically, it is suggested that we reflect upon the emergence of personality as an outcome of the interaction of cultural agents and the individual child. In the space here available only a brief summary statement is permissible of the major aspects of this process in which we may distinguish an individual organism, with an organic inheritance, slowly growing, developing, and maturing under the tutelage of parents and teachers intent upon patterning him to the culturally prescribed and socially sanctioned modes of action, speech, and belief.

As elsewhere stated,[2] the child is not passive clay but a re-acting organism with feelings, as are the parents, nurses, and teachers who are rearing him. He therefore receives training in the prescribed cultural and social norms of action, speech, and belief, according to their personal bias and feelings, and he accepts this training with varying degrees of observance, always idiomatically and with feelings toward these instructors. What we can observe then is the dual process of *socialization,* involving sufficient conformity in outer conduct to permit participation in the common social world, and of *individuation,* involving the progressive establishment of a private world of highly idiosyncratic meanings, significances, and feelings that are more real and compelling than the cultural and physical world.

The foregoing does not imply any subjective duality or other traditional dichotomy; it is an attempt at a simple statement of the well-known and generally accepted view that in all events

[2] *Cf.,* Frank, L. K. Fundamental needs of the child. *Men. Hyg.,* 1938, **22,** 353–379; Frank, L. K. Cultural coercion and individual distortion. *Psychiatry,* 1939, **2,** 11–27.

we may observe both similarities or uniformities and also individual deviations. We may concentrate upon the larger uniformities and ignore the individual components that are participating, as we do in measuring the temperature, pressure, and other properties of a gas, or we may look beyond the aggregate uniformities to the individual, discrete molecules and atoms and electrons which, as we now are realizing, are highly erratic, unpredictable, and far from that uniformity of behavior described statistically. Thus, we may observe a similar antithesis between the group uniformities of economic, political, and social affairs and the peculiar personal conduct of each of the citizens who collectively exhibit those uniformities and conformities.

Culture provides the socially sanctioned patterns of action, speech, and belief that make group life what we observe, but each individual in that group is a personality who observes those social requirements and uses those patterns idiomatically, with a peculiar personal inflection, accent, emphasis, and intention.[3] Strictly speaking, there are only these individuals, deviating from and distorting the culture; but with our traditional preoccupation with uniformities we have preferred to emphasize the uniformity of statistical aggregates of all activities as the real, and to treat the individual deviation as a sort of unavoidable but embarrassing failure of nature to live up to our expectations. These deviations must be recognized, but only as minor blemishes on and impediments to the scientific truths we seek!

Those ideas flourished in all scientific work up to about 1900 or 1905 when x-rays, quantum physics, relativity, and other new insights were developed that made these earlier ideas obsolete, except in a number of disciplines which still cling to the nineteenth century. Thus it is scientifically respectable, in some circles, to recognize that uniformity is a statistical group concept

[3] *Cf.*, Benedict, R. *Patterns of culture.* New York: Houghton Mifflin, 1934; Mead, M. *Sex and temperament.* New York: Morrow, 1935; Bateson, G. *Naven.* Cambridge: Cambridge Univ. Press, 1936.

that overlays an exceedingly disorderly, discontinuous array of individual, discrete events that just won't obey the scientists' laws! It is also respectable to speak of organization and processes "within the atom," although it is recognized that no direct measurements or even observations can be made within the atom; inferences being drawn from activities and energy transformations that are observable and frequently measurable.

For purposes of discussion it is convenient to see individuals (a) as organisms existing in the common public world of nature, (b) as members of their group, carrying on their life careers, in the social world of culturally prescribed patterns and practices, but living (c) as personalities in these *private worlds* which they have developed under the impact of experience. It is important to recognize these three aspects of human behavior and living because of their implications for scientific study.

As organisms reacting to the environmental impacts, overtly and physiologically, human activity presents a problem of observation and measurement similar to that of all other organisms and events. The human body moves or falls through geographical space, captures, stores, and releases energy and so on. As members of the group, individuals exhibit certain patterns of action, speech, and belief that may be aggregated into larger categories of uniformity or cultural and group norms; at least we find certain pronounced, often all inclusive modes in their observed activities in which they tend to conform to social and cultural prescriptions.

When we examine the personality process or *private worlds* of individuals we face a somewhat peculiar problem because we are seeking not the cultural and social norms of the uniformities of organic activity, but rather the revelation of just that peculiar, individual way of organizing experience and of feeling which personality implies.

In this context we may emphasize then that personality is approachable as a *process* or operation of an individual who organizes experience and reacts affectively to situations. This process is dynamic in the sense that the individual personality imposes upon the common public world of events (what we call nature) his meanings and significances, his organization and patterns, and he invests the situations thus structured with an affective meaning to which he responds idiomatically. This dynamic organizing process will of necessity express the cultural training he has experienced so that until he withdraws from social life, as in the psychoses, he will utilize the group sanctioned patterns of action, speech, and belief, but as he individually has learned to use them and as he feels toward the situations and people to whom he reacts.

If it were not liable to gross misunderstanding, the personality process might be regarded as a sort of rubber stamp which the individual imposes upon every situation by which he gives it the configuration that he, as an individual, requires; in so doing he necessarily ignores or subordinates many aspects of the situation that for him are irrelevant and meaningless and selectively reacts to those aspects that are personally significant. In other words the personality process may be viewed as a highly individualized practice of the general operation of all organisms that selectively respond to a figure on a ground,[4] by reacting to the configurations in an environmental context that are relevant to their life careers.

It is interesting to see how the students of personality have attempted to meet the problem of individuality with methods and procedures designed for study of uniformities and norms that ignore or subordinate individuality, treating it as a troublesome deviation which derogates from the real, the superior, and only important central tendency, mode, average, etc. This is not the occasion to review these methods and the writer is not competent to assess them critically, but it is appropriate to point out

[4] *Cf.*, Frank, L. K. The problem of learning. *Psychol. Rev.*, 1926, **33**, 329–351.

some aspects of the present methodological difficulty we face in the accepted quantitative procedures.

Since individuals, as indicated earlier, learn to conform to the socially sanctioned patterns of action, speech, and belief (and with individual bias and flavor of their own), it is possible to establish the social norms appropriate for *groups* of like chronological age, sex, and so on and to construct standardized tests and to calculate statistically their validity, i.e., do they measure or rate what they are expected to measure or rate for each group, and their reliability, i.e., how well or reliably do they measure or rate the performance of the groups?[5]

While standardized tests are generally considered to be measures of individual differences, it would be more appropriate to say that they are ratings of the degree of likeness to cultural norms exhibited by individuals who are expected, as members of this society, to conform to those group patterns. In other words, the standardized test does not tell very much about the individual, *as an individual,* but rather how nearly he approximates to a normal performance of culturally prescribed tasks for which a more or less arbitrary, but internally consistent, scheme of quantitative ratings is utilized.[6] By the use of an all-over total figure for an individual, it becomes possible to assign numerical evaluations to individuals in various categories of achievement, skill, conformity, and so forth, such as accelerated, average, or retarded mentally; manual or verbal proficiency, etc. Having assigned him to a rank order in a group or class according to the standardized test, the individual is disposed of and adequately explained.[7] The history of the use of standardized tests shows how they are used to place individuals

[5] *Cf.,* Frank, L. K. Comments on the proposed standardization of the Rorschach method. *Rorschach Res. Exch.,* 1939, **3.**

[6] *Cf.,* Kent, G. H. Use and abuse of mental tests in clinical diagnosis. *Psychol. Rec.,* 1938, **2,** 391–400.

[7] *Cf.,* Lewin, K. *A dynamic theory of personality.* New York: McGraw-Hill, 1935. (Especially Chapter 1 on Aristotelian and Galilean modes of thought, and the class theory of investigation.)

in various classifications that are convenient for administration, for remedial work and therapy, or for segregation for purposes of social control, with little or no concern about understanding the individual so classified or placed, or discovering his characteristics *as an individual.*

It would seem fair to say, therefore, that standardized tests offer procedures for rating individuals in terms of their socialization and how nearly they approximate to the acceptance and use of the culturally prescribed patterns of belief, action, and speech for which statistical norms can be calculated from actual observations of performance of *groups* of individuals, according to age, sex, etc.

In order to apply these and more recently developed quantitative methods to the study of personality it has been necessary to adopt a conception of the personality as an aggregation of discrete, measurable traits, factors, or other separable entities which are present in the individual in differing quantity and organized according to individual patterns. But since the personality is more than overt activity, some way of getting at the underlying personality is necessary. The need for quantitative data has led to the use of the culturally standardized, socially sanctioned norms of speech and belief and attitudes in and through which the individual has been asked to express his personality, as in questionnaires, inventories, rating scales, etc.

If time allowed, it would be desirable to examine more fully the implications of this procedure which attempts to reveal the individuality of the person by using the social stereotypes of language and motives that necessarily subordinate individuality to social conformity, emphasizing likeness and uniformity of group patterns. This point becomes more significant when we recall that almost identical actions and speech may be used in extraordinarily different senses by each individual using them; while conversely the widest diversity of action and speech may have almost identical sense and significance for different individuals exhibiting them. Moreover the conventional traits and motives and objectives, derived from traditional concepts of human nature and conduct, carry meanings often alien to the investigator using them as data. Words are generalized symbols, are usually obscuring of, when not actually misleading about, the idiomatic personality using them.[8]

It should be further noted that many procedures for study of personality rely upon the subject's self-diagnosis and revelation of his *private world* of personal meanings and feelings which the social situation compels the individual to conceal, even if, as is unusual, he had any clear understanding of himself. When we ask an individual to tell what he believes or feels or to indicate in which categories he belongs, this social pressure to conform to the group norm operates to bias what he will say and presses him to fit himself into the categories of the inventory or questionnaire offered for self-diagnosis.[9] Moreover, as Henry A. Murray has observed, the most important things about an individual are what he cannot or will not say. The law has long recognized testimony as unreliable, to be accepted only after many checks and tests as formulated in the law of evidence.

At this point there may be a feeling of dismay, if not resentment, because the discussion has led to a seeming impasse, with no road open to study the personality by the accepted methods and procedures of present-day quantitative psychology. Moreover, the insistence upon the unique, idiomatic character of the personality appears to remove it from the area of scientific study conceived as a search for generalizations, uniformities, invariant relationships, etc. It is proposed, therefore, to discuss a few recent developments in scientific concepts and methods and the new problems they have raised in order to indicate a way out of this apparent impasse.

[8] *Cf.*, Willoughby, R. P., & Morse, M. E. Spontaneous reactions to a personality inventory. *Amer. J. Orthopsychiat.*, 1936, **6**, 562–575.

[9] *Cf.*, Vigotsky, L. S. Thought and speech. *Psychiatry*, 1939, **2**, 29–54.

## RECENT CONCEPTS AND METHODS IN SCIENCE

It is appropriate to recall that the uniformity and laws of nature are statistical findings of the probable events and relationships that occur among an aggregate of events, the individuals of which are highly disorderly and unpredictable. Theoretical physics has adjusted itself to the conception of a universe that has statistical regularity and order, and individual disorder, in which the laws of aggregates are not observable in the activity of the individual making up these aggregates. Thus quantum physics and statistical mechanics and many other similar contrasts are accepted without anxiety about scientific respectability. The discrete individual event can be and is regarded as an individual to whom direct methods and measurements have only limited applicability. We can therefore acknowledge an interest in the individual as a scientific problem and find some sanction for such an interest.

Another recent development is the concept of the *field* in physics and its use in biology. The field concept is significant here because it offers a way of conceiving this situation of an individual part and of the whole, which our older concepts have so confused and obscured.[10] Instead of a whole that dominates the parts, which have to be organized by some mysterious process into a whole, we begin to think of an aggregate of individuals which constitute, by their interaction, a field that operates to pattern these individuals. Parts are not separate, discrete, independent entities that get organized by the whole, nor is the whole a superior kind of entity with feudal power over its parts, e.g., a number of iron filings brought close to a magnet will arrange themselves in a pattern wherein each bit of iron is related to the other bits and the magnet and these relations constitute the whole; remove some bits and the pattern shifts as

[10] *Cf.*, Burr, H. S., & Northrop, F. S. C. An electro-dynamic theory of life. *Quart. Rev. Biol.*, 1935, **10**, 322–333.

it does if we add more filings, or bits of another metal. Likewise, in a gas, the gas may be viewed as a field in which individual molecules, atoms, and electrons are patterned by the total inter-actions of all those parts into the group activity we call a gas. Ecology studies this interaction of various organizations in the circumscribed life zone or field which they constitute.[11]

This field concept is highly important because it leads to the general notion that any "entity" we single out for observation is participating in a field; any observation we make must be ordered to the field in which it is made or, as we say, every observation or measurement is relative to the frame of reference or field in which it occurs.

There are many other far-reaching shifts in concepts and methods that should be discussed here, but the foregoing will suffice to indicate that the study of an individual personality may be conceived as an approach to a somewhat disorderly and erratic activity, occurring in the field we call culture (i.e., the aggregate interaction of individuals whose behavior is patterned by participation in the aggregate). Moreover, the observations we make on the individual personality must be ordered to the field of that individual and his life space. We must also regard the individual himself as an aggregate of activities which pattern his parts and functions.

Here we must pause to point out that the older practice of creating entities out of data has created many problems that are unreal and irrelevant and so are insoluble. In by-gone years it was customary to treat data of temperature, light, magnetic activity, radiation, chemical activity, and so on as separate entities, independent of each other. But the more recent view is to see in these data evidences of energy transformations which are transmitted in different magnitudes, sequences, etc., and so appear as heat, light, magnetism, etc. This has relevance to the

[11] *Cf.,* du Nouy, P. L. *Biological time.* New York: Macmillan, 1937. (Other part-whole fields are a candle flame, a fountain jet, a stream of water, etc.)

study of personality since it warns us against the practice of observing an individual's actions and then reifying these data into entities called traits (or some other discrete term), which we must then find some way of organizing into the living total personality who appears in experience as a unified organism.

With this background of larger, more general shifts in scientific procedures, let us examine some more specific developments that are relevant to our topic.

Within recent years new procedures have been developed for discovering not only the elements or parts composing the whole, but also the way those parts are arranged and organized in the whole, without disintegrating or destroying the whole. The x-rays are used, not merely for photographs or to show on a fluorescent screen what is otherwise invisible within an organism or any object, but also for diffraction analysis, in which the x-rays are patterned by the internal organization of any substance to show its molecular and atomic structure. Spectographic analysis reveals the chemical components qualitatively, and now quantitatively, and in what compounds, by the way light is distributed along a continuous band of coarse and fine spectral lines, each of which reveals a different element or isotope. The mass spectroscope offers another exceedingly delicate method for determining the composition of any substance that gives off radiations whereby the electrons or their rate of travel can be measured and the composition of the substance inferred.

X-rays, however, are only one of the newer methods whereby any complex may be made to reveal its components and its organization, often quantitatively, when approached by an appropriate procedure. Recently, it has been found that the chemical composition of various substances, especially proteins, can be ascertained by the reflection of a beam of light upon a thin monomolecular film of the protein substance spread on a film of oil on water over a metallic surface. Again it has been found that metallic ores and coal may be analyzed, i.e., be made to reveal their chemical composition and other properties by the "angle of wetability," the angle of reflection, or the color of light reflected from a liquid film that adheres to the surface of the unknown material.

Polarized light has also become an instrument for revealing the chemical composition of substances without resort to the usual methods of disintegration or chemical analysis. Electrical currents may also be passed through substances, gaseous, liquid, or solid, and used to discover what they contain and in what form. Indeed, it is not unwarranted to say that these indirect methods that permit discovery of the composition and organization of substances, complexes, and organisms, seem likely to become the method of choice over the older destructive analytical procedures, because these methods do not destroy or disturb the substance or living organism being studied.

In this connection reference should also be made to the development of biological assays, whereby a living organism, plant, or animal, is used for assaying the composition of various substances and compounds and determining their potency, such as vitamins, hormones, virus, drugs, radiation, light, magnetism, and electrical currents (including electrophoresis for separating, without injury or change, the different sub-varieties of any group of cells, chemical substances, etc.). In these procedures the response of the living organism is utilized as an indicator, if not an actual measurement, of that about which data are sought, as well as the state, condition, maturation, etc., of the organism being tested. It is appropriate to note also that physicists are using such devices as the Wilson Cloud Chamber and the Geiger Counter to obtain data on the *individual* electrical particle, which reveals its presence and energy by the path traced in water vapor, or by activation of the Counter, although never itself observable or directly measurable.

These methodological procedures are being refined and extended because they offer possibilities for ascertaining what is either unknowable by other means or is undeterminable because the older analytic methods destroyed part or all of that which was to be studied. They are being accepted as valid and credible, primarily because they are more congruous with the search for undivided totalities and functioning organisms are more productive of the data on organization on which present-day research problems are focused. They are also expressive of the recent concepts of whole-and-parts and their interrelations, which no longer invoke the notion of parts as discrete entities upon which an organization is imposed by a superior whole, but rather employ the concept of the field. Finally they offer possibilities for studying the specific, differentiated individuality of organized structures and particulate events which are ignored or obscured by the older quantitative determinations of aggregates.

Since the threshold task in any scientific endeavor is to establish the meanings and significances of the data obtained by any method of observation and measurement, it should be noted that these indirect methods for revealing the composition and organization of substances and structures rely upon experimental and genetic procedures to establish reliability and validity, not statistical procedures. That is to say, these newer procedures establish the meaning of any datum by employing the procedure upon a substance or structure of known composition, often made to order, so that it is possible to affirm that the resulting bending, patterning, arrangement of light, radiation, and so on, are reliable and valid indicators of the substance or structure when found in an unknown composition. These methods for establishing reliability and validity are therefore genetic in the sense of observing or tracing the origin and development of what is to be tested so that its presence or operation may be historically established; they are also dependent upon the concurrent use of other procedures which will yield consistent data on the same composition which therefore are validated by such internal consistency and congruity of findings.

Psychology developed the statistical procedures for establishing reliability and validity because the only data available were the single observations or measurements taken at one time on each subject. Since no other data were available on the prior history and development of the subjects, reliability had to be determined by statistical manipulation of these test data themselves; also since no other data were available on the subject's other functions and activities only statistical validity could be established. It would appear that these tests of reliability and validity devised to meet the difficulty presented by absence of other data now act as barriers to the use of any other procedures for personality study in which reliability and validity for each subject is tested through these other non-statistical methods.

Methods of *temporal validation* offer great promise because they permit testing of the validity of data for a *specific subject* over a period of time, and the method of congruity among data obtained by different procedures from the same subject offer large possibilities for testing the reliability of any data for a *specific subject*.[12] It is appropriate to recall here that the accepted methods for testing reliability and validity of tests, inventories, etc., offer indices only for the *group,* not for any individual subject in that *group.*

We may therefore view the problem of personality in terms of these more recent ideas and conceptions and consider the application of these indirect procedures for revealing the composition and organization of substances and energy complexes.

As indicated earlier the personality may be viewed as a dynamic process of organizing experience, of "structuralizing the life space" (Lewin) according to the unique individual's

[12] *Cf.,* Bateson, G. *Naven.* Cambridge: Cambridge Univ. Press, 1936. In which appears a discussion of diachronic and synchronic procedures.

*private world.* This conception may be made precise and operational by seeing the individual and his changing environment as a series of fields which arise through the interaction of the individual personality with his selective awareness, patterned responses, and idiomatic feelings, with the environmental situations of objects, events, and other persons. A field organization or configuration arises out of this interaction wherein, as suggested, the personality distorts the situation, so far as it is amenable, into the configurations of its *private world,* but has to adjust to the situation in so far as it resists such distortion and imposes its necessities upon the personality. What we have called personality and fumblingly have tried to formulate as the total responses of the whole individual and similar additive conceptions becomes more understandable and approachable for investigation when conceived as the living process in this field created by the individual and the environing situation.

The objective world of objects, organisms, and events likewise may be seen as fields of interacting object-situations, upon which cultural patterns operate in the conduct of human beings who, by very reason of behaving in these learned patterns, create the cultural fields of interacting human conduct. What is highly important to note is that every observation made must be ordered—given its quantitative and qualitative interpretation—to the field in which it occurs, so that the idea of pure objectivity becomes meaningless and sterile if it implies data not biased, influenced, relative to the field in which observed. Likewise the conception of a stimulus that may be described and measured apart from the field and the organism in that field is untenable.[13] The "same" stimulus will differ in every field, and

[13] *Cf.,* Vigotsky, L. S. Thought and speech. *Psychiatry,* 1939, **2,** 29–54. "The investigator who uses such methods may be compared to a man, who, in order to explain why water extinguishes fire, analyzes the water into oxygen and hydrogen and is surprised to find that oxygen helps the process of burning and hydrogen itself burns. This method of analyzing a whole into elements is not a true analysis which can be used to solve concrete problems" (p. 29).

for every field and for every organism which selectively creates its own stimuli in each situation. Indeed, this dynamic conception of the personality as a process implies that there are no stimuli to conduct (as distinct from physical and physiological impacts) except in so far as the individual personality selectively constitutes them and responds to them in its idiosyncratic patterns. In other words the stimuli are functions of the field created by the individual interacting with the situation.

Thus the movement in various areas of scientific work is toward recognition of the field concept and the devising of methods that will record not merely data but the fields in which those data have been observed and find their significance. Those who are appalled by the seeming anarchy thus threatening scientific work may be reminded that the present-day standards of scientific work and of methods are part of a development that will inevitably make today's ideas and procedures obsolete. It is well to recall how proud (justly so) chemistry was to achieve quantitative determinations of the composition of substances and now, how crude those early quantitative methods and findings now appear, when they now are seeking to find out not merely what and how much, but the spatial arrangement of the constituents as in stereochemistry where the same atoms in the same quantity produce different substances according to their spatial arrangement. It is likewise worth recalling that, about 1900, young physicists could find no problems except the more precise measurement of the pressure, temperature, etc., of a gas and were content with such crude quantitative findings. Furthermore, biologists today are accepting as common-place that the same nutritive components, amino-acids, carbohydrates, fats, minerals, and vitamins are selectively digested, assimilated, and metabolized in different ways by each species and by each individual. Moreover, it is conceded that the proteins of each species are different as are those of each individual with the possibility of an almost unlimited number of different protein molecules, in which the same basic elements are organized into unique spatial-temporal configurations appropriate to the organic field of the individual organism.[14]

## THE EXPLORATION OF THE PRIVATE WORLD

Coming directly to the topic of projective methods for personality study,[15] we may say that the dynamic conception of personality as a process of organizing experience and structuralizing life space in a field, leads to the problem of how we can reveal the way an individual personality organizes experience, in order to disclose or at least gain insight into that individual's *private world* of meanings, significances, patterns, and feelings.

Such a problem is similar to those discussed earlier where indirect methods are used to elicit the pattern of internal organization and of composition without disintegrating or distorting the subject, which is made to bend, deflect, distort, organize, or otherwise pattern part or all of the field in which it is placed—e.g., light and x-rays. In similar fashion we may approach the personality and induce the individual to reveal his way of organizing experience by giving him a field (objects, materials, experiences) with relatively little structure and cultural patterning so that the personality can project upon that plastic field his way of seeing life, his meanings, significances, patterns, and especially his feelings. Thus we elicit a projection of the individual personality's *private world* because he has to

[14] The concepts of individuality and of individuation are being used by biologists because they find themselves confronted with individual organic activities and idiomatic processes.

*Cf.,* Blumenthal, H. T. Effects of organismal differentials on the distribution of leukocytes in the circulating blood. *Arch. Path.,* 1939, **27,** 510–545; Coghill, G. E. Individuation versus integration in the development of behavior. *J. gen. Psychol.,* 1930, **3,** 431–435; Coghill, G. E. Integration and motivation of behavior as problems of growth. *J. genet. Psychol.,* 1936, **48,** 3–19.

[15] References to the projective techniques discussed in this section appear in the bibliography at the end of the paper.

organize the field, interpret the material and react affectively to it.

More specifically, a projection method for study of personality involves the presentation of a stimulus-situation designed or chosen because it will mean to the subject, not what the experimenter has arbitrarily decided it should mean (as in most psychological experiments using standardized stimuli in order to be "objective"), but rather whatever it must mean to the personality who gives it, or imposes upon it, his private, idiosyncratic meaning and organization. The subject then will respond to *his* meaning of the presented stimulus-situation by some form of action and feeling that is expressive of his personality.

Such responses may be *constitutive* as when the subject imposes a structure or form or configuration (Gestalt) upon an amorphous, plastic, unstructured substance such as clay, finger paints, or upon partially structured and semi-organized fields like the Rorschach cards; or they may be *interpretive* as when the subject tells what a stimulus-situation, like a picture, means to him; or they may be *cathartic* as when the subject discharges affect or feeling upon the stimulus-situation and finds an emotional release that is revealing of his affective reactions toward life situations represented by the stimulus-situation, as when he plays with clay or toys. Other expressions may be *constructive* organizations wherein the subject builds in accordance with the materials offered but reveals in the pattern of his building some of the organizing conceptions of his life at that period, as in block-building.

The important and determining process is the subject's personality which operates upon the stimulus-situation as if it had a wholly private significance for him alone or an entirely plastic character which made it yield to the subject's control. This indicates that, as suggested earlier, a personality is the way an individual organizes and patterns life situations and effectively responds to them, "structuralizes his life space," so that by projective methods we are evoking the very process of personality as it has developed to that moment.[16] Since the way an individual organizes and patterns life situations, imposes his *private world* of meanings and affectively reacts upon the environing world of situations and other persons and strives to maintain his personal version against the coercion or obstruction of others, it is evident that personality is a persistent way of living and feeling that, despite change of tools, implements, and organic growth and maturation, will appear continuously and true to pattern.

When we scrutinize the actual procedures that may be called projective methods we find a wide variety of techniques and materials being employed for the same general purpose, to obtain from the subject "what he cannot or will not say," frequently because he does not know himself and is not aware what he is revealing about himself through his projections.

In the following statement no attempt has been made to provide a complete review of all the projective methods now being used, since such a canvass would be beyond the present writer's competence and intention. Only a few illustrations of projective methods are offered to show their variety and their scope, in the hope of enlisting further interest in and creating a better understanding of, their characteristics and advantages.[17]

The Rorschach ink blots, to which the subject responds by saying what he "sees" in each of a number of different blots, are perhaps the most widely known of these procedures. They have been utilized in Europe and in the United States, frequently in connection with psychiatric clinics and hospitals, for revealing

---

[16] *Cf.*, Dunbar, H. F. *Emotions and bodily changes.* New York: Columbia Univ. Press, 1938. (2nd Ed.) An individual may express his feelings, otherwise blocked, in illness or physiological dysfunctions.

[17] *Cf.*, Horowitz, R., & Murphy, L. B. Projective methods in the psychological study of children. *J. exp. Educ.*, 1938, **7**, 133–140, for further discussion of different procedures and their use.

the personality configurations and have been found of increasing value. In so far as life histories and psychiatric and psychoanalytic studies of the subjects who have had the Rorschach diagnosis are available, the ink blot interpretations are being increasingly validated by these clinical findings. Such comparative findings are of the greatest importance because they mutually reinforce each other and reveal the consistency or any conflicts in the different interpretations and diagnosis of a personality.

Another similar procedure is the *Cloud Picture* method, developed by Wilhelm Stern to evoke projections from a subject upon more amorphous grounds, with advantages, he believed, over the Rorschach blots. The more amorphous or unstructured the ground, the greater the sensitivity of the procedure which however loses in precision as in most instruments. Hence the Rorschach may be less sensitive than *Cloud Pictures* or clay but more precise and definite. Both the ink blots and the *Cloud Pictures* offer a ground upon which the subject must impose or project whatever configural patterns he "sees" therein, because he can only see what he personally looks for or "perceives" in that ground. The separate details of the responses, however, are significant only in the context of the total response to each blot and are meaningful only for each subject. This does not imply an absence of recurrent forms and meanings from one subject to another but rather that the same letters of the conventionalized alphabet may recur in many different words and the same words may be utilized in a great variety of sentences to convey an extraordinary diversity of statements, which must be understood within the context in which they occur and with reference to the particular speaker who is using them on that occasion.[18]

[18] Since each personality must use socially prescribed cultural patterns for his conduct and communications he will exhibit many recurrent uniformities but these are significant only for revealing the patterns or organizations or configurations which the personality uses to structuralize his life space.

Play techniques are being increasingly employed for clinical diagnosis and for investigation of the personality development of children. As materials almost any kind of toy or plaything or plain wooden building blocks may be presented to the subject for free play or for performance of some designated action, such as building a house, sorting into groups, setting the stage for a play, or otherwise organizing the play materials, into some configuration which expresses for the subject an affectively significant pattern. In children, it must be remembered there are fewer disguises and defenses available to hide behind and there is less sophisticated awareness of how much is being revealed in play. The investigator does not set a task and rate the performance in terms of skill or other scale of achievement, since the intention is to elicit the subject's way of "organizing his life space" in whatever manner he finds appropriate. Hence every performance is significant, apart from the excellence of the play construction or activity, and is to be interpreted, rather than rated, for its revelation of how the subject sees and feels his life situations that are portrayed in the play constructions and sequences.

The question of how to decide whether a particular activity is or is not meaningful is to be decided, not by its frequency or so-called objective criteria, but by the total play configuration of that particular subject who, it is assumed, performs that particular action or uses that specific construction, as an expression of his way of seeing and feeling and reacting to life, i.e., of his personality. But the degree of relevance is to be found in the context, in what precedes and what follows and in the intensity of feelings expressed. If these criteria appear tenuous and subjective and lacking in credibility, then objections may be made to the use of various methods for discovering the composition and structure of an unknown substance through which light, electric current, or radiations are passed, to give patterned arrangements or a spectrum photograph in which the position, number, intensity of lines, and the coarse and fine structure indicate what the unknown substance is composed of, how organized internally and so on. Personality studies by projective methods have not, of course, been as extensively studied nor have the patterns used by subjects been so well explored. The important point is that the way is open to the development of something similar to spectroscopic and diffraction methods for investigation of personality.

If the foregoing appears far-fetched it may be recalled that the lines on the spectroscopic plate were established, not by statistical procedures, but by experimental procedures through which a known chemically tested substance was spectroscopically tested so that its identifying line could be precisely located and thereafter confidently named. In much the same fashion it is being established that a child who is known to be undergoing an affective experience will express that feeling in a play configuration that can be so recognized. Thus, children who have lost a beloved parent or nurse, who have been made anxious by toilet training, are insecure and hostile because of sibling rivalry, etc., will exhibit those feelings in their play configurations. Experimentally produced personality disturbances can be established and their severity investigated by subsequent play forms and expressions. Moreover, the insights derived from play configurations yield interpretations that are not only therapeutically effective but often predictive of what a child will show in the near future.

Not only play toys and objects are utilized but also various plastic amorphous materials such as modelling clay, flour, and water, mud and similar substances of a consistency that permits the subject to handle freely and manipulate into various objects. In these play situations, the subject often finds a catharsis, expressing affect that might otherwise be repressed or disguised, or symbolically releasing resentments and hostility that have been long overlaid by conventionally good conduct. Dolls, capable of being dismembered, can be used to evoke repressed hostility and aggression against parents and siblings. Dramatic stage play with toy figures and settings have also provided occasions in which a subject not only revealed his personality difficulties but also worked out many of his emotional problems. Clay figures are modelled by child patients in which they express many of their acute anxieties and distortions. Reference should be made to eidetic imagery which, as Walther Jaensch in his constitutional studies has shown, indicates one aspect of the subject's way of expressing what enters into his personality make-up or way of organizing his life space.

Artistic media offer another series of rich opportunities for projective methods in studying personality. Finger-painting has given many insights into child personality make-up and perplexities. Painting has been found very fruitful for study of personality make-up and emotional disturbances. Other clinical uses of painting have been reported that indicate the way paintings and drawings supplement the clinician's interviews and evoke responses, that are exceedingly revealing, often more so than the verbal responses. Puppet shows elicit responses from child patients that are both diagnositic and therapeutic because the intensity of the dramatic experience arouses the child to a vehement expression of his feelings toward authority and toward parents and of his repressed desires to hurt others. Roles have been assigned to individuals who are then asked to act out these roles impromptu, thereby revealing how tangled and repressed his or her feelings are and how release of pent-up emotion leads to insight into one's personality difficulties. Dramatics teachers are finding clues to personality in the way individuals portray the characters assigned them in a play. Music offers similar and often more potent possibilities for expression of affects that are revealing of the personality. It is interesting to note that as psychotherapy proceeds to free the patient, his art expressions, painting, modelling, music, and dramatic rendition become freer and more integrated.

As the foregoing indicates, the individual rarely has any understanding of himself or awareness of what his activities signify. In the Thematic Perception methods this unawareness offers an opportunity to elicit highly significant projections from subjects who are asked to write or tell stories about a series of pictures showing individuals with whom they can identify themselves and others of immediate personal concern. Likewise the subjects project many aspects of their personality in the completion of stories and of sentences, in making up analogies, sorting out and grouping objects, such as toys, and similar procedures in which the subject reveals "what he cannot or will not say."

Expressive movements, especially handwriting, offer another approach to the understanding of the personality who reveals so much of his characteristic way of viewing life in his habitual gestures and motor patterns, facial expressions, posture and gait. These leads to the study of personality have been rejected by many psychologists because they do not meet psychometric requirements for validity and reliability, but they are being employed in association with clinical and other studies of personality where they are finding increasing validation in the consistency of results for the same subject when independently assayed by each of these procedures. In this group of methods should be included observations on tics of all kinds and dancing as indications of tension, anxiety, or other partially repressed feelings.

## CONCLUSIONS

If we will face the problem of personality, in its full complexity, as an active dynamic process to be studied as a *process* rather than as entity or aggregate of traits, factors, or as a static organization, then these projective methods offer many advantages for obtaining data on the process of organizing experience which is peculiar to each personality and has a life career. Moreover, the projective methods offer possibilities for utilizing the available insights into personality which the prevailing quantitative procedures seem deliberately to reject.

Here again it may be re-emphasized that the study of personality is not a task of measuring separate variables on a large group of individuals at one moment in their lives and then seeking, by statistical methods, to measure correlations, nor is it a problem of teasing out and establishing the quantitative value of several factors.[19] Rather the task calls for the application of a multiplicity of methods and procedures which will reveal the many facets of the personality and show how the individual "structuralizes his life space" or organizes experience to meet his personal needs in various media. If it appears that the subject projects similar *patterns* or *configurations* upon widely different materials and reveals in his life history the sequence of experiences that make those projections psychologically meaningful for his personality, then the procedures may be judged sufficiently valid to warrant further experimentation and refinement. In undertaking such explorations the experimenter and clinicians may find reassurance and support in the realization that they are utilizing concepts and methods that are receiving increasing recognition and approval in scientific work that is today proving most fruitful.

## BIBLIOGRAPHY

1.  Abel, T. M. Free designs of limited scope as a personality index. *Charact. & Pers.*, 1938, **7,** 50–62.
2.  Ackerman, N. W., with the technical assistance of V. Rehkopf. Constructive and destructive tendencies in children. *Amer. J. Orthopsychiat.*, 1937, **7,** 301–319.

[19] *Cf.,* Jersild, A. T., & Fite, M. D. The influence of nursery school experience on children's social adjustments. *Child Devel. Monog.*, No. 25, 1939. See especially page 102.

3. Allport, G. W., & Vernon, P. E. *Studies in expressive movement.* New York: Macmillan, 1933.

4. Anderson, H. H. Domination and integration in the social behavior of young children in an experimental play situation. *Genet. Psychol. Monog.,* 1937, **19,** 343–408.

5. Barker, R. G. The effect of frustration upon cognitive ability. *Charact. & Pers.,* 1938, **7,** 145–150.

6. Barker, R. G., Dembo, T., & Lewin, K. Experiments in frustration and regression: studies in topological and vector psychology. *Univ. Iowa Child Wel. Res. St. Monog.,* 1939.

7. Beck, S. J. Autism in Rorschach scoring: a feeling comment. *Charact. & Pers.,* 1936, **5,** 83–85.

8. Beck, S. J. Psychological processes in Rorschach findings. *J. abnorm. soc. Psychol.,* 1937, **31,** 482–488.

9. Beck, S. J. Introduction to the Rorschach method. *Amer. Orthopsychiat. Assoc. Monog.,* No. 1, 1937.

10. Beck, S. J. Personality structure in schizophrenia. *Nerv. & Ment. Dis. Monog.,* 1938, No. 63.

11. Bender, L., & Woltmann, A. The use of puppet shows as a psychotherapeutic method for behavior problems in children. *Amer. J. Orthopsychiat.,* 1936, **6,** 341–354.

12. Bender, L., Keiser, S., & Schilder, P. Studies in aggressiveness. *Genet. Psychol. Monog.,* 1936, **18,** 357–564.

13. Bender, L., & Schilder, P. Form as a principle in the play of children. *J. genet. Psychol.,* 1936, **49,** 254–261.

14. Bender, L., & Woltmann, A. Puppetry as a psychotherapeutic measure with problem children. *Monthly Bull., N. Y. State Assoc. Occup. Therap.,* 1937, **7,** 1–7.

15. Bender, L. Art and therapy in the mental disturbances of children. *J. Nerv. & Ment. Dis.,* 1937, **86,** 229–238.

16. Bender, L. Group activities on a children's ward as methods of psychotherapy. *Amer. J. Psychiat.,* 1937, **93,** 1151–1173.

17. Bender, L., & Woltmann, A. The use of plastic material as a psychiatric approach to emotional problems in children. *Amer. J. Orthopsychiat.,* 1937, **7,** 283–300.

18. Bender, L. A visual motor gestalt test and its clinical use. *Amer. Orthopsychiat. Assoc. Monog.,* 1938, No. 3.

19. Booth, G. C. Personality and chronic arthritis. *J. Nerv. & Ment. Dis.*, 1937, **85,** 637–662.

20. Booth, G. C. The use of graphology in medicine. *J. Nerv. & Ment. Dis.*, 1937, **86,** 674–679.

21. Booth, G. C. Objective techniques in personality testing. *Arch. Neur. & Psychiat.*, 1939.

22. Cameron, N. Individual and social factors in the development of graphic symbolization. *J. Psychol.*, 1938, **5,** 165–183.

23. Cameron, N. Functional immaturity in the symbolization of scientifically trained adults. *J. Psychol.*, 1938, **6,** 161–175.

24. Cameron, N. Reasoning, regression, and communication in schizophrenics. *Psychol. Monog.*, 1938, **50,** 1–34.

25. Cameron, N. Deterioration and regression in schizophrenic thinking. *J. abnorm. soc. Psychol.*, 1939, **34,** 265–270.

26. Conn, J. H. A psychiatric study of car sickness in children. *Amer. J. Orthopsychiat.*, 1938, **8,** 130–141.

27. Curran, F. F. The drama as a therapeutic measure in adolescents. *Amer. J. Orthopsychiat.*, 1939, **9,** 215–231.

28. Despert, J. L., & Potter, H. W. The story, a form of directed phantasy. *Psychiat. Quart.*, 1936, **10,** 619–638.

29. Erikson, E. H. Configurations in play: clinical notes. *Psychoanal. Quart.*, 1937, **6,** 139–214.

30. Fite, M. D. Aggressive behavior in young children and children's attitudes toward aggression. *Genet. Psychol. Monog.*, 1939.

31. Gerard, M. W. Case for discussion at the 1938 symposium. *Amer. J. Orthopsychiat.*, 1938, **8,** 1–18.

32. Gitelson, M., *et al.* Section on "play therapy," 1938. *Amer. J. Orthopsychiat.*, 1938, **8,** 499–524.

33. Gitelson, M. Clinical experience with play therapy. *Amer. J. Orthopsychiat.*, 1938, **8,** 466–478.

34. Griffiths, R. *Imagination in young children.* London: Kegan Paul, 1936.

35. Hanfmann, E. Social structure of a group of kindergarten children. *Amer. J. Orthopsychiat.*, 1935, **5,** 407–410.

36. Hanfmann, E., & Kasanin, J. A method for the study of concept formation. *J. Psychol.*, 1937, **3,** 521–540.

37. Hanfmann, E., & Kasanin, J. Disturbances in concept formation in schizophrenia. *Arch. Neur. & Psychiat.*, 1938, **40**, 1276–1282.

38. Hanfmann, E. Analysis of the thinking disorder in a case of schizophrenia. *Arch. Neur. & Psychiat.*, 1939, **41**, 568–579.

39. Hertz, M. R. The method of administration of the Rorschach ink blot test. *Child Devel.*, 1936, **7**, 237–254.

40. Hertz, M. R., & Rubinstein, B. B. A comparison of three "blind" Rorschach analyses. *Amer. J. Orthopsychiat.*, 1939, **9**, 295–314.

41. Holmer, P. The use of the play situation as an aid to diagnosis. *Amer. J. Orthopsychiat.*, 1937, **7**, 523–531.

42. Horowitz, R. E., & Murphy, L. B. Projective methods in the psychological study of children. *J. exp. Educ.*, 1938, **7**, 133–140.

43. Horowitz, R. E. Racial aspects of self-identification in nursery school children. *J. Psychol.*, 1939, **7**, 91–99.

44. Hunter, M. The practical value of the Rorschach test in a psychological clinic. *Amer. J. Orthopsychiat.*, 1939, **9**, 287–294.

45. Jaensch, E. R. *Eidetic imagery and typological methods of investigation.* New York: Harcourt, Brace, 1930.

46. Kasanin, J., & Hanfmann, E. An experimental study of concept formation in schizophrenia: I. Quantitative analysis of the results. *Amer. J. Psychiat.*, 1938, **95**, 35–48.

47. Kelley, D. M., & Klopfer, B. Application of the Rorschach method to research in schizophrenia. *Rorschach Res. Exch.*, 1939, **3**, 55–66.

48. Klopfer, B. *Rorschach Research Exchange.* September, 1936, to date.

49. Klüver, H. The eidetic child. *Handbook of child psychology.* Worcester: Clark Univ. Press, 1931.

50. Levy, D. M. Use of play technique as experimental procedure. *Amer. J. Orthopsychiat.*, 1933, **3**, 266–277.

51. Levy, D. M. Hostility patterns in sibling rivalry experiments. *Amer. J. Orthopsychiat.*, 1936, **6**, 183–257.

52. Levy, D. M. "Release therapy" in young children. *Psychiatry*, 1938, **1**, 387–390.

53. Levy, J. The use of art techniques in treatment of children's behavior problems. *Proc. Amer. Assoc. Ment. Def.,* 1934, **58,** 258–260.

54. Levy, J. The active use of phantasy in treatment of children's behavior problems. (Unpublished paper presented at a meeting of the American Psychiatric Association.)

55. Lewin, K. Environmental forces. *Handbook of child psychology.* Worcester: Clark Univ. Press, 1933.

56. Lewin, K. *A dynamic theory of personality.* New York: McGraw-Hill, 1935.

57. Lewin, K. *Principles of topological psychology.* New York: McGraw-Hill, 1936.

58. Lewin, K. Psychoanalysis and topological psychology. *Bull. Menninger Clin.,* 1937, **1,** 202–211.

59. Liss, E. Play techniques in child analysis. *Amer. J. Orthopsychiat.,* 1936, **6,** 17–22.

60. Liss, E. The graphic arts. *Amer. J. Orthopsychiat.,* 1938, **8,** 95–99.

61. Lowenfeld, V. *The nature of creative activity.* London: Kegan Paul, 1938.

62. Masserman, J. H., & Balken, E. R. The clinical application of phantasy studies. *J. Psychol.,* 1938, **6,** 81–88.

63. Moreno, J. L. Who shall survive? *Nerv. & Ment. Dis. Monog.,* 1934, No. 58.

64. Moreno, J. L., & Jennings, H. Spontaneity training, a method of personality development. *Sociomet. Rev.,* 1936.

65. Moreno, J. L. Psychodramatic shock therapy—a sociometric approach to the problem of mental disorders. *Sociometry,* 1939, **2,** 1–30.

66. Moreno, J. L. Creativity and cultural conserves—with special reference to musical expression. *Sociometry,* 1939, **2,** 1–36.

67. Morgan, C. D., & Murray, H. A. Method for investigating fantasies—the thematic apperception test. *Arch. Neur. & Psychiat.,* 1935, **34,** 289–306.

68. Murphy, L. B. *Social behavior and child personality: an exploratory study of some roots of sympathy.* New York: Columbia Univ. Press, 1937.

69. Murray, H. A., *et al.* Papers in *J. soc. Psychol.*, 1933, **4;** *J. abnorm. soc. Psychol.*, 1934, **28;** *J. Psychol.*, 1937, **3,** 27–42.

70. Murray, H. A. Techniques for a systematic investigation of fantasy. *J. Psychol.*, 1937, **3,** 115–143.

71. Murray, H. A. *Explorations in personality.* New York: Oxford Univ. Press, 1938.

72. Newman, S., & Mather, V. G. Analysis of spoken language of patients with affective disorders. *Amer. J. Psychiat.*, 1938, **94,** 913–942.

73. Newman, S. Personal symbolism in language patterns. *Psychiatry*, 1939, **2,** 177–184.

74. Piotrowski, Z. The methodological aspects of the Rorschach personality method. *Kwart. Psychol.*, at Poznan, 1937, **9,** 29.

75. Piotrowski, Z. The *M, FM,* and *m* responses as indicators of changes in personality. *Rorschach Res. Exch.*, 1937, **1,** 148–156.

76. Plant, J. S. Personality and the culture pattern. *J. soc. Philos.*, 1938, **3.**

77. Porter, E. L. H. Factors in the fluctuation of fifteen ambiguous phenomena. *Psychol. Rec.*, 1937, **2,** 231–253.

78. Rosenzweig, S., & Shakow, D. Play technique in schizophrenia and other psychoses: I. Rationale; II. An experimental study of schizophrenic constructions with play materials. *Amer. J. Orthopsychiat.*, 1937, **7,** 32–35; 36–47.

79. Sapir, E. The emergence of the concept of personality in a study of culture. *J. soc. Psychol.*, 1934, **5,** 408–415.

80. Sender, S., & Klopfer, B. Application of the Rorschach test to child behavior problems as facilitated by a refinement of the scoring method. *Rorschach Res. Exch.*, 1936, **1,** 1–17.

81. Shaw, R. F. *Finger painting.* Boston: Little, Brown, 1934.

82. Stein-Lewinson, T. An introduction to the graphology of Ludwig Klages. *Charact. & Pers.*, 1938, **6,** 163–177.

83. Troup, E. A comparative study by means of the Rorschach method of personality development in twenty pairs of identical twins. *Genet. Psychol. Monog.*, 1938, **20,** 465–556.

84. Vaughn, J., & Krug, O. The analytic character of the Rorschach ink blot test. *Amer. J. Orthopsychiat.*, 1938, **8,** 220–229.

85. Werner, H. William Stern's personalistics and psychology of personality. *Charact. & Pers.*, 1938, **7,** 109–125.

# CHAPTER 6

## Idiodynamics in Personality Theory with Special Reference to Projective Methods

### BY SAUL ROSENZWEIG

Though, as an eminent psychologist recently remarked, "New projective methods are a dime a dozen," the conceptualization of these techniques still remains a scarce commodity. Only an occasional writer (4, 6) has recognized the conceptual difficulties and suggested possible solutions. The reasons for this lack are not far to seek. The projective methods of psychodiagnosis present unprecedented problems in psychological measurement, and these problems, in turn, arise from certain new conceptions of personality and of psychodynamics. Until these latter concepts have been systematically absorbed, the principles of test construction and standardization applicable to the projective techniques cannot be formulated.

From *Psychological Review*, 1951, **58**, 213–223. Reprinted by permission of the author and the publisher. Presented at the annual meeting of the American Orthopsychiatric Association in 1950.

## THE INDIVIDUAL AND NORMS IN PSYCHOLOGICAL THEORY

Part, if not the central aspect, of the new orientation in personality theory concerns the fate of the individual in the psychologist's perspective.[1] Elsewhere (9) an attempt has been made to delineate three stages in the history of psychology: the first, in which the individual has figured as the representative of the generalized human being to whom universal principles of segmental behavior could be applied; the second, in which he has been viewed as a more or less indivisible component of a statistically conceived group; the third, in which he emerges as a world of events constituting a population subject to both statistical analysis and dynamic conceptualization.

Closely tied to these conceptual destinies are three species of norms typically employed in psychological measurement and interpretation. Corresponding to the search for general laws of segmental behavior are certain implicit *universal* norms; in differential psychology—the psychometric approach—*group* norms on a statistical basis are explicitly employed; where, finally, the person in his intra-individual dynamics is taken into account, *individual* norms are recognized as crucial.

It is comparatively easy to illustrate the three kinds of norms by following the association method through its historical vicissitudes. After Galton invented it, Wundt and his students used the method to derive certain general laws of stimulus-response relationship in the tradition of the generalized human being and of universal norms. In the descriptive psychiatric province the technique was developed for purposes of diagnostic differentiation, e.g., the work of Kent and Rosanoff, with group norms as the objective. With the advent of psychoanalysis and Jung's attempt to validate its concepts experimentally, the word-

[1] The obvious influence of G. W. Allport (*Personality*. New York: Holt, 1937), who has so effectively stressed the role of the individual in the science of psychology, will be recognized by any informed reader. The emphasis in the present account is, however, explicitly psychodynamic.

The Individual and Norms in Psychological Theory

| Theoretical Matrix | General-Experimental | Statistical-Psychometric | Psychoanalytic-Projective (Idiodynamic) |
|---|---|---|---|
| Objective | To establish principles of stimulus-response relationship applicable to the generalized human mind. | To allocate the individual in the group according to the distribution of various individual differences. | To reveal intra-individual (response-response or need-response) relationships for understanding the given case and for deriving principles of personality functioning. |
| Role of the Individual | An exemplar of responses in segmental stimulus-response behavior. | A constituent part or component of the group, the group being the basic unit. | A universe of events (idioverse) subject to analysis as a population. |
| Species of Norms | *Universal:* functional criteria of behavior, usually implicit, conceived as operating, under the required conditions, without exception for all individuals. | *Group:* statistical standards, usually explicit, for measuring the individual's conformity to the average of the group or for placing him otherwise in the range of its distribution. | *Individual:* implicit or explicit terms of reference for understanding the behavior of the person in the context of what is characteristic or idiomatic of him. |
| Criterion of Normality | Frequency of the conditions that initiate lawful sequences of behavior, the infrequent being the pathological. | Frequency of end-product behavior in a given social group or culture, the infrequent being the abnormal. | Economy or efficiency in intra-individual organization, the uneconomical being the unhealthy. |

association method came to be employed as a probe for individual norms, called by Jung "complexes." The survey indicates that a single psychological tool can be employed with quite different objectives as regards the role of the individual and related norms. Furthermore, this example may serve to demonstrate that all projective methods, despite their indigenous bias toward individual norms, allow as well for group and universal norms in a complete conceptualization.

The accompanying chart summarizes the varying roles of the individual and the attendant, typical norms encountered in the history of psychology and in contemporary psychological theory. As has already been implied, and as will appear later in further detail, the objective of each theoretical matrix is different and in each the individual assumes an appropriately modified conceptual role. The norms that implicitly or explicitly prevail in the making of interpretations vary similarly and, as the chart indicates, the criteria of normality or abnormality conform to pattern in each approach. The intended implication of the survey is that, while it is theoretically possible to take consistently different views of the individual, the current trend is toward an idiodynamic formulation in which the person is studied with the dual purpose of understanding him as an individual and of deriving general principles of intra-individual functioning. Despite this emerging emphasis, the other two orientations are by no means obsolete and must be taken seriously into account.

## IDIODYNAMIC PERSONALITY POSTULATES

To appreciate how the projective methods can combine the various concepts of the individual, full recognition must first be accorded the "idiodynamic" approach to personality. The projective techniques embody this approach in at least three closely related aspects: response dominance, configuration dominance, and idioverse dominance. These postulates are not only implicit in the methods of psychodiagnosis but are rooted in psychodynamic theory generally.

## 1. Response dominance

Experimental psychology, as well as the psychometric clinical approach, has always proceeded on the assumption that stimulus-response relationships provide the key to the understanding of behavior. In order to build a science of psychology the stimulus had to be a public matter, externally defined, whether by the experimenter or by the examiner. The formulation of behavior principles in which such externally defined stimuli were co-ordinated to certain regularly expected responses constituted the goal of the traditional experimentalist. Similarly the psychometric examiner effected his measurements by relating the responses of his subject to certain standardized stimuli for which there were pre-defined expectancies of response. With the introduction of the psychodynamic point of view came a revolution in the conception of the stimulus and of its relation to the response. The stimulus was dethroned; the dominance of the response ensued. The relationship of responses to each other in a given individual was now the matter of primary interest.

To the traditional psychologist this new state of affairs represented a decided threat to the objective nature of science. In the new regime he saw the degeneration of psychology into a subjective, impressionistic game whose proponents were at best clinicians and at worst charlatans. To the psychodynamic theoretician and to the projective diagnostician, however, the new approach to the stimulus was imperative since it thus became possible to accord the individual personality its proper place in psychological study and theory. What is the answer? The difference between the older, traditional approach and the newer, psychodynamic one is not a matter of objectivity but of objective. The psychophysicist, the behaviorist, and the psychometrician assume certain constant stimulus-response relationships and operate accordingly; the psychodynamic theoretician is interested in response-response relationships to be found in the given individual. The change is from a search for stimulus-response relationships to the study of response-response relationships. Concurrently the generalized human being yields place to the unique individual in central interest for the psychologist.

Thurstone long ago recognized this shift and discussed it under the heading "stimulus-response fallacy" (14). Writing in 1924, he appealed in his exposition to the "New Psychology"—psychoanalysis—and credited it with cogently emphasizing relationships between the impulse or need and the response of the individual, in contrast with the more academic practice of concentrating upon relationships of stimulus and response. In the light of this statement the postulate of response dominance may be more sharply defined. Response-response relationships are significant not only in their own frame of reference but because they also reflect need-response relationships. The translation of manifest to latent content in Freudian dream analysis and the similar interpretations in the projective methods illustrate this type of inference.

The role of the external stimulus may also now be clarified. In the formulations which stress response-response or need-response relationships, the stimulus is often merely a trigger, sometimes only an "excuse," for evoking prepared reactions that have already been set in motion by the inner stimulation of an impulse. It is on this basis that the external stimulus is frequently regarded as being *selected* by the individual or by his impulse-nature from a multiplicity of possible external stimuli. Past stimuli, in so far as they have modified the inner organization of the personality, may thus be far more influential in determining present behavior than any environmental stimulus acting at the moment. Roles are thus assigned to need or impulse, inner stimulation, past stimuli, present external stimulus, and response.

To the projective methods the postulate of response dominance is applicable with one important qualification. While in the free-association method of the psychoanalyst no regard for a standardized stimulus of any kind is necessary, the concern being exclusively with relationships between the subject's earlier and later associations, in the field of the projective techniques there are usually certain common stimuli that are employed consistently with all subjects. One of the advantages of the projective method lies precisely in this qualification. But this difference between the projective techniques and other psychodynamic methods of study complicates the problem of measurement and demands the recognition not only of individual norms but of group norms—stimulus-oriented—as well. The difference between the word-association test as a projective method and the free-association method as the psychoanalyst employs it illustrates the point.

Another way of recognizing the qualified application of response dominance to the projective techniques is to observe that the examiner presents his standard stimuli primarily as a means of eliciting responses. The interrelationships of these responses contain the essence of what he is seeking—the organization of the so-called "inner personality." The stimulus as such is more or less negligible—*more* in so far as the unique responses of the individual subject delineate him psychodiagnostically, *less* in so far as the stimulus itself is a standard one applied to all subjects and related, within certain limits, to group-standardized responses that permit a certain amount of prediction about the subject's relationships to other subjects. The nub of the problem again lies in the interplay of individual and group norms and their mutual definition.

It should further be noted that universal norms are by no

means ruled out in the psychodynamic approach. Concepts like repression and displacement are obviously considered to have a universal application under the appropriate conditions. But there is a difference between such general principles and the corresponding behavioristic stimulus-response formulations. In the last analysis the conditions for repression and the threat to the ego which makes for the operation of this form of defense are to be found in the individual's definition of the stimulus situation according to his own past experience and present attitudes. Moreover the principle itself is mainly a statement of intra-individual dynamics rather than of any systematic relationship between externaly defined stimulus and internally mustered response. For the very distinction between external and internal has largely disappeared and is gradually being replaced by a phenomenological frame of reference in which the "stimulus" and the "response" are interdependent aspects of the subject's universe. Since the stimulus is regarded as ultimately defined by the response, the former can no longer serve as an infallible determiner of the latter.

## 2. Configuration dominance

The twilight of the stimulus is matched by the similar subordination of the part to the whole in the idiodynamic approach. The phenomenological relationship between stimulus and response is paralleled by the absorption of parts into wholes. The important influence of Gestalt psychology is here recognized as complementing the already indicated influence of psychoanalysis. The wholeness of the subject's behavior lies both in the pattern of his responses and in that of the standard stimuli projectively employed. The essential totality is, of course, the world of the individual in which "responses" and "stimuli" are mutually definitive.

Stated thus baldly the postulate of configuration dominance is as much a threat to the traditional psychologist as is the postulate of response dominance. Both signalize the eclipse of scientific "objectivity." Increasingly, however, empirical work has demonstrated both in Gestalt psychology and in experimental psychoanalysis, if not as yet in the field of the projective methods, that these postulates are denotatively stable, not merely a confession of faith in the uniqueness of the individual. A new conception of objectivity is perhaps implicit in recent approaches to the person, but the fact that the new objectivity differs from the old is in itself no criterion of adequacy. It must in the end be recognized that the conception of objectivity inherited from nineteenth century science rests upon a one-sided, if not prejudiced, view of the individual and his place in nature. The final test must, as always in scientific method, rest with the evidence. When it becomes possible in the course of time and experience to compare the effectiveness of the older and newer approaches in terms of their capacity to allow prediction and control, the relative merits of each can be determined.

An important aspect of the part-whole problem as applied to psychodynamics and the projective methods is found in the conception of personality levels (7). In attempting to understand the individual as such, it is essential to recognize various levels or layers of personality, either in terms of conscious and unconscious, as id, ego, and super-ego, or, perhaps more demonstrably, as opinion, overt, and implicit levels of response. In whatever terms the formulation is made, it becomes incumbent upon those working with projective methods and psychodynamic concepts to distinguish the interplay of personality levels in any observed behavior. Interpretation, as the concept is employed in psychodynamics, rests largely upon this distinction, e.g., in Freud's differentiation of manifest and latent dream content or in Lewin's distinction between phenotypical and genotypical levels of explanation.

## 3. Idioverse dominance

This third postulate has been partially anticipated and exemplified in the previous argument. In fact all three of the postulates here outlined are aspects of a single reorientation. But each aspect deserves separate emphasis.

*Idioverse* is the name here given to an *individual's universe of events*. The concept is implicit in psychoanalytic theory and has been advanced in more than one independent version (1, 11, 13); the term is new. Idioverse dominance highlights the standpoint of the individual in any attempt to understand him. At the same time, as has already been noted, the individual is conceived not to exist in a world completely separated from the worlds of others. Thus individual norms, e.g., complexes, play an important part in the assessment of personality but, at the same time, group norms, in terms of shared experiences of a common stimulus, also play a part. Universal norms and general principles based upon them contribute to idiodynamic theory, though—to repeat—these general principles differ from the traditional ones of experimental psychology in the extent to which intra-individual organization is emphasized and in the way in which the stimulus is defined "subjectively" by the individual's own performance. The inclusion of group and universal norms, as well as individual ones, is wholly compatible with idioverse dominance. Frequently the error is made both by opponents and proponents of the projective techniques of identifying these tools with the approach of individual norms alone.

It follows from the postulate of idioverse dominance that the projective technique is not to be conceived as a "test" in the usual sense.[2] The test, as it has become known in the field of

---

[2] If the reader notes the sedulous avoidance of "test" as a substantive following "projective" and a consistent preference for "method," "technique" or "procedure," the reason is apparent at this point. The projective *method* is not to be confused with the psychometric *test*. The term "test" has been pre-

psychometrics, exists for the measurement of individual differences in a group, the norms being statistical or group norms. To place the individual in the group becomes the aim of the procedure. External standards, pre-established by the examiner or by his colleagues who standardized the test, determine right and wrong responses—just as certain expected responses to objectively defined stimuli figure in the principles of behavioristic, general psychology.

In the projective technique, as contrasted with the psychometric test, the approach is shifted from an emphasis upon group norms to an emphasis upon individual norms—the more or less unique ways in which the subject structures or interprets the eliciting stimuli. As has been pointed out elsewhere (10), however, it is still necessary to employ group norms, wherever feasible, in order to demarcate the individual from the group. If, for example, one does not know what is commonly given as a response to a particular TAT card, it becomes impossible to say what is unique. Group norms thus play a part in the detection of individual responses and of the individual norms implicit in them. Moreover the delineation of individual norms serves not only to show how the person functions in his particular universe but also to prefigure the inner organization of his personality according to the relatively universal principles of psychodynamics. The universal norms of psychodynamics thus combine with the individual norms adumbrated in the projective methods to prepare the way for laws applicable to the population of events in the individual universe.

The conceptualization of the projective techniques is possible only on the basis of the foregoing postulates. Response dominance, configuration dominance, and idioverse dominance involve a complete revolution of thinking in psychological meas-

---

empted for use in the orientation of the stimulus, the segment, and the external universe of the person as something imposed upon the subject from without. To respect this usage promotes clarity.

urement. The familiar concepts of test construction and of experimental design are obviously incompatible with such a radical reorientation even though, as in all revolutions, the past is to a certain extent implicit in and serves as an evolutionary foundation for the over-emphasized present.

## THE CONCEPTUALIZATION OF PROJECTIVE TECHNIQUES

From the foregoing exposition of personality theory as related to the projective methods it should be easier to appreciate the difficulties which these techniques present, as compared with the usual psychometric test, when problems of test construction and standardization are posed. The present discussion of these difficulties will be limited to the two chief dimensions in respect to which the traditional test has had to prove itself. These dimensions are, of course, *reliability* and *validity*.

### I. Reliability

The inapplicability of the traditional reliability concept to projective techniques can be readily appreciated if the previous discussion of configuration dominance is recalled. The standard stimuli in the projective method are almost always considered to constitute a configuration that cannot be analyzed into its separate parts or segments without significant loss of meaning. Thus the Rorschach cards have certain relationships to each other on the basis of which it is possible to detect so-called "color shock." Changes in the reaction time from card to card and differences in the quality of response, all of which derive from the fact that the subject has first seen certain cards and is then shown others, depend upon the configurational unity of the total series. Once this fact is recognized it becomes obvious that the reliability of a projective technique cannot be determined by either the split-half or alternate-item methods.

Not only are the parts or aspects of these psychodiagnostic instruments interdependent, but even when separable they differ from the parts of a psychometric test in being of unequal psychological import. This inequality is, moreover, not merely a quantitative but is rather a qualitative matter. The inequality of units refers not to differences in the difficulty of items or in the capacity of the subject to solve them, but to differences in the kind of psychological reaction the stimuli may be expected to elicit. Under these circumstances any attempt to divide the total series of cards into a first half and a second half or to equate odd and even items for the purpose of determining reliability would violate the essence of the procedure. Any two "halves" of the method are simply not intended to be equal and hence should not correlate with each other if the projective technique lives up to its configurational design.

One might then maintain that it should at least be possible to use alternate forms of a projective technique and establish reliability by this means. To a certain extent the suggestion has been borne out in practice. Thus one finds for the Rorschach method not one but two alternate forms—the Behn and the Harrower. In theory the solution is less simple. If one is to examine the same subject on two different occasions with either the same or alternate versions of a particular projective technique, it is still necessary to consider the possibility that the experience of participation on the first occasion may affect the second performance. The temporal configuration of the subject's total experience here manifests itself in a new form. The nearest equivalent to this dilemma in the psychometric test of capacity is the effect of practice on performance, but since ability is presumably static over a brief period of time, such effects are negligible or can be statistically corrected. In the projective methods such solutions are not available, for one is there attempting to evaluate subtle personality processes with a temporal dimension that includes the configurational effect of earlier upon later experience.

Moreover any theory of personality must take into account the general fact that a person is not identically the same from the time of one experimental or diagnostic session to that of another. To be sure, there are presumably stable aspects of personality which have a certain degree of permanence and should be measurably equal from one day to the next. However, these stable and basic aspects are not yet easy to define or to tap. Mood changes are sometimes noted to affect the results even of the venerable Rorschach. In other words, to study the subject's performance on several occasions is not merely to assess the reliability or stability of an instrument—as is true for the psychometric test; one is inevitably committed to the measurement of personality consistency. The familiar reliability concept is, therefore, too narrow for the projective field.

In some of the writer's experimental work the foregoing considerations as to the repeatability of a subject's performance have led to a novel concept—"the range of personal variability." The concept is intended to allow for the scope which any personality must be permitted if it is to maintain its constantly changing and dynamic character. On the assumption that personality is constituted of a population of events (the idioverse), the range of variability here in question corresponds to the standard deviation or some other measure of dispersion around the mean performance. A statistical analysis of the intra-individual population is thus envisaged as part of any reliability determination. It is hoped that by concepts of this kind it will be possible eventually to adapt or replace the traditional techniques of test construction and standardization. In such efforts the theory of personality and of psychodynamics will, of course, have to be closely coordinated with the statistical methods evolved.

In the meantime it is well to bear in mind that the reliability dimension has its own limitations. Reliability as such is no un-mixed blessing, especially in the field of personality assessment. It is self-evident that a high degree of re-test reliability, demon-strated for a particular personality inventory, may have been achieved by virtue of an equal degree of invalidity on both occasions. If the subject commits the same "opinion errors" both times, the scores of his tests will, of course, correlate highly. The important conclusion will, however, not then be that the inventory has proved to be reliable but rather that it has proved—if we can prove it—to be equally *invalid* on the two occasions. Validity thus becomes a far more basic matter than reliability—a point to which it will be necessary to return.

A confusingly related consideration is the reliability of scor-ing. In psychometric tests, e.g., the Stanford-Binet, response samples and other means of making it possible for different examiners to score identically have played an obvious part. When, however, a projective technique is under scrutiny, the reliability of scoring becomes more problematic, since here the variety of possible responses is so much greater and their an-chorage to the stimulus is so much looser. In this context Harrison and Rotter (5) have attempted to show that the TAT can be consistently scored by two independent workers. A similar project has been devoted to the Picture-Frustration Study (2). Reliability of scoring as here recognized, should not, how-ever, be confused—as Harrison and Rotter tend to do—with test reliability in the usual sense.

## 2. Validity

Far more intricate than the problems associated with re-liability are those associated with validity. As Ellis (3) has shown in his critical review, the validity of personality in-ventories is notoriously weak as compared with their reliability. In fact, it almost appears as if the student of personality has

consoled himself with high reliability coefficients in compensa-
tion for any adequate degree of validity. In contrast to this
state of affairs it should be noted that proponents of the projective methods have always put validity ahead of reliability.
Their demonstrations of validity have not, however, always convinced others. Clinicians are apt to be too easily satisfied with
the consistency of their own experience as a proof of validity.
Some of them even make a fetish of the fact that the methods
they use do not need, or at least cannot benefit from, the time-
honored techniques for establishing validity. Anyone who has
had clinical experience in the appraisal of personality by projective and cognate methods can testify to this temptation.

The student of personality theory and measurement cannot
afford to be so sanguine. He requires systematic evidence, carefully controlled. At the same time he takes issue with those
investigators from the psychometric field who, not being con-
versant with the psychodynamic basis of the projective techniques, tend to ignore the postulates reviewed above. The most
common error of this kind involves the use of segmental "objective" methods of determining both reliability and validity.
Vernon (15) early recognized the limitations of such approaches
to the Rorschach and offered the matching method as one cor-
rective.

In keeping with this orientation the first aspect of the validity
problem in the projective methods concerns their configurational properties. To be completely consistent one might even
question whether the scoring of projective productions, segment
by segment, does not violate their Gestalt character. The insistent need for analytic scoring if one is to come to grips with
the data has denied this point the systematic attention it deserves. Perhaps this partial blindness implies a recognition that
no alternative exists except a frankly impressionistic and suspect
approach to the subject's total productions. But before the
alternative is dismissed, it might be useful to consider with Sara-

son (12) the possibility of putting so-called *subjectivity* or impressionistic interpretation (as opposed to scoring) on an objectively phenomenological basis. There is nothing to prevent empirical studies of the comparative validity of impressionistic interpretations with others arrived at by the more usual analytic-synthetic procedures.

Closely related to the scoring issue is the problem of interpreting particular quantities or values of an isolated scoring factor. Beck, for example, has repeatedly emphasized that identical quantitative values for any one of the Rorschach factors may have quite different psychological meanings depending upon the total pattern of scores in which that quantity is embedded. If, therefore, one is to validate a projective technique, it is necessary theoretically to consider this multi-potentiality of the isolated factor. One must take into account the shifting meaning of its whole range of quantities, each of which can, in turn, have a multiplicity of meanings according to whether it is found in any one of a multiplicity of scoring patterns. As can readily be seen from this rather appalling, but not exaggerated, statement of the case, the prospect involves an almost limitless number of situations to be validated.

But it is necessary to validate more than the individual factors of a projective technique; the various patterns of such factors lie even closer to the configurational approach which these methods espouse. According to the previous exposition of idiodynamic postulates, it could even be maintained that individual scores or measures have a partial, if not misleading, significance psychologically and that only the total record or protocol should be interpreted. Some hope is perhaps to be found in following this line of thought to its logical conclusion. Are there possibly certain qualitatively unitary aspects of personality—certain qualitative quanta—that are more or less finite in number and that may be isolable in the various patterns that a projective technique discloses? If such a hypothesis is justified, the aim of validating various separate quantities of a particular scoring category would be abandoned. Only configurations of scores would be considered as having possible significance, and a subject's record would be scrutinized as a whole or as a constellation of wholes with certain possible unitary meanings.

Having considered the special properties of the projective technique as they affect validation, it is necessary to examine next the broader issues of the validation procedure in its entirety. The first of these issues is the definition of the validity objective. To ask in general terms whether a projective method is valid or not is relatively meaningless. It is always essential to decide for what particular purpose—for what specific predictive or heuristic use—the validity of the procedure is to be assessed. Far too often this obvious caution is not observed, and the results obtained are then bound to be confusing and inconclusive.

The definition of the independent validity criterion is another frequent source of confusion. In particular, the problem of levels of personality expression (7) is here noteworthy. Whether the subject is manifesting the opinion (self-critical), overt, or implicit level of behavior, or some combination of them, is not easy to determine. Yet if a projective method is tapping one level, say the implicit, and the judgment of personality with which the technique is to be correlated for purposes of validation is made at another level, say the overt, the fact that little agreement between these two assessments was found to exist would in no way reflect upon the validity of the instrument. Unless this difference in levels had been taken into account, false conclusions might be drawn regarding the validity of the technique.

The problem of validating the independent criterion is a further aspect of its proper definition. When one resorts to an independent criterion, one turns inevitably to one or another of three main sorts of evidence: one may make or ask for certain observations of the subject in situations independent of the projective method; one may obtain ratings from some judge who has observed the subject under favorable conditions; or one may apply other measuring instruments with the intention of correlating their results with those of the instrument to be validated. The hazards connected with each of these courts of appeal are readily apparent and have been repeatedly described. Observations made on a subject are inevitably colored by the situation in which he was observed or by the personality of the observer, and such evidence is therefore often as dubious as the evidence of the projective method to be validated. Ratings are similarly apt to be subjectively contaminated, even when the judge is highly motivated and conscientious in the performance of his task. Measures from other instruments, especially if projective, are themselves apt to be questionably valid. To validate one unvalidated projective technique by means of another involves the investigator in a circular type of argument, with the blind leading the blind. It may be concluded that no investigation of validity can be more than suggestive or preliminary unless precautions are taken in it to establish the validity of the independent criterion.

To accomplish the above goals in respect to validation new investigative procedures may be indicated. One example is the method of validation by successive clinical predictions (8).

### 3. Relative values of reliability and validity

Up to this point reliability and validity have been considered more or less separately. It may now be useful to cast a glance at their interrelated significance. As has been indicated above, reliability without validity can be a doubtful virtue. If one must make a choice, it is obviously validity that is fundamental.

It can be convincingly maintained that validity demonstrated on repeated occasions implies reliability. To put the matter in these terms has a certain advantage from the standpoint of personality theory since stress is here placed upon the importance of measuring what one purports to measure. Reliability as such is more a property of an instrument than it is a reflection of the relationship between an instrument and the personality one seeks to assess. The only merit in getting the same answer twice with a particular measuring rod lies in the fact that the measure actually reflects some property of that which is to be measured. In so far as personality is itself inconsistent or subject to change with time, room is rightly left for a certain degree of psychometric "unreliability" without any contradiction to the validity of a projective technique or to its *essential* reliability.

## SUMMARY

In the history of psychology the theoretical fate of the individual and the attendant norms for interpreting his behavior have evolved in an idiodynamic direction. The essential postulates of the idiodynamic approach are response dominance, configuration dominance, and idioverse dominance. Personality theory of this type is fundamental to any compelling conceptualization of the projective techniques, but cannot be used in isolation from the relevant aspects of the general-experimental and psychometric points of view. In thus integrating personality theory with the newer methods of psychodiagnosis, the traditional concepts and methods of test construction and standardization, notably reliability and validity, must be recast.

## REFERENCES

1.  Allport, F. H. Teleonomic description in the study of personality. *Charact. & Pers.*, 1937, **5,** 202–214.
2.  Clarke, H. J., Rosenzweig, S., & Fleming, E. E. The reliability

of the scoring of the Rosenzweig Picture-Frustration Study. *J. clin. Psychol.*, 1947, **4**, 364–370.

3. Ellis, A. The validity of personality questionnaires. *Psychol. Bull.*, 1946, **43**, 385–440.

4. Frank, L. K. *Projective methods.* Springfield, Ill.: Charles C. Thomas, 1948.

5. Harrison, R., & Rotter, J. B. A note on the reliability of the Thematic Apperception Test. *J. abnorm. soc. Psychol.*, 1945, **40**, 97–99.

6. Macfarlane, J. W. Problems of validation inherent in projective methods. *Amer. J. Orthopsychiat.*, 1942, **12**, 405–410.

7. Rosenzweig, S. Levels of behavior in psychodiagnosis with special reference to the Picture-Frustration Study. *Amer. J. Orthopsychiat.*, 1950, **20**, 63–72.

8. Rosenzweig, S. A method of validation by successive clinical predictions. *J. abnorm. soc. Psychol.*, 1950, **45**, 507–509.

9. Rosenzweig, S. Norms and the individual in the psychologist's perspective. In *Feelings and emotions* (M. L. Reymert, Ed.). New York: McGraw-Hill, 1950.

10. Rosenzweig, S. Apperceptive norms for the Thematic Apperception Test. I. The problem of norms in the projective methods. *J. Personality*, 1949, **17**, 475–482.

11. Rosenzweig, S. Projective techniques: their progress in the application of psychodynamics. In *Orthopsychiatry 1923–1948: retrospect and prospect.* New York: Amer. Orthopsychiatric Assoc., 1948. Pp. 456–469.

12. Sarason, S. B. The TAT and subjective interpretation. *J. consult. Psychol.*, 1948, **12**, 285–299.

13. Snygg, D., & Combs, A. W. *Individual behavior.* New York: Harper, 1949.

14. Thurstone, L. L. *The nature of intelligence.* New York: Harcourt, Brace, 1924.

15. Vernon, P. E. The significance of the Rorschach test. *Brit. J. med. Psychol.*, 1935, **15**, 199–217.

# Part III

---

**THE SELF AND OTHERS**

## CHAPTER 7

........................................................................................................

# The Phenomenological Approach to
# Social Psychology

---

## BY ROBERT B. MACLEOD

Social psychology today is both one of the most challenging and one of the least disciplined fields of psychological research. The rapidly growing interest in the psychological study of the individual in society reflects a healthy moral awakening on the part of psychologists to their social responsibilities. Yet, as we review some of the great issues toward which psychology should contribute understanding, e.g., the causes of national, racial, and class tension, the possibility of individual freedom in a tightly organized society, we cannot but be appalled by the discrepancy between what we can now assert as established fact or principle and the insights which society rightly expects us to provide.

The simple fact is that the sudden expansion of the field of social psychology finds us with conceptual and methodological

From *Psychological Review*, 1947, **54**, 193–210. Reprinted by permission of the author and the publisher.

tools which are inadequate to the new task. Social psychology must either rest content with present concepts and methods, which have proved useful in restricted contexts, and run the risk of producing obvious or trivial results, or make a fresh start, reviewing its basic assumptions, redesigning old tools and inventing new ones, and developing a science equal to the task which confronts us.

The writer believes that in this connection the social psychologist can profit from a glance at recent developments in the psychology of perception. In some respects social psychology to-day resembles the psychology of perception of thirty-five years ago. At that time the systematic application of the phenomenological method liberated the psychology of perception from its traditional bonds and launched it on a new and productive course. Whether or not an analogous method can be successfully applied to social problems remains to be seen. The present thesis is that it must be tried. The systematic application of a social phenomenology holds forth the promise of a new definition of the field of social psychology, of a more adequate social psychological methodology, and ultimately of an integration of the laws of social psychology with those of perception.[1]

## PHENOMENOLOGY IN THE PSYCHOLOGY OF PERCEPTION

By the phenomenological method,[2] as applied to psychology,

[1] The direct application of perceptual principles to problems of social psychology has already proved fruitful, e.g., in the work of Sherif (8). The importance of a phenomenological approach to social problems has been stressed by various authors, e.g., Köhler (6, 7), Koffka (5), Heider (3).

[2] Psychological phenomenology must be clearly distinguished from philosophical phenomenology (2). While the former derived historically from the latter, and can continue to profit from the developments in philosophical phenomenology, it has remained and must continue as an approach rather than as a theory. Phenomenology in psychology can never be a substitute for psychophysics and psychophysiology. Its function is rather to set the initial problem, to define the psychological datum which must then be envisaged in the setting of its physical and physiological correlates. Whereas philosophical

is meant the systematic attempt to observe and describe in all its essential characteristics the world of phenomena as it is presented to us. It involves the adoption of what might be called an attitude of disciplined naivete. It requires the deliberate suspension of all implicit and explicit assumptions, e.g., as to eliciting stimulus or underlying mechanism, which might bias our observation. The phenomenological question is simply, "What is there?", without regard to Why, Whence, or Wherefore.

In a sense every psychologist is at times a phenomenologist, and no psychologist ever achieves the ideal. Nevertheless it is an ideal which can be approached; and it was the application in systematic and rigorous form of the phenomenological method to the study of perception that marked a turning-point, about thirty-five years ago, in the history of that branch of psychology. Although the importance of a psychological phenomenology had been recognized long before by Hering (1878), had been expounded by Husserl (1900), and was reflected in the early researches from the laboratories of Stumpf, G. E. Müller and Külpe, it can scarcely be disputed that the publication of Katz' *Erscheinungsweisen der Farben* (4) and of Wertheimer's study of movement (10) demonstrated for the first time how a careful phenomenology could lead to a thoroughgoing reformulation of the whole problem of perception.

The psychology of perception of thirty-five years ago had

---

phenomenology began with an attempt at an unbiased description of psychological data and proceeded therefrom toward an account of ultimate reality in terms of its essences, the psychological phenomenologists have endeavored merely to liberate their science from some of its theoretical biases, and to focus attention on problems which might otherwise be neglected. Thus, for example, the phenomenal properties of subjectivity and objectivity, of reality character, of psychological distance, which tend to escape the notice of the seeker for simple physical and physiological correlates of experience, are seen by the phenomenologist in their proper perspective. And there is no reason to doubt that, in due course, we shall have a psychophysics and psychophysiology of these properties analogous to our present psychophysics and psychophysiology of color.

notable achievements to its credit. With methods adapted from physics and sensory physiology it had demonstrated that mental phenomena can be studied under controlled laboratory conditions. It had successfully challenged the age-old assumption that psychological data cannot be measured. It had succeeded, within limits, in refining out of the older association psychology, with its confusion of logical with psychological analysis, a set of constructs which could serve as a framework for a validly psychological description. And it had formulated and tested a set of principles which promised, if systematically applied, to lead eventually to a complete and scientific account of perceptual experience.

The achievements of Titchener, of Wundt or of Helmholtz should not be disparaged. Yet it was in a sense the very excellence of their work which hampered the forward movement of the psychology of perception. They had provided a neatly hewn set of building blocks with which the edifice of perceptual experience was to be reconstructed. Elementary sensations were the building blocks. These elementary sensations had been studied in the laboratory, their properties described, their physical and physiological correlates measured. One cannot condemn the faith that every perceptual experience, however complex, could finally be reduced to terms of elementary sensations combined in a particular way. It was natural that Helmholtz, for instance, should insist that the apparent discrepancy between physical change and phenomenal change in what has subsequently been called color constancy involved no real change of sensation, but was due rather to an elaborate system of unconscious inferences. The hypothesis of a simple point-to-point correlation between stimulus and sensation had proved satisfactory in the laboratory study of elementary sensation. When a more complex phenomenon was presented it was easier to maintain the original hypothesis, and to add to it the postulate of certain secondary psychological processes, than it was to take a fresh look at the phenomena and redesign the hypothesis accordingly.

The phenomenologically minded students of perception had three interrelated biases to combat: (1) the belief that something small is more fundamental than something large—*the atomistic-reductive bias;* (2) the belief that a differentiable variable in the physical world or a differentiable receptor in the organism implies the existence of a correspondingly differentiated unit of experience—*the stimulus-receptor bias;* and (3) the belief that that which is genetically early is more fundamental than that which is genetically late—*the genetic bias.*

The atomistic-reductive bias was assimilated directly from 19th century physical science. In an atmosphere dominated by the search for physical elements it was natural that psychologists should seek for the elements of mind and attempt to reduce complex mental phenomena to terms of those elements. It is equally intelligible, if less pardonable, that even after physics had in large part given up its elementarism psychologists should continue to believe that only by reductive analysis can psychological phenomena be explained.

The stimulus-receptor bias was in part a by-product of the laboratory method, in part merely an unchallenged consequence of the Aristotelian doctrine of the senses. Throughout the history of psychology the senses, at first five and later many more, have been accepted as the mediators between the mind and the external world. Succeeding studies of the anatomy and physiology of the sense organs have permitted closer and closer correlations between physical stimulus variable and elementary sensory reaction. Granted the search for elements, it is understandable that that experience was considered elementary which seemed to be the direct result of the activation of a simple receptor mechanism. By the same logic, any experience which evinced no such simple correlations was accorded a secondary status. Thus there was imposed on the perceptual world a theoretical structure which did not necessarily correspond to the structure of direct experience.

The genetic bias is, if possible, even more tenacious than the other two. The 19th century emphasis on evolution is merely a vigorous expression of a much older belief that if we are to understand we must seek origins. The search for origins frequently involves the implicit assumption that an earlier form of a phenomenon is somehow or other a truer form. In perception the assumption was that the perceptions of everyday life are tainted with past experience, that the only true immediacy is found in a perception which is occurring for the first time. Hence the tendency to regard generalizations based on meaningful material as suspect; hence the unwillingness of psychologists in their study of perception to deal with phenomena of everyday life.

The genius of the phenomenological psychologists lay simply in their ability to suspend these biases while they took a fresh look at the world of perceptual phenomena. And the results were impressive. One need only recall the early contributions of Bühler, Gelb, Jaensch, Katz, Koffka, Köhler, and Wertheimer—to mention only the leading names—to realize that new and challenging problems were emerging in fields which had been rendered inaccessible by the older point of view. Color constancy is a good example. The basic facts had been observed by Helmholtz, and both he and Hering had advanced alternative explanations. It was Katz, however, who recognized that an adequate treatment of the problem required a revision of the descriptive methods of color psychology.

The simple categories of hue, brightness, and saturation afford no basis for an intelligible characterization of surface quality, film quality, bulkiness, shininess, transparency, or luminosity. Some colors, for example, are perceived as properties of objects (the whiteness of a sheet of paper), others as properties of media through which objects are seen (the redness of a stained glass through which the paper is seen), and still others as properties of empty space (the blueness or greyness of the sky); and the behavior of such colors depends on their mode of appearance. The whiteness which inheres phenomenally in a sheet of paper is more resistant to change than is the brightness which appears as a property of the illumination. If conditions of observation permit, a decrease in the intensity of the light reflected by the paper will tend to be seen as a darkening of the illumination rather than as a darkening of the color of the paper. The "true" color of the paper will tend to maintain itself as long as possible.

Thus visual perception responds selectively to changes in physical stimulation. It is as though the organism in its perceptual activity were attempting to resist the disrupting influence of change by referring changes to the functionally less important parts of the field. The same generalization is supported by observations in other fields of perception, notably the perception of the size and shape of objects, of position in space, of induced movement, and even of such object properties as temperature and apparent loudness.

The theory of the constancies need not be discussed here.[3] There are, however, a few general facts worth noting: (1) the problem can receive no constructive formulation as long as psychological thinking is dominated by the reductive-atomistic, the stimulus-receptor, and the genetic biases. From the traditional point of view it represents merely a set of perceptual anomalies, analogous to the optical illusions, which must be "explained away." (2) Once the problem has been accepted as legitimate, phenomenological observation reveals as relevant a

[3] For a fuller discussion of the problem see Koffka (5) and Woodworth (11).

series of perceptual properties which have been disregarded in traditional psychological analysis. (3) These "new" perceptual properties—which, in fact, are all familiar phenomena of everyday observation—prove in the main to be properties of field organization which disappear under traditional conditions of laboratory observation. To study them in a scientific way the experimenter is consequently required to revise his experimental methods. (4) Any analysis of the field determinants of an individual phenomenon leads to a new appreciation of the interdependence of different parts of the perceptual field, and ultimately to the formulation of principles of field organization which, in turn, (5) make new demands on psychophysical and psychophysiological theory.

The constancies represent only one group of problems which, formulated first as a result of phenomenological analysis, have contributed to the development of a field theory of perception the implications of which extend far beyond phenomenology. The whole configurational emphasis in psychology presents a similar history—first an attempt at an unbiased description of phenomena, then systematic experimentation designed to reveal the essential determinants of these phenomena, and finally revision of existing theory in the light of the new principles discovered. A phenomenological emphasis in psychology does not restrict the psychologist to the description of phenomena. It requires him, however, to look first at the world of things-as-they-are in its entirety before deciding which aspects of this world are to be considered important for theory, and at every stage in his investigation to keep checking back to phenomena to make sure that they have not been distorted by the very process of investigation. In essence the phenomenologist asks the question "What?" before he asks the questions "Why?", "Whence?", or "Wherefore?", and his answers to the latter question are guided by his answer to the first.

## IMPLICIT ASSUMPTIONS IN
## SOCIAL PSYCHOLOGICAL THINKING

How should one proceed with a phenomenological analysis of the social world? The first fact to be noted is that there is no social world different from or superimposed upon the world of perception. We are dealing with a single set of phenomena, and we shall presumably discover a single set of laws. We are striving merely to complete a phenomenological analysis which has hitherto recoiled from some of the more difficult phenomena. In the second place, the phenomena which we call "social" are intrinsically more difficult to describe, both because of the poverty of our language (which is in itself of great phenomenological significance) and because the phenomenologist here meets in its most acute form the old difficulty of being at the same time both subject and observer. In the third place, these very descriptive difficulties make it even more necessary than in standard perceptual analysis that the descriptions of one observer be checked against those of other observers.

If we are to follow the pattern of perceptual phenomenology, our descriptive analysis must be preceded by an attempt to uncover and temporarily to suspend the implicit assumptions, or biases, which govern our social psychological thinking. The following list of biases is offered with no claim to completeness or originality, and without any suggestion that they necessarily represent unsound approaches. No science can proceed without systematic assumptions. What is important, however, is that our assumptions be held up to scrutiny before they are accepted as a basis for scientific thinking. The following biases are presented in simple and dogmatic form as representative ways in which the subject-matter and methods of social psychology may be predetermined by a set of implicit assumptions.

1. *The organism centered bias.* The essential determinants of social behavior are defined as conditions of the organism or

as forces emerging from the organism. The language of instincts, drives, needs, interests, attitudes, and other inherited or
acquired dispositions of the organism, accords primary significance to directive and regulative factors of a biological or
quasi-biological order, and relegates to a position of secondary importance extra-organismic direction and regulation. In
Lewin's terms this is to recognize vectors from within as more
fundamental than vectors from without; in Murray's terms it is
to make need more important than press. In a very general
sense it is to found our social psychology on a psychology of
motivation. Such a tendency is recognizable, for instance, in the
explanation of social behavior as the expression of a gregarious
instinct or an instinct of imitation, or in the acceptance of a
postulated trait of suggestibility as the basis for responsiveness
to propaganda.

2. *The genetic bias.* The explanation of a present state, e.g.,
a conflict, a prejudice, a loyalty, is sought in the forces which
operated at an earlier period in time rather than in the forces at
present operative. Although the enthusiastic search for social
origins which characterized the social anthropology of the late
19th century has been generally replaced by a more functional
approach, and the animal psychologists have long since lost
their conviction that human social behavior can be seen in its
"raw" form in the animal world, the ontogenetic bias is still
strong. The question "Why?", applied to present behavior, suggests a "because" which points back to early childhood. The
implication is that the true pattern of behavior is revealed in
the child, and that present behavior is composed of the original
plus modifications or accretions.

Without disparaging genetic studies we must insist that continuity does not necessarily imply identity in any essential respect. When I say that I still possess my great-grandfather's
axe, which incidentally has had two new heads and five new
handles since my great-grandfather's time, the historic reference

has little bearing on the present properties or functions of the axe. The significance of present behavior in its present context, e.g., the anarchist's resistance to political authority, may be obscured by a too ready identification of it with a similar pattern, e.g., an Oedipus conflict, in the context of childhood.

3. *The sociological bias.* This is somewhat analogous to the stimulus-receptor bias in the psychology of perception. In its most common form it involves the acceptance of the structures and processes of society as defined by the sociologist as the true coordinates for the specification of social behavior and experience. From this point of view, for instance, the church or the political party in which the individual possesses membership is regarded as an institution of society, possessing the manifold properties and functions which a many-sided sociological investigation reveals, rather than as the church or political party as it is apprehended and reacted to by the individual. The process of social adjustment, of socialization, or of attitude formation thus becomes defined in terms of a set of norms which have reality for the scientific observer, but not necessarily for the individual concerned.

4. *The logical bias.* Although this is most commonly found in the psychology of motivation it may, by virtue of that fact, affect social psychological observation and thinking. The most obvious example is found in the characterization of the directedness of motivated behavior in terms of a goal which is a logically implied outcome of the behavior but which is not in any sense psychologically contained within the behavior. Thus to assert that the goal of an act is to attain a final state of equilibrium or of maximum happiness, or to preserve the species, or even to escape from a conflict, is to impute a directedness to behavior which may not be present as such to the individual.

Granted that the problem of unconscious motivation, and consequently of unconscious goals, is not to be lightly brushed aside, it would seem plausible that the attack on the problem of directedness should begin with the study of goals which are phenomenally present. To argue from correlational studies, for instance, that anti-Negro prejudice is based on the desire to eliminate the Negro as an economic competitor is to translate a set of relevant conditions into a possibly fictitious goal structure. This may or may not be a real goal, or it may be one of a number of equivalent goals subordinate to a more general goal. We cannot solve the problem of prejudice until we discover what goals are actually present and how they are related to one another.

5. *The reductive-atomistic bias* may affect social psychological thinking as it does every other kind of psychological thinking. Although the sensation units of the traditional theory of perception are no longer relevant, it is still easier to break social behavior down into small parts, into response mechanisms, into discrete attitudes, or into cultural patterns, and to treat these parts as independent existents with their own inherent properties and functions, than it is to preserve the more cumbersome language of functional interdependence. We are tempted to assume, for instance, that because our language is studded with familiar names for social objects—races, nations, classes, and so forth—and because meaningful reactions can be elicited by these names, that therefore there must exist an attitude corresponding to each name, each attitude constituting a separately measurable entity. Such an assumption can lead to a *Stückhaftigkeit* fully as dangerous as that contained in associationism. Although this danger has been clearly recognized (1, 9), the prevalence of the bias cannot be overlooked.

6. *The relativistic bias* might be considered as the logical opposite of the reductive-atomistic bias. This has gained support in recent years from anthropological studies. The demonstration that particular customs or particular personality traits become fully intelligible only in the light of a particular cultural pattern leads readily to the conclusion that there are no "absolutes" in

human nature. Insofar as this represents a recognition of the facts of functional interdependence it can be accepted as a healthy reaction against atomism. In its extreme form, however, it may lead to an equally untenable assumption, namely, that no thing, process, or situation possesses any inherent properties. The fact that what we condemn as "stealing" may be applauded in another culture suggests a relativistic interpretation of crime. What is relative to the culture, however, is merely the particular act which is condemned as criminal, not the fact of criminal behavior as such. The term "crime" represents a pattern, found in all societies, in which certain acts are condemned as bad. It has meaning which is independent of any particular cultural setting.

Both atomism and relativism can be avoided if we take another look at phenomena. The fact is that the phenomenal world contains things which possess properties phenomenally inherent in the things, but it also has characteristics which are accidental and extraneous to thinghood. It is neither an array of arbitrarily definable entities nor an infinitely complex network of relationships. An adequate phenomenology should give us, at least as a basis for further inquiry, an indication as to which phenomena represent tough and resistant entities or systems to which causal significance can be attributed and which phenomena represent fleeting functions of field conditions.

## SOME SAMPLE PROBLEMS
## FOR A SOCIAL PHENOMENOLOGY

The listing and scrutinizing of biases is only a first step, preparatory to the phenomenologist's attempt, with these biases held temporarily in abeyance, to give a systematic account of all the social phenomena of his world—describing, classifying, analyzing, abstracting, generalizing, and so forth, and eventually emerging with a conceptual scheme which will serve as a framework for empirical investigation. It is obvious that this is not the way in which a social phenomenology will be worked out. The phenomenologist must begin with specific problem areas, and gradually extend the scope of his inquiry. The following paragraphs will briefly annotate three such problem areas, namely, (1) the self as phenomenal datum, (2) the other person as phenomenal datum, and (3) society as phenomenal datum. In each case the lack of an adequate phenomenology has seriously crippled the advance of social psychology.

1. *The self as phenomenal datum.* The term "subjective" is, of course, to be encountered everywhere in the literature of psychology and philosophy, ranging in its use from an epithet connoting "unscientific" or "unreliable" to a technical term designating a school of philosophy. In the classic arguments of the British empiricists the perceptual properties of objects were variously considered as inherent in the object, i.e., really there, or dependent on the perceiver, i.e., subjective. Thus the distinctions among primary qualities (e.g., extension, duration), secondary qualities (e.g., color, sound) and subsequently tertiary qualities (e.g., beauty, ugliness), were based on their presumed degree of dependence on the perceiving mind, or subject. Such a dependence was, however, an inferred dependence, and the resultant confusion in epistemology has never been completely dispelled.

In recent psychology the problem has been more frequently stated in terms of degree of dependence on the organism—with the same resultant confusion. It becomes speedily clear that any act or experience of an organism is dependent on the organism, and that any attempt to differentiate exactly between the contributions of the organism and those of the environment is doomed. Thus, in the traditional sense, all psychological data become "subjective."

Let us, however, suspend for a moment our concern about dependency on the organism (or the perceiver) and look at the phenomena themselves. What, for instance, are the phenomenal differences between a color and a pain? The color is usually "out there" in space; it is usually a property of an object; I am convinced that it is still there even when I close my eyes; I cannot apprehend it as a property of me. On the other hand, my headache is mine; the pain of the pin-prick is felt in me, not in the pin; and try as I may I can only seldom and with difficulty "push out" the pain and regard it as something independent of me. From a psychophysiological point of view, both color and pain are in pretty much the same sense dependent on the organism. From the phenomenological point of view, there is a clear and inescapable difference. The color is objective; the pain is subjective. Thus objectivity and subjectivity are phenomenal facts; they represent a dimension of variation in the phenomenal world just as valid as those of brightness and loudness. Every perceptual experience can be rated in this way, although no perceptual quality considered in abstraction can be assigned a fixed place on the scale. Thus the perceptual result of patterned cutaneous stimulation may change rapidly from objective roughness or smoothness to subjective pressure.

Subjectivity and objectivity are properties of an organized perceptual field in which the points of reference are selves (subjects) and objects, and the degree of articulation in this dimension may vary greatly. It is probably true that no object-organization can exist without a self as a point of reference, and that no feeling of selfhood can be maintained without at least some degree of organization in the area of the not-self. There are, nevertheless, conditions, as for example in extreme drowsiness, in which the distinctions are blurred, and it is probable that the world of the child is less differentiated and stabilized in this respect than in the world of the adult. It may be, in fact, that a line of psychological development could be traced, along which self and object could be represented as becoming progressively differentiated out of a more primitive state of consciousness in which neither exists in its characteristic adult form. Whether or not this be true, it is clear that self and object have many characteristics in common. Each constitutes a segregated entity in the same perceptual field, oriented and extended in space, persisting in time, maintaining its identity in spite of changes in the field, and so forth. In traditional language, each possesses primary and secondary qualities, many of which are similar. It is in the category of the tertiary qualities that the differences are greatest; but even here most of the differences are differences of degree. A phenomenal object may be attractive or repellent; objects may interact with each other in a way which is perceived (not merely inferred) as causal; the behavior of another person may be perceived (not merely inferred) as directed toward a goal. Such properties are validly objective. In the ordinary perceptual situation, however, they pale before the corresponding properties of the self. Perceived causality in its most impressive form is found in the experience of self-determination; perceived purpose in the experience of striving. In hate, fear, and curiosity the properties of the object are far from neutral; but the self is by far the liveliest component of the field.

It is this very predominance of the dynamic properties of the self which leads us so readily to the assumption that all dynamic and directive characteristics of experience are in essence subjective, that the world of objects is a neutral screen upon which we project our own hopes and fears. In the psychology of perception this is a serious error; in social psychology it is fatal. Let us consider, for example, what is commonly called a race prejudice. In colloquial language, I dislike the members of another race. I consider them intellectually and morally inferior, I shun their society, and I actively resent and resist any suggestion that they be considered as my equals. Let us assume that a careful investigation reveals no significant differences between the disliked race and my own. The prejudice must, ergo, be a matter of my own "subjective" attitude, and any effort to eliminate the prejudice must accordingly be focussed on "my" attitude. Such an effort will usually take a form varying from moral exhortation to forthright denunciation. The implicit assumption is that "my attitude" is a possession of me, and that pressure on me will change it. The actual result of such pressure may be to create an attitude which is genuinely "mine" and which will consequently be protected with all the resources of my self.

Even a superficial phenomenological analysis will throw light on the problem. How much of the prejudice is validly subjective, in the phenomenological sense, and how much objective? When we see an apple as red and appetizing, we apprehend the redness and the appetizingness as in the apple, not in ourselves. These are objective properties. Furthermore we may apprehend redness as related to appetizingness in a way in which brownness would not be; and whether or not that relation is historically connected with previous experiences with apples is irrelevant so far as the present objectivity of the percept is concerned. If we wish to change the redness or the appetizingness of the apple we must change the context within which it is seen. Similarly we may apprehend another person as brown-faced, dishonest, and stupid, and all these properties may be as validly objective as are the properties of the apple. Our dislike will be felt as caused by, not as causing, the perceived properties of the person; and our dislike will continue until the person is apprehended in the kind of context which will present him with a different set of phenomenal properties.

What we call an attitude is thus, phenomenologically considered, not a state of the self but a state of the "field," of which the self is a part; and it may well be that the most important components of the attitude are in this sense objective rather than subjective. It is clear that the relative prominence of subjectivity and objectivity may vary considerably from attitude to attitude and from person to person. We are all familiar with the "pet prejudice" which becomes almost a possession of the self. It would seem probable, however, that most of our attitudes have developed, and still exist, as objective, cognitive structures, or even as ill-defined cognitive properties which have not yet become structures. If this be true, the first task of the psychology of attitudes must be cognitive analysis. The psychologist must first seek to determine, without regard to conventional attitudinal categories, exactly what is there for the person, what structures with what properties and related in what ways. What we need is thus a kind of descriptive analysis of the objective field which is unbiased by hypotheses about our deeper motivation.

2. *The other person as phenomenal datum.* The other person is, first of all, a segregated object in the perceptual field. He can be seen, heard, touched, recognized as familiar, differentiated from other objects. To this extent he presents no new problem. Other objects can be attractive, mobile, threatening. At first glance it might appear as though persons could be classified merely as a sub-category of objects-in-general, differentiated from other objects by their possession of a particular combination of dynamic properties, all of which are present in lesser degree in other objects. And a strong case might be made for such a thesis. For the child the distinction between person and thing is less clear than it is for the adult. For the savage the inanimate world may be highly charged with dynamic properties. Rather than assume that the child and the savage have projected their own feelings into the inanimate world, it would make more developmental sense to say that as we have become sophisticated we have depersonalized an originally animate world.

For a preliminary analysis, however, the *origin* of the "personal" properties of the other person is an irrelevant question. The fact remains that as a person he may have a unique status among objects in the psychological field. The other person is, more or less, "like me"; he can be apprehended as an "other self." Regardless of the specific ways in which he may differ from me, in what are commonly called personality traits, he may appear to me irresistibly as someone who can initiate action, who can be kindly or cruel, who can rightly be praised or blamed for what he does. The stubbornness with which the problem of the freedom of the will maintains its challenge is testimony not only to the experienced fact of self-determination but also to the experienced fact of other-self-determination. Inanimate objects can be apprehended as causes and can be believed to incorporate immanent or transcendent purposes, but the other person is there for us as an object which can generate its own purposes. In the context of the other person, purpose may thus be a phenomenologically objective property. Recognition of this fact need not force us into a teleological position.

Within the general category of "other persons" we can distinguish great differences in the degree to which other persons can be apprehended as "other selves." The patient in a catatonic stupor, for instance, is apprehended indubitably as a person, but we cannot easily apprehend him as in the same class with ourselves. The same applies to the new-born child. To a lesser but significant degree we have difficulty in accepting as an "other self" a New Guinea native or a member of another national group; and we may even experience this difficulty with a member of our own sociologically defined community whose habits, beliefs, and tastes differ widely from our own. This general fact has been widely recognized, for instance, in the studies of social distance, in such distinctions as that between in-group and out-group, in the psychological treatments of sympathy and antipathy and of the sentiment of self-regard; but it deserves a more elaborate phenomenological analysis.

The way in which we apprehend the other person is basic to the dynamics of interpersonal relations, to the group-structure of the world of people as we see it, and, very practically, to the way in which social tensions develop and are resolved. Consider, for instance, the mechanism of guilt projection. However we may characterize it in detail, it involves a reorganization of the psychological field of such a nature that the self remains relatively intact and the responsibility for our reprehensible conduct is assumed by some entity in the field other than the self. But all objects in the field are not equally receptive to the projected guilt. The ideal recipient is that object which possesses the characteristics of another self. The factors which determine "other selfhood" are thus factors which determine the direction of the projection. The same holds true for the experience of collective responsibility. When my colleague behaves badly I am ashamed. I am ashamed when my congressman casts a cowardly vote, when a scientist of another nation yields to fascist pressure. When the New Guinea native strangles his wife, however, I am not ashamed; for there is no psychologically real way in which I can include the New Guinea native with me in a common category of "we." The experience of collective responsibility can extend itself only within whatever limits are indicated by the term "we"; and "we" can refer only to myself and other persons who are apprehended as other selves.

Such examples could be easily multiplied. Our immediate concern, however, is merely to point out: (1) that within the category of psychologically apprehended persons there is a range of variation which extends from persons who are relatively neutral or indifferent to us to persons who are highly charged with selfhood; (2) that these phenomenal differences betoken crucially important determinants of our behavior with reference to other persons and, ultimately, of the way in which the social world becomes organized for us; and (3) that a thoroughgoing phenomenology of the other person is consequently basic to social psychology.

3. *Society as phenomenal datum.* Society is composed of people; but the social world as we apprehend it is only in small measure composed of persons. In face-to-face social situations, it is true we deal directly with other persons; the individual to whom we address a letter may appear to us as a person; and so may the leading statesman of another country as we reflect upon the tension between his country and ours. Such persons may be objects of admiration or contempt, hate or reverence, or indifference, and whether or not they are perceptually present, they may regulate our behavior in a personal way. But for most of our social behavior other persons as segregated phenomenal objects constitute little more than anchorage points, the most vividly presented components of vague and fluctuating social structures. When I tremble before public opinion I may have a particularly spiteful spinster lady in mind; but the public opinion as such has for me an undeniable, if somewhat intangible, reality which extends beyond the spinster lady. When I resent the interference of the church in political affairs I may have fleeting memories of good and bad priests whom I have known, which may correspondingly allay or reinforce my anxiety; but beyond the priests is a social structure which is "there" for me and which has properties of its own.

The sociologist in his analysis of society may recognize such structures as family, occupational group, political association, religious organization, nation, or racial group, or he may specify social constraints in terms of custom, tradition, or law. It would be ridiculous to expect that every sociologically definable institution or function must have its counterpart in the social world of the individual, or even that the formal pattern of psychological analysis should coincide with that of sociological analysis. What is important for social psychology, however, is the fact that the social world of the individual is structured. Thus our basic phenomenological question, "What is 'there' for the individual?", becomes in this context "What is the social structure of the world he is living in?"

The practical importance of this kind of social phenomenology is so evident that it should need no demonstration. The individual for whom China is represented by the corner laundryman and Russia by the bewhiskered terrorist of the cartoons is living in a world quite different from that of the student of Chinese literature and Russian military strategy. Any attitudes which they evince toward China and Russia cannot be adequately understood until we know what cognitive structures are represented by these words. The methodological difficulties, however, are formidable. Is it possible to give a disciplined yet unbiased description of the psychological structure of the social world? In what terms should such an analysis be made? Where should one begin? Disturbing as these questions may sound, they are in principle no different from the questions which one must ask in connection with any phenomenology; and one must answer them in the same way. Predisposing biases cannot be excluded from the psychology of perception, but by becoming aware of them we can partially control them. When we describe a perceptual object or event we do in fact lift it partially from its context and thereby run the risk of suppressing or distorting the very phenomena which we wish to observe; but we can guard against the danger by systematically shifting from one level of description to another.

All phenomenology inevitably involves analysis, but we can always distinguish, in principle at least, between an analytic procedure which is arbitrary and destructive and one which is dictated by the phenomena themselves. Social phenomenology is in this respect no different from perceptual phenomenology. When we open our eyes and look upon the world immediately about us, we find objects, events, and relationships thrusting themselves upon us. These are the subject matter of perception psychology. When we look beyond our immediate surroundings, we find larger contexts of objects, events, and relationships which less vividly but equally truly thrust themselves upon us. Their organization may be unclear and unstable, and they may almost defy description. Yet these are facts, and they constitute an essential part of the subject-matter of social psychology.

Social phenomenology presents two special difficulties, however, which deserve mention. In the first place, although the analysis of perceptual phenomena requires no hypothesis about the physical counterparts of those phenomena, we do in fact believe that the phenomenal rests on the physical, and we use our knowledge of the physical to create or to modify the phenomena which we wish to observe. Thus the constructs of physics provide us with a base-line on which to plot our phenomenal variables. For a social phenomenology there is no such base-line. We may believe, as we all in fact do, that nations, political parties, and churches, have real existence, but their precise definition is still a matter of dispute, and we cannot manipulate them as we do lightwaves and electric currents. It can be argued, of course, that the constructs of sociology are strictly analogous to those of physics, since each science represents a transcendence of the world of phenomena; but sociology is still in the descriptive stage, and part of that description rests on the very social phenomenology which we are now trying to develop.

The second difficulty is more serious. The content of the perceptual world can be defined roughly as that which is here and now, and it is usually anchored to a physical reality which affects us directly in a physical way. The social world may include the here and now, but it extends far beyond both in time and in space. In functional terms the social world is a product of memory and imagination rather than of perception. This does not mean that it may not be stably structured. When we say that we have firm convictions about the proper settlement of the Arab-Jewish question we are indicating the existence of a stable structure in our social world, although none of the components of the situation may be present in a perceptual sense. Purely fictitious objects, events, and relationships can be just as truly determinative of our behavior as are those which are anchored in physical reality.

Our difficulty lies, however, in the fact that social phenomena are for the most part present to us only partially or in symbolic form. The social world is too large to be encompassed in a single act of apprehension. As it becomes articulated during the course of our development its various structures become salted away in the form of linguistic symbols. The fact of linguistic stereotyping of social structures is, of course, not to be deplored. It is the basis upon which we maintain ourselves in a world which extends beyond the perceptual. But by the same token we run the risk in our social phenomenology of mistaking a set of linguistic stereotypes for a description of what is genuinely there, of accepting, for instance, an expanded definition of the formal concept of "country" as a substitute for the psychological structure "our country" which is there for us in our social world.

Granted that linguistic categories may serve to select, strengthen, and even at times to create the structures of our social world, and that for this reason linguistic analysis may contribute richly to social phenomenology, the fact nevertheless remains that the word can indicate but never completely represent the phenomenon. We may apprehend phenomena for which we have no adequate linguistic symbols; and we may use language with formal correctness but without any clearly articulated field of reference. Our almost paradoxical task is, while of necessity using language in our analysis, to penetrate through language to real psychological structures, yet all the while recognizing that some linguistic artifacts are psychologically real.

Social psychology must simply recognize these two difficulties and make the best of the situation. We have no independently established social categories for which we can find psychological counterparts. Nor can we simply sit back and describe the social field as we would describe an array of colors, permitting the natural organization of the field to dictate our descriptive categories. Our necessary compromise is on the one hand to accept the conventional social categories simply as points of departure for an analysis of the psychological structures which roughly correspond to them, and by a process of descriptive elaboration and correction to work toward a more valid set of psychologically defined categories; on the other hand to select deliberately social situations which do not fit readily into the conventional categories of social analysis and from these to glean hunches as to principles and patterns of organization which are ordinarily overlooked. The two approaches are complementary. If followed systematically they will eventually give us an analysis of the social world which is validly psychological. A few examples may clarify the point.

We may attempt, for instance, to construct a psychological geography. An orthodox geographic analysis will give us as units continents, countries, subdivisions of countries, cities, rivers, etc., with each structure formally comparable with any other structure of its class. But what is actually there for the individual? Certainly not all the facts discussed in the school text on geography; and, even if we remember as many facts about Bolivia as we do about Sweden, this has little bearing on the relative importance of these two countries in our psychological world. What we must find out is how clearly Bolivia exists for us as a structure, what properties it possesses, to what extent it is differentiated from or grouped with other countries; in short, what Bolivia means to us. Thus if we go systematically through the categories of the geographer we can gradually construct a useful, if partial, picture of the geographic world as we apprehend it. It will be something like the famous "New Yorker's map of the United States," but it will be closer to the psychological truth than any geographer's map will be.

Similarly we may try to construct a psychological history, linking the past with the present in terms of developments not as they "really" occurred but as they are apprehended by us. "1066 and All That" is an essay in psychological history which can be read with profit as well as with amusement. Our present attitudes toward the UN, Russia, Great Britain, are embedded not in "real" history, but in history as we know it, the history of the League of Nations, of World War I, of the Russian revolution, of the American Revolution, constructed in terms of personalities, events, causes, and consequences as we apprehend them. In the same way the concepts of local community, Negro race and owner class are represented in the social field by structures which may resemble only crudely the institutions and groups as defined by the sociologist. Nevertheless it is these, and not the hypothetically "real" structures, which actually regulate our social behavior, which constitute the objective components of our loyalties, our prejudices, and our resentments.

Such an inventory of social structures would in itself, however, be inadequate; for it would fail to indicate which of the structures are functionally important, and it would not reveal psychological structures for which there is no conventional symbol. The fact, for instance, that psychological structures can be found which correspond roughly to "Bolivia" or "ownership class" may be quite misleading, for they may have little importance as regulators of behavior, and they may indeed by crystallized into structures for the first time by the question which is asked.

Thus as a supplement to the inventory analysis we must have an approach which is less constrained by conventional categories. Such an approach might, for instance, be a variant of the free interview method. If we ask a child to compare his Negro and white playmates we may elicit a Negro stereotype, echoed from his parents, which in fact does not constitute an important structure in his field. If, instead, we ask him who his playmates are, which he prefers, and why, we may discover groupings which are far more important for the child than those defined by the color line, e.g., children who are bullies, children who know how to play baseball.

Similarly, if we ask a member of the surface gang in a nickel mine what he understands to be the essential differences between capital and labor, we may momentarily crystallize for him a class structure which ordinarily plays no role as a determinant of his behavior. His significant memberships may be with the native-born as opposed to the immigrant groups, with the Evangelical Methodists as opposed to all other religious sects, or with the old-timers as opposed to the newcomers. Or it may be that a class-structured society, which we accept as a sociological fact, is utterly unintelligible to him.

The social field of any individual is inevitably structured. We can easily see how the salience of structures which are known to us may vary from person to person, and how structures which at a given time lack salience are nevertheless deeply embedded and capable of becoming powerfully determinative. It is more difficult for us to realize, however, that structures which have no meaning for us may be exceedingly powerful for other people, and that structures which are obvious and unchallengeable to us may be unintelligible to others. The best examples of this are to be found in the anthropological literature. The strange tabus, the peculiar religious rites, the weird beliefs of the savages, which are at first incomprehensible to us, are indicators of a psychological structure which is radically different from ours.

We cannot ask the savage to phenomenolize for us, or even to explain the structures which we point out to him, since he regards them as self-explanatory. Similarly, we cannot be expected in our first attempt to give a complete account of the structures in our own field, since our description may be governed by those very structures. Nevertheless a modest achievement in this direction is possible. By deliberately attempting to step outside the context of our own culture, by attempting to adopt the point of view of another culture or of another period in our own culture and in this way seeing our own field in a new perspective, we may be able to discern as determinative psychological structures certain relationships which have hitherto gone unheeded because of their very commonplaceness. We frequently speak of the values inherent in a culture. "The Christian emphasis on the ultimate worth of the individual," "the twentieth century acceptance of the Horatio Alger myth," "the white man's burden," "the age of the common man"— these are convenient clichés; but their very prevalence betokens in at least some of their users a way of apprehending the social world which must be specified if we are to understand the individuals in question.

## CONCLUSIONS

1. The phenomonological method, in social psychology as in the psychology of perception, can never be more than an approach to a scientific inquiry. It is the attempt to view phenomena in their entirety and without prejudice, to distinguish the essential from the non-essential, to let the phenomena themselves dictate the conceptual framework and the further course of the inquiry. Social psychology today is suffering from confusion—as to subject-matter and as to method—and this confusion is enhanced by the sudden demands which are being placed on social psychology by an insistent post-war world. It is the contention of this paper that this confusion can be considerably reduced if we profit from the history of the pychology of perception, suspend for the time being our present theoretical constructs and take a fresh look at the phenomena which are there for us. The phenomenal world is, in fact, a social world, structured in terms of selves, other persons,

groups, nations, as well as in terms of simple objects and events ordered in space and time. Social psychology must go far beyond the psychology of perception; but it deals initially with the same field, its phenomena must be describable in the same way, and its laws must be of the same kind.

2. Our immediate need is clearly for improved methods of observation. In this connection the products of casual, uncontrolled observation must not be scorned. The alert psychologist is always in touch with his subject-matter, and much can be gained from the persistent attempt to note and describe the social phenomena which occur incidentally in one's own experience. It is notoriously difficult, however, to maintain a disciplined naivete about oneself, and for this reason, if for no other, the social psychologist must improve his methods of studying the social field of the other person. Although most of the existing methods of social psychology, clinical, biographical, experimental, etc., can be adapted to this end, it is suggested that the most promising method is that of the intensive interview. In the hands of the clinicians the interview has been developed as an effective technique for the untangling of confused motives. More recently the value of the intensive interview has been demonstrated in the sampling of public attitudes. In each case, although the interviewer has a limited objective, the interview permits a high degree of insight into the world of the person interviewed. For purposes of social psychology the two methods can be profitably combined, the thoroughness of the clinical interview with the objective emphasis of the survey. What we require is nothing less than a complete account of the individual's world in terms of its essential social structure.

This is, of course, an unattainable ideal; but even a partial achievement will mean progress. If we can discover some of the structures that are there for the individual, e.g., what his picture of Russia is or whether he apprehends religion as a moral compulsive, we can begin to find out why they are there, i.e., the factors which determine the development and the potency of a given structure. But in every case our point of reference must be, not some pre-established category which may be real for us, but the person whom we are interviewing. Only in this way can we establish the relation between one structure and another, and thus proceed towards the formulation of general laws of field structuring.

3. The full implications of this approach for social psychological theory can become clear only as investigation proceeds. In the psychology of perception it has led us inevitably away from a reductive atomism towards a field theory. It is to be expected that it will have similar consequences for social psychology, providing us eventually with a set of field constructs in terms of which all social processes can be envisaged, and ultimately with a set of constructs which will unify all psychology.

The immediate implication, however, is that we must undertake a critical revaluation in the light of phenomenological evidence of such concepts as need, attitude, and value. This is not to suggest that a social phenomenology will invalidate the current research on these topics. Recent advances in the psychology of perception have not invalidated the correlations established by traditional psychophysics; they have given these correlations a new and broader significance. Similarly, many of the current measurements of attitude will stand as valid; but they may require reinterpretation.

An attitude cannot be regarded either as a property of a person or as a possession of a person, any more than a perceived object can be so regarded. An attitude is a structure which has both objective and subjective components. If we are to characterize adequately an "attitude towards religion," we must specify both what is objectively there as symbolized by the term "religion" and what is subjectively felt in relation to that objective structure. For some people the only clear objective structure may be the linguistic symbol, for some it may be an attractive or repulsive person, and for some it may be an elaborately organized authoritarian system which offers comfort or threatens persecution; and the degree of subjective participation may vary within an equally wide range. A need is by definition a predominantly subjective structure, a value a predominantly objective structure, but neither can be considered as exclusively subjective or objective. Thus the concepts of need, attitude, and value may be ordered within a single continuum of subjectivity-objectivity.

Subjectivity-objectivity is, however, only one of many ways in which the social field must be characterized. Some structures are more tightly organized than others, more resistant to influences from the rest of the field; some are transitory, others enduring; some have a high degree of reality-character; some are strongly dynamic, are directive rather than regulative. Such concepts as purpose, belief and doubt, conservatism, loyalty, and anxiety may have their phenomenal counterparts as structures, as properties of structures, or as relations between structures in the phenomenal world; or they may prove to be linguistic artifacts without meaningful phenomenal reference. The first test of their validity must come from phenomenology. As new descriptive categories emerge the traditional terms will either find their place or drop out of use.

4. Can a social phenomenology lead to a social psychology which is useful? The answer to this question is a matter of faith. The goal of science as science is not prediction and control but understanding. Prediction is merely the test of understanding and control the practical reward. For social psychology, however, understanding itself is of immense practical value. If we can understand the world as it is structured for the other person— for the national of the country we fear, for the member of the minority group, for the revolutionary, for the reactionary, for

the "average American"—we shall have made one small step towards the resolution of the conflicts that beset us.

This is, however, a mere knowledge of acquaintance, an answer to the question "What?". Social psychology must also answer the question "Why?". Having described and defined the social structures which exist for us and for the other person, social psychology must proceed to the formulation of laws which govern the formation, the maintenance and the change of social structures as such. It has proved possible to formulate such laws for the field of perceptual phenomena. It should be possible for this larger field of social phenomena.

# REFERENCES

1.  Allport, G. W. Attitudes. In *A Handbook of social psychology* (C. Murchison, Ed.). Worcester: Clark Univ. Press, 1935. Pp. 798–844.

2.  Farber, M. *The foundations of phenomenology.* Cambridge: Harvard Univ. Press, 1943.

3.  Heider, F. Social perception and phenomenal causality. *Psychol. Rev.*, 1944, **51**, 358–374.

4.  Katz, D. *Die Erscheinungsweisen der Farben.* Leipzig: Barth, 1911; *Der Aufbau der Farbwelt* (rev. ed.). Leipzig: Barth, 1930; *The world of colour* (trans.). London: Kegan Paul, 1935.

5.  Koffka, K. *Principles of Gestalt psychology.* New York: Harcourt, Brace, 1935.

6.  Köhler, W. *Gestalt psychology.* New York: Liveright, 1929.

7.  Köhler, W. *The place of value in a world of facts.* New York: Liveright, 1938.

8.  Sherif, M. *The psychology of social norms.* New York: Harper, 1936.

9.  Sherif, M., & Cantril, H. The psychology of "attitudes." *Psychol. Rev.*, 1945, **52**, 295–319; 1946, **53**, 1–24.

10. Wertheimer, M. Experimentelle Studien über das Sehen von Bewegung. *Z. f. Psychol.*, 1911, **61,** 161–265.
11. Woodworth, R. S. *Experimental psychology.* New York: Holt, 1938.

## CHAPTER 8

..................................................................................................

# Perception and Interpersonal Relations

─────────────────────────────────────

## BY   HADLEY   CANTRIL

It is with a very profound feeling of humility that I, as a psychologist, offer any comments for the consideration of psychiatrists on the subject of perception and interpersonal relations. For the more one studies perception, the more one sees that what we label "perception" is essentially a process which man utilizes to make his purposive behavior more effective and satisfying, and that this behavior always stems from and is rooted in a personal behavioral center. Thus perception involves numerous aspects of behavior which we artificially and necessarily differentiate in order to get a toe-hold for understanding, but which, in the on-going process of living, orchestrate together in a most interdependent way.

This means, then, that the nature of perception can only be understood if somehow we manage to start off with what some of us call a "first person point of view" as contrasted to the

From the *American Journal of Psychiatry*, 1957, **114**, 119–126. Reprinted by permission of the author and the publisher. Presented at the Montreal meeting of the American Psychiatric Association in 1956.

"third person point of view" represented by the traditional psychological investigator. And so my very genuine feeling of humility in accepting an invitation of psychiatrists derives from the fact that the psychiatrist, perhaps more than any other specialist concerned with the study of human beings, is primarily concerned with the first-person point of view, is skilled in the art of uncovering what this may be for his patient, and knows from his own experience the wide gap that exists between this first-person experience and the abstractions we have created as scientists in order to analyze, conceptualize, and communicate. A very nice expression of this last state of affairs was, incidentally, recently made by Aldous Huxley in his book *The Genius and the Goddess:*

"What a gulf between *im*pression and *ex*pression! That's our ironic fate—to have Shakespearian feelings and (unless by billion-to-one chance we happen to *be* Shakespeare) to talk about them like automobile salesmen or teen-agers or college professors. We practice alchemy in reverse—touch gold and it turns to lead; touch the pure lyrics of experience, and they turn into the verbal equivalents of tripe and hogwash."

## BACKGROUND

Most of you are probably familiar to some extent with a point of view that has developed rather recently in psychology and has been dubbed "transactional psychology." While I do not want to spend time here repeating what has been published in a variety of sources, I might at least very briefly note some of the major emphases of transactional psychology before discussing certain aspects and some experimental results which may be of particular interest to psychiartists (2, 3, 5, 7).

Here, then, are some of the emphases of transactional psychology which may give us a take-off for discussion:

Our perception depends in large part on the assumptions we bring to any particular occasion. It is, as Dewey and Bentley long ago pointed out, not a "reaction to" stimuli in the environment but may be more accurately described as a "transaction with" an environment.

This implies that the meanings and significances we assign to things, to symbols, to people, and to events are the meanings and significances we have built up through our past experience, and are not inherent or intrinsic in the "stimulus" itself.

Since our experience is concerned with purposive behavior, our perceptions are learned in terms of our purposes and in terms of what is important and useful to us.

Since the situations we are in seldom repeat themselves exactly and since change seems to be the rule of nature and of life, our perception is largely a matter of weighing probabilities, of guessing, of making hunches concerning the probable significance or meaning of "what is out there" and of what our reaction should be toward it, in order to protect or preserve ourselves and our satisfactions, or to enhance our satisfactions. This process of weighing the innumerable cues involved in nearly any perception is, of course, a process that we are generally not aware of.

## CREATING CONSTANCIES

Since things in the world outside us—the physical world and more especially the social world—are by no means static, are not entirely determined and predictable, experience for most of us often carries at least some mild overtone of "concern" which we can label "curiosity," "doubt," or "anxiety" depending on the circumstances involved.

One of my favorite illustrations of this point is an incident by Carl Sandburg in his autobiography, *Always the Young Strangers.*

"I have always enjoyed riding up front in a smoking car, in a seat back of the 'deadheads,' the railroaders going back to the home base. Their talk about each other runs free. . . . Once I saw a young fireman in overalls take a seat and slouch down easy and comfortable. After a while a brakeman in blue uniform came along and planted himself alongside the fireman. They didn't say anything. The train ran along. The two of them didn't even look at each other. Then the brakeman, looking straight ahead, was saying, 'Well, what do you know today?' and kept looking straight ahead till suddenly he turned and stared the fireman in the face, adding, 'For sure.' I thought it was a keen and intelligent question. 'What do you know today—for *sure?*' I remember the answer. It came slow and honest. The fireman made it plain what he knew that day for sure: 'Not a damn thing!' . . ."

Thus we seldom can count on complete 100% surety in terms of a perfect correspondence between our assumptions concerning the exact experience we may have if we do a certain thing and the experience we actually do have as the consequence of the action we undertake.

In an attempt to try to minimize our potential lack of surety concerning any single occasion and thereby maximize our sense of surety concerning the effectiveness of our action in achieving our intent, we build up "constancies" and begin to count on them. While a great deal of experimental work has been done on "constancies" in the psychological laboratory, we still have much more to learn. And above all, we have a great deal to learn about constancy as we extend this concept into the field of our interpersonal relations.

Parenthetically, one of the most important things we have to learn is that the "constancy" we create and that we describe usually by means of some word, symbol, or abstract concept *is* man's creation, the validity of which can only be tested and the meaning of which can only be experienced in terms of some behavior which has consequences to us and signals to us what the concept refers to.

We create these constancies by attributing certain *consistent* and *repeatable* characteristics to what they refer to, so that we can guess with a fair degree of accuracy what the significances and meanings are of the various sensory cues that impinge upon us. We do this so that we will not have to make fresh guesses at every turn.

These significances we build up about objects, people, symbols, and events, or about ideas all orchestrate together to give us what we might call our own unique *"reality world."* This "reality world" as we experience it includes, of course, our own fears and hopes, frustrations and aspirations, our own anxiety and our own faith. For these psychological characteristics of life—as the psychiatrist knows better than anyone else—are just as real for us in determining our behavior as are chairs, stones or mountains or automobiles. It seems to me that anything that takes on significance for us in terms of our own personal behavior center *is* "real" in the psychological sense.

## ASSIGNING SIGNIFICANCES

Let me illustrate with reference to a few recent experiments the way in which the significance we attach to others "out there" seems to be affected by what we bring to the situation. Incidentally but important: I do want to underscore that the experiments mentioned here are only exploratory; are only, I believe, opening up interesting vistas ahead. I am in no sense attempting to indicate what their full theoretical implications may be. But I mention them to show how experiments designed to get at the first person point of view may suggest to the experienced psychiatrist ways of using experimental procedures in his diagnosis and possibly even in therapy. And I also mention them because of my deep conviction that psychology can be both humanistic and methodologically rigorous.

A whole series of most promising experiments now seems possible with the use of a modern adaptation of an old-fashioned piece of psychological equipment, the stereoscope. Dr. Edward Engel who devised the apparatus has already published a description of it and reported some of his findings (4). As you know, the stereoscope in a psychological laboratory has been used to study binocular rivalry and fusion but the material viewed almost always consisted of dots and lines or geometrical patterns. Engel was curious to see what would happen if meaningful figures were used instead of the traditional material.

The results are really most exciting. In Engel's experiments he prepares what he calls "stereograms" consisting of photographs 2 x 2 inches, one of which is seen with the left eye, the other with the right. The photographs he used first were those of members of the Princeton football team just as they appeared in the football program. Although there were slight differences in the size and position of the heads and in the characteristics of light and shadow, still there was sufficient superimposition to get binocular fusion. And what happens? A person looks into the stereoscope and sees one face. He describes this face. And it almost invariably turns out that he is describing neither the face of the man seen with the left eye nor the face of the man seen with the right eye. He is describing a new and different face, a face that he has created out of the features of the two he is looking at. Generally the face seen in this particular case is made up of the dominant features of the two individuals. And generally the face created by the observer in this situation is more attractive and appealing that either of those seen separately. When the observer is shown the trick of the experiment by asking him to close first one eye and then the other and to compare the face he originally saw with the other two, he himself characterizes the face he created as more handsome, more pleasant, a fellow he'd like better, etc.

I hasten to add, however, that we should by no means jump to the conclusion that an individual picks out the "best" or "most attractive" features of figures presented to him in a situation of binocular fusion. For example, Professor Gordon Allport recently took one of Engel's stereoscopes with him to South Africa and initiated some experimental work there, using photographs of members of the different racial groups which make up that complex community.

While the experiments in South Africa have only just begun and no conclusion should be drawn, it is significant to note that in recent letters communicating the early results, Allport reported that when the stereograms consist of a European paired with an Indian, a colored person compared with an Indian, etc. the Zulus see an overwhelming preponderance of Indians. For the Zulu is most strongly prejudiced against the Indian who represents a real threat to him. Allport also reports that when Europeans in South Africa view the stereogram they tend to see more colored faces than white. It would seem, then, that a person sees what is "significant," with significance defined in terms of his relationship to what he is looking at.

One pair of slides we use in demonstrating this piece of equipment consists of two stereograms, each a photograph of a statue in the Louvre. One of the statues is that of a Madonna with Child, the other a lovely young female nude. While I am unable so far to predict what any given individual will "see," no doubt such a prediction might be made after some good psychiatric interviewing. But let me describe what happened in a typical viewing of these stereograms. The viewers happened to be two distinguished psychologists who were visiting me one morning, one from Harvard, the other from Yale. The first looked into the stereoscope and reported that he saw a Madonna with Child. A few seconds later he exclaimed, "But my God, she is undressing." What had happened so far was that somehow she had lost the baby she was holding and her robe had slipped down from her shoulders and stopped just above the breast line. Then in a few more seconds she lost her robe completely and became the young nude. For this particular professor, the nude never did get dressed again. Then my second friend took his turn. For a few seconds he could see nothing but the nude and then he exclaimed, "But now a robe is wrapping itself around her." And very soon he ended up with the Madonna with Child and as far as I know still remains with that vision. Some people will never see the nude; others will never see the Madonna if they keep the intensity of light the same on both stereograms.

In the situation described above, we do not have conditions for genuine fusion, but rather a condition which introduces conflict and choice in the possible meaning of the content represented. In order to learn whether or not there might be differences in choice that would be culturally determined, a cross cultural comparison was made by Dr. James Bagby (1). He constructed pairs of stereograms that would create binocular rivalry: in one stereogram of each pair he had a picture of some individual, object, or symbol that would be of particular interest to Mexicans; in the other stereogram he had a picture that would be of particular significance to Americans. For example, one pair of slides consisted of a picture of a bull fighter matched with a stereogram picturing a baseball player. When these pairs were shown to a sample of Mexican school teachers, an overwhelming proportion of them "saw" the Mexican symbol; when the same slides were presented to a group of American school teachers, the overwhelming proportion "saw" the American symbol.

Incidentally, the Engel stereoscope is so constructed that one can get some idea of the relative "strength" of each of the stereograms by adjusting the intensity of the lighting on each. Hence, if the lighting is equivalent on two stereograms in a rivalry situation, one can reduce the amount of lighting on the one that originally predominates, increase the amount of light on the one that was not "seen" and find the point where the first one disappears and the second one "comes in."

A modification of the stereoscope has just been completed by

Mr. Adlerstein in the Princeton laboratory. Our thought was that it might be extremely useful both in the clinical and social areas, if instead of having to use photographs of objects or people, a person could view the real thing—that is, the faces of real, live individuals or pairs of actual objects. So by means of prisms and mirrors, this device was constructed and I have only very recently had the opportunity of experiencing the resulting phenomena. I must say it is strange and wonderful. For example, when I viewed Mr. Adlerstein and Mrs. Pauline Smith, Curator of our Demonstration Center, I seemed to be looking at a very effeminate Mr. Adlerstein who was wearing Mrs. Smith's glasses. Though weird, he was extremely "real." At one point while I was observing them Mrs. Smith began to talk yet it was Adlerstein's lips that were moving! Tingling with excitement and with a certain amount of anxiety, I drove home and asked my wife and daughter to come down to the laboratory so that I could take a look at them. I was, of course, fearful that I might see only one or the other. But fortunately, again I got an amazing fusion—a quite real and lovely head composed of a blending of my daughter's hair and chin and my wife's eyes and mouth—an harmonious composition that would do justice to any artist and which I created almost instantaneously and without any awareness of what was going on.

These pieces of apparatus seem to me to have enormous potential usefulness for studying the way in which we create the world around us. I am hoping, for example, that before long someone in a position to do so may use this sort of equipment in a study of disturbed children. The child—having two eyes and two parents—might in some situations and in a very few seconds reveal a good bit about his inner life and his interpersonal family relations.

An interesting series of experiments on perception and interpersonal relations began systematically a few years ago after an observation I made one Sunday morning in our laboratory. An old friend of mine, who was a distinguished lawyer in New York and has since died, called me at home to say that he and his wife had been in town for the weekend and would I be willing to show them some of the Ames' demonstrations about which they had heard. It is important for this story to emphasize the fact that the gentleman in question was really a most unusual man in terms of his ability, charm, accomplishments, and his devotion to his family and friends.

Many of you are familiar, I am sure, with the "distorted room" designed by Adelbert Ames, Jr. which produces the same image on the retina as a regular square room if it is viewed monocularly from a certain point. Since the room is seen as square, persons or objects within the room or people looking through the windows become distorted. I had shown this room to hundreds of individuals and among other phenomena had demonstrated that when two people look through the back windows, the head of one individual appeared to be very large, the head of the other to be very small. When the individuals reversed the windows they were looking through, the size of their heads appeared to the observer to change. But on this Sunday morning when my friend's wife was observing him and me, she said, "Well, Louis, your head is the same size as ever, but Hadley your head is very small." Then we changed the windows we were looking through and she said, "Louis, you're still the same, but Hadley you've become awfully large." Needless to say this remark made a shiver go up my spine and I asked her how she saw the room. It turned out that for her—unlike any other observer until then—the room had become somewhat distorted. In other words, she was using her husband—to whom she was particularly devoted—as her standard. She would not let him go. His nickname for her was "Honi" and we have dubbed this the "Honi phenomenon."

This observation was followed systematically in a series of experiments on married couples by Dr. Warren Wittreich. He found that if couples had been married less than a year there was a very definite tendency not to let the new marital partner distort as quickly or as much as was allowed by people who had been married for a considerable time (8). But, again, I hasten to add that it is not a simple matter of how long one has been married that determines how willing one is to distort the size or shape of one's marital partner! The original observation was made on a couple who were already grandparents. Preliminary investigation also seems to show that parents of young children will not allow their children to distort as readily as will parents of older children.

We could continue at some length reporting experiments which seem to show that what we "perceive" is, as already emphasized, in large part our own creation and depends on the assumptions we bring to the particular occasion. We seem to give meaning and order to sensory impingements in terms of our own needs and purposes and this process of selection is actively creative.

## SOCIAL CONSTANCIES AND SELF-CONSTANCY

It is clear that when we look for constancies in other people either as individuals or as members of a group a variety of complications is introduced. For when people are involved, as contrasted to inorganic objects or most other forms of life, we are dealing with purposes, with motives, with intentions which we have to take into account in our perceptual process—the purposes, motives, and intentions of other people often difficult to understand. The purposes and intentions of these other people will, of course, change as conditions change; and they will change as behavior progresses from one goal to another. Other people's purposes will be affected by our purposes, just as our purposes will be affected by theirs.

It is by no means a quick and easy process, then, to endow

the people with whom we participate in our interpersonal relations with constancies and repeatabilities that we can always rely on. And yet we must, of course, continue to do so, so that our own purposeful action will have a greater chance of bringing about the satisfying consequences we intended. So we try to pigeonhole people according to some role, status, or position. We create constancies concerning people and social situations. These provide us with certain consistent characteristics that will ease our interpretation and make our actions more effective so long as there is some correspondence between the attribution we make and the consequence we experience from it in our own action.

The "social constancies" we learn obviously involve the relationships between ourselves and others. So if any social constancy is to be operational, there must also be a sense of "self-constancy." The two are interdependent. Since the human being necessarily derives so much of his value satisfaction from association with other human beings, his conception of his "self," his own "self-constancy" and "self-significance" is determined to a large extent by the significance he has to other people and the way they behave toward him. The point is, of course, a familiar one to the psychiatrist and has been eloquently illustrated in literature as, for example, in Shaw's *Pygmalion*.

But it seems to me of paramount importance in any discussion of perception and interpersonal relations that we should not slip into the error of positing an abstract "self" or "ego" that can somehow be isolated, pointed to, analyzed, or experienced apart from any social context. It is only through the life setting and the process of participation with others that meaning and continuity are given to the "self." If the constancy of "self" is upset, it becomes difficult for us to assess changes in our interpersonal relations and accommodate to them. We lose the compass that keeps us going in a direction. "We" are lost.

This does not mean in any sense that for self-constancy to be maintained there can be no development or growth. On the contrary, self-development and growth are themselves aspects of social constancy. But this development must, as the psychiatrist knows better than anyone, flow from form if it is to be recognized, if there is to be continuity, and if there is to be a standard for comparison. Obviously, each of us surrounds himself with anchoring points of one kind or another which help to maintain this self-constancy in the process of ceaseless change around us. In this connection I think, for example, of Konrad Lorenz' interpretation of why people like dogs. In his book *King Solomon's Ring,* he writes that we should "not lie to ourselves that we need the dog as a protection for our house. We *do* need him, but not as a watch-dog. I, at least in dreary foreign towns, have certainly stood in need of my dog's company and I have derived, from the mere fact of his existence, a great sense of inward security, such as one finds in a childhood memory or in the prospect of the scenery of one's own home country, for me the Blue Danube, for you the White Cliffs of Dover. In the almost film-like flitting-by of modern life, a man needs something to tell him, from time to time, that he is still himself, and nothing can give him this assurance in so comforting a manner as the 'four feet trotting behind.' "

This interdependent problem of social constancy and self-constancy has been submitted to some preliminary investigation. For example, when a person is wearing a pair of aniseikonic spectacles, which greatly distort the shape of the environment when familiar monocular cues are ruled out, he will generally see another person as distorted if that person is standing in an environment which has itself already become distorted. With a certain pair of these spectacles for example, an individual will be seen as leaning forward with the upper and lower half of his body distorted in length. Dr. Wittreich set up such a situation at the Naval Training Center at Bainbridge, Maryland to see what might happen when the relationship of the person who was doing the viewing and the person being viewed was altered. His subjects were 24 white male Navy recruits. They first observed an authority figure dressed up as a first class petty officer and, second, a non-authority figure dressed up in a white enlisted uniform with the marks of a recruit. Wittreich found that the authority figure did not distort nearly as much as the non-authority figure. In other words, the disciplinary training imposed in an organization that depends for effective functioning on the rigid acceptance of roles had produced a "constancy" which overpowered physiological changes in the optical system.

Another finding using the aniseikonic spectacles may be of interest to psychiatrists: namely, that a person tends to report much less distortion of his own image when he looks at himself in a full-length mirror while wearing aniseikonic spectacles than he reports when he is looking at a stranger. When one looks at one's self, the changes that appear seem to be minor and detailed—for example, slight distortions in the hands or feet; when one looks at a stranger, there is the more general bodily distortion plus the leaning one way or another, depending on the kind of spectacles used.

A subsequent study by Wittreich and one which I emphasize is only suggestive, was made comparing 21 subjects obtained from the patient roster of the neuro-psychiatric unit at the Bethesda Naval Hospital. When these disturbed individuals were wearing aniseikonic spectacles and saw their own image in the mirror, they tended to see the gross distortions that the "normal" population attributed to others; and, conversely, when the disturbed clinic population looked at others, they tended to see the more detailed and minor distortions which the "normal" population had seen in themselves. All I should like to conclude about this particular experiment so far is that there seems to be some difference between the normal individual and the clinical patient in the functional importance assigned to his bodily image; the patient may conceivably be operating in terms of a relatively fixed and homogeneous image of himself which does not alter readily with the demands of the environment.

## PERCEPTUAL CHANGE

Laboratory experimentation as well as research in the field of opinion and attitude change seems to demonstrate beyond a shadow of a doubt that the major condition for a change in our perception, our attitudes or opinions is a frustration experienced in carrying out our purposes effectively because we are acting on the basis of assumptions that prove "wrong." For example, Dr. Kilpatrick has demonstrated that apparently the only way we can "learn" to see our distorted room distorted is to become frustrated with the assumption that the room is "square" in the process of trying to carry out some action in the room (6). It is clear that an "intellectual," "rational," or "logical" understanding of a situation is by no means sufficient to alter perception. The psychotherapist has taught us how successful reconditioning requires a therapy which simplifies goals so that their accomplishments can be assured through an individual's action as he experiences the successful consequences of his own behavior and thereby rebuilds his confidence in himself.

In this connection I recall a conversation I had in 1948 in Paris with an extremely intelligent woman who was at that time a staff member of the Soviet Embassy in Paris. We were at some social gathering and she began to ask me about American elections and the two-party system. She just couldn't understand it. She wasn't trying to be "smart" or supercilious. She was simply baffled. She couldn't "see" why we had to have two parties. For, obviously, one man was better than another and why wasn't he made President and kept as President as long as he proved to be the best man? It was a difficult argument for me to understand, just as my argument was impossible for her to understand. It was much more than a matter of opinion, stereotype, or prejudice on either side. We were simply living in different reality worlds, actually experiencing entirely different significances in happenings which might appear to an "objective," "outside" observer to be the same for both of us.

Parenthetically, while one of the outstanding characteristics of man is often said to be his amazing capacity to learn, it seems to me that an equally outstanding characteristic is man's amazing capacity to "unlearn" which is, I think, not the exact opposite. Because man is not entirely a creature of habit, he has the fortunate ability to slough off what is no longer of use to him.

## THE REALITY OF ABSTRACTIONS AND THE COMMONNESS OF PURPOSES

In order to ease our interpersonal relations and to increase the commonness of the significances we may attribute to the happenings around us, man has created abstractions in his attempt to find more universal guides for living no matter what the unique and individual purposes and circumstances of an individual may be. Such abstractions are represented by our scientific formulations, our ethical, political, legal, and religious systems. The abstractions can be recalled and repeated at will. They can be communicated. They are repeatable because they are static and have fixed characteristics.

The value of these abstractions for us in our interpersonal relations seems to be that when the tangibles of our personal reality world break down, we can turn to the intangible—to the abstractions we have learned that have been created by others and have presumably proved useful to them. We can begin to check our own particular situation, possibly a frustrating one, against the abstraction and thereby, perhaps experience for ourselves what the abstraction is referring to. Only then will the abstraction become real for us. For when it does become functional for us in our own individual lives, it *is* real as a determinant of our experience and behavior.

I will close this discussion of perception and interpersonal relations with a story which seems to sum a good deal of what I have been talking about. The story concerns three baseball umpires who were discussing the problems of their profession. The first umpire said, "Some's balls and some's strikes and I calls 'em as they is." The second umpire said, "Some's balls and some's strikes and I calls 'em as I sees 'em." While the third umpire said, "Some's balls and some's strikes but they ain't nothin' till I calls 'em."

## REFERENCES

1.  Bagby, J. A cross cultural study of perceptual predominance in binocular rivalry. 1956 (to be published).
2.  Cantril, H. *The "why" of man's experience.* New York: Macmillan, 1950.
3.  Cantril, H. Toward a humanistic psychology. *Etc. Rev. gen. Semant.,* 1955, **12**, 278–298.
4.  Engel, E. The role of content in binocular resolution. *Amer. J. Psychol.,* 1956, **69**, 87–91.
5.  Kilpatrick, F. P. (Ed.) *Human behavior from the transactional point of view.* Hanover, N. H.: Institute for Associated Research, 1952.
6.  Kilpatrick, F. P. Two processes in perceptual learning. *J. exp. Psychol.,* 1954, **47**, 362–370.
7.  Kilpatrick, F. P. Recent transactional perceptual research, a summary. Final Report, Navy Contract N60nr 27014, Princeton University, May, 1955.
8.  Wittreich, W. The Honi phenomenon: a case of selective perceptual distortion. *J. abnorm. soc. Psychol.,* 1952, **47**, 705–712.

# CHAPTER 9

........................................................................................................

# Autistic Hostility and Social Reality

# BY THEODORE M. NEWCOMB

I want to present a rather simple thesis concerning the changing of certain kinds of interpersonal attitudes. It is a thesis which, I believe, applies to attitudes toward others as members of groups—e.g., racial or class groups—as well as to attitudes toward others simply as individuals—e.g., a wife's attitude toward her husband. I should like to make it perfectly clear that I am primarily interested in hostile attitudes which are more or less conscious.

The thesis has to do with the conditions under which hostile impulses develop into persistent attitudes. Briefly, it is this: the likelihood that a persistently hostile attitude will develop varies with the degree to which the perceived interpersonal relationship remains autistic, its privacy maintained by some sort of barriers to communication.

Such a thesis has an immediate plausibility. Attitudes, after

From *Human Relations*, 1947, **1**, 69–86. Reprinted by permission of the author and the publisher. Presented as the Chairman's address at the annual meeting of the Society for the Psychological Study of Social Issues in 1946.

all, are matters of judgment and perception which must take place within a frame of reference. If communication with others is cut off, the initial framework responsible for the perception of hostility is less likely to be modified than if interpersonal give-and-take is continued.

Such a thesis, I believe, is a special application of a more inclusive principle, to the effect that idiosyncratic fixations of any kind may owe their persistence to the fact that they are safely barricaded against interpersonal communications. Before elaborating the application of this principle to the special area of hostile attitudes, I should like to point out how recent psychotherapeutic theory has moved in the general direction of this principle.

## PERSONALITY DISTURBANCES AS AUTISMS

Mental hygienists commonly discuss personality disturbances in terms of the evasion of "reality." Whatever is meant by the term "reality," I submit that it must be defined in social terms. I refer not only to the frequency with which disturbances in interpersonal relations are found among individuals who present personality problems—a point to which I shall soon return. Beyond this, however, the distortions of meanings which invariably characterize such patients are acquired in a social matrix. As Benedict, Mead, Horney, and others have shown, it is some aspect of a cultural norm, not an absolute standard, the distortion of which characterizes a personality deviant. "Reality" thus refers to something which is not only social, but which is defined by particular cultural standards.

It would seem to be a necessary corollary that the processes by which people normally maintain the normativeness (or reality) of their meanings and perceptions have, in the case of personality deviants, somehow been interfered with. Since it is by interpersonal communication that such a process of maintaining normativeness occurs, some distortion in communication must be involved.

The Freudians, of course, have never emphasized such matters. In the individual's Oedipus attitudes, for example, they have seen only a backdrop for intra-individual conflict, and personality disturbances are traced to repression stemming from such conflict. And yet, as I peruse the case material presented in the Freudian literature, I seem always to find, by implication at least, that barriers to communication have been erected so that autisms develop, uncorrected if not unchallenged. It can scarcely be an accident that Freud found repression to be so common in precisely that area in which, in his time and place, communication between parents and children was least possible, i.e., in the area of sex. Perhaps it would not be too outrageous a hypothesis to assume that it is the impossibility of communication which is responsible for repression. Perhaps, it would be too outrageous to suggest that, whether or not repression occurs, it is in the area of the defensively private that personality disturbances breed. In any case, the fact remains that that which is repressed is cut off from communication.

If it is true, as I think we all assume, that we learn most about the nature of things when we try to change them, then perhaps we can learn more from Freudian practice than from Freudian theory. It was Freud himself who insisted upon the crucial part played by the transference, as he sought to change personalities. The point which I stress is that, regardless of repression, certain areas of the patient's life are restored to communication during psychonalalysis. The defensively private ceases to be private as defense becomes less necessary. It is pointless to argue which is the essential feature—overcoming defensiveness or resorting to communication; apparently both must occur.

More recent psychotherapists, though borrowing heavily from Freud, have dealt with interpersonal relations as central rather than peripheral. When a psychiatrist like H. S. Sullivan can define psychiatry as "the field of personal relations" (33), the social psychologist takes notice; after checking his impulse to cry "plagiarist," he concludes that psychiatry must be simply the individual pathology of his own discipline. J. L. Moreno subtitles the publication in which so much of his psychiatric theory has appeared, "a journal of interpersonal relations." He refers to the area of the private as "the abode where . . . trouble . . . may blossom" (20). Horney sees "the basic conflict of the neurotic in the fundamentally contradictory attitudes he has acquired towards other persons" (11). Erich Fromm, in stressing the loneliness and isolation of "modern man," is obviously dealing with some sort of disturbances in communication (8).

In keeping with their theoretical formulations, such practitioners as those just mentioned stress the actual process of interpersonal communication as a central part of their therapeutic procedures. Thus (if I may paraphrase him freely) Sullivan strives to aid the patient to bring under control those "parataxic" forms of communication which are private in the sense of not being intentional communication at all. I think it is not too great a simplification to say that for him the goal of therapy is to enable the patient to communicate without distortion.

Moreno's "psycho-dramatic" procedures are directly aimed at the area of the private. For him, indeed, the patient closeted alone with the therapist is only half escaping from privacy. And so Moreno brings onto his very literal therapeutic stage not only the co-partners in misunderstanding (such as a married couple); he also employs various "auxiliary egos," and at a certain stage in the procedure spectators observe the various role-enactments.

Parallel with Moreno's work have appeared various other developments in the nature of treating individual personality disturbances by means of group therapy. The successful recovery of many members of Alcoholics Anonymous, for example, as reported by Bales (3) and others, is quite obviously dependent upon a kind of interpersonal relationship that is characterized by "reality" rather than by autistic pretense. A somewhat similar movement is that of Recovery, Inc., whose members are convalescent psychoneurotics. As reported by Abraham Low (17), it is the group relationship, into which the patient is introduced before leaving the hospital, which prevents him from lapsing into a solipsistic state in which he becomes defeatist concerning his own recovery.

Future historians of psychotherapy may perhaps conclude that it was in the area of group therapy that most conspicuous advances were made in World War II. Here, as so often, new discoveries were mothered by necessity; demands for time-saving methods of treatment led to new understanding of social reality. Thus, for example, Nathan Ackerman, a psychoanalyst who has used group procedures with veterans, describes the psychoanalytic procedure as one in which "it is part of the analyst's role to personify reality . . . But," he adds, "this special role of the analyst in personifying reality does not always work satisfactorily. In the analytic situation there is no actual social reality against which a patient may measure the impact of his impulses. It is in this respect that group psychotherapy offers a special advantage . . . In the group setting, the impact with concrete forms of social reality is immediate. Group therapy," he continues, "is a more real experience than individual therapy. It is less bound to the irrationalities of the unconscious and is weighed on the side of allegiance to social reality" (1).

And so we may conclude, I think, that just as psychiatry earlier became less purely medical and more individual-psychological, so it is now becoming more interpersonal. And one of the things to be learned from this development, it seems to me, is that personalities are more likely to become distorted when barriers to communication encourage autistic frames of reference for perceiving interpersonal relations.

## INTERPERSONAL HOSTILITIES AS AUTISMS

My major concern, however, lies in the area of interpersonal attitudes of hostility. Assuming the essential correctness of the frustration-aggression hypothesis as presented by Dollard, *et al.* (7), hostile *impulses* may be aroused by the blocking of any goal-directed behavior. A hostile *attitude* is such an impulse directed against a given individual or kind of individual. Or, in Gordon Allport's phrase, it is a "state of readiness" for such hostile impulses.

Privacy—that is, some degree of isolation behind barriers to interpersonal communication—is not a necessary condition for the development of hostile impulses into persistent attitudes. But it is, I believe, a common condition, and a particularly important one if we distinguish between two aspects of hostility. One of these is a state of readiness to injure another; the other is a state of readiness to view another person as threatening injury. The two are commonly associated.

It seems to me a truism that no interpersonal behavior can be understood without a knowledge of how the relationship is perceived by the persons involved. The "meaning" of another person—I am following Muenzinger's terminology (21)—is the manner in which he is related to the behavior-direction of the perceiver. No interpersonal relationship is ever perceived, presumably, without assigning such meaning to the other persons involved. I do not care to argue that a meaning of threat is always assigned to others toward whom one has a hostile attitude; I am not sure. But I do believe that it is the meaning of the threat which, when it becomes autistic, is responsible for much of the persistence of hostile attitudes.

We now have abundant evidence (31) that persistent attitudes presuppose certain frames of reference, and are most likely to change if and as the frames are shifted. The evidence upon which this conclusion is based does not have to do primarily with interpersonal relations, but I see no reason for exempting this particular kind of attitude from the generalization. The frame of reference which determines interpersonal attitudes presumably has to do with perceived status-relationship. (I am using the term not in Linton's sense of culturally prescribed status, but simply as interpersonal position.)

Hostile impulses commonly arise, then, when status-relationship is so perceived that another is viewed as threat. Such a perception arises through interaction, and it is likely to persist until modified by further interaction. If, as a result of a hostile attitude, emerging from the newly perceived status-relationship, communication with the other person is avoided, the conditions necessary for eliminating the hostile attitude are not likely to occur.

For the sake of concreteness, let me illustrate—at first anecdotally; I shall return later to more reliable sources of evidence. A rather egotistical man—let us say a professor—is affably recounting some minor successes to an acquaintance who maliciously hints at greater triumphs to come. The unsuspecting victim of the teasing grows more and more expansive, then suddenly realizes that the encouragement is overdone, and turns bitter. He has never since exchanged more than formal words with his malefactor, though they have repeatedly met during the intervening years; he hates him to this day. The incident is a true one, though admittedly extreme.

In such an instance, the impulse to hostility is inevitable. A less "sensitive" man, no doubt, would have continued normal relations with his teasing acquaintance, and would have developed no persistent attitude of hostility. Too often, however, the initial impulse creates those conditions, i.e., barriers to further communication, which perpetuate the hostile frame of reference. The attitude perpetuates itself not just because attitudes are by nature persistent, but if and as something about the attitude prevents a modification of its frame of reference.

I am obviously using the term "barriers to communication" in a rather extended sense. Many forms of interaction may continue even though a hostile attitude has developed. Employees continue to work under supervisors long resented; spouses may spend years together in a state of mutual mistrust; children who are convinced that they are unloved and unwanted continue to live with their parents. Mere opportunity for exchange of words and gestures is not enough to prevent the perpetuation of hostile attitude. A fixated frame of reference may persist in spite of ample opportunity for this behavioral kind of communication. But, after all, it is meanings, not the words and gestures which are their vehicles, which are the essense of communication. If an individual's frame of reference is so fixed that certain meanings are simply inaccessible to him, he is to that extent cut off from communication.

There are thus two senses in which a hostile impulse may give rise to barriers to communication behind which a persistent attitude is protected. *Overt* communication may be cut off, either entirely (for example, by avoidance of the other person), or in part (as by avoiding certain topics of conversation, or by limited spontaneity). *Covert* communication may also be limited by a fixed frame of reference which renders inaccessible certain meanings concerning status relationship. Limitation of either kind of communication is apt to be associated with limitation of the other. One might speak of them as interlocking barriers, each giving support to the other.

Whatever the exact nature of the limitations of communication, their consequence is that revised meanings concerning status relationship become less probable—revised, that is, in such manner as to reduce hostility.

I have been using rather freely the terms "private" and "autistic." Obviously an individual may develop toward another a hostile attitude in which he is supported by a circle of his own. The frame of reference involved in such an instance is not strictly private, but shared by others. I suspect that most attitudes of interpersonal hostility involve some sharing. They are private only in the sense that communication with the object of hostility is restricted. For the moment, however, I should like to keep my eye on privacy of this sort, for present purposes regarding shared support of the hostile attitude merely as social reinforcement of privacy. I shall return to this aspect of the matter.

Autistic hostility is thus based upon a more or less fixed perception of self-other relationships, the persistence of which is maintained by barriers to communication (overt and/or covert) with the object of hostility, whether or not it is also reinforced by communication with other individuals.

Again, because we know most about things when we try to change them, I should like to refer to certain psychotherapeutic procedures as sources of evidence. Turning first to Freud, among the few of his doctrines which deal directly with interpersonal relationships, those concerning the Oedipus complex are most conspicuous—relationships which, of course, include attitudes of persistent hostility. Assuming, with Freud, that sexual components are involved in such attitudes, we have adequate grounds for believing that there are barriers to communication between father and son, or mother and daughter—at least among the kinds of families from which Freud's patients came. Or even if one is skeptical about the sexual components, there still remains abundant evidence, I think, that between hostile fathers and sons in our society there are apt to be barriers to communication which tend to perpetuate their perceptions of their status-relationship.

Freud's practice, if not his preaching, lends support to this position. I refer specifically to his use of the transference during psychoanalysis. The correctness of Freud's practice at this point has been notably confirmed, it seems to me, and its implications carried a good deal further, by Otto Rank (26). For both of them, the essence of the matter is the role of the therapist as substitute; insofar as hostile Oedipus attitudes are involved, he functions as the parent toward whom hostility is felt.

In short, a man's Oedipus hostilities, if successfully treated, are removed by a process of communication with the (substitute) object of hostility. The patient expresses attitudes which, having been unconscious, were beyond communication in the full sense; i.e., he may have communicated hostile meanings, but, being unaware of the fact, he could not have interpreted others' responses to such expressions of his own. Under analysis, however, full two-way communication becomes possible. As the patient becomes aware of the meanings he is communicating to the father-analyst (the temporary object of hostility), he becomes more realistic—i.e., less autistic—in his interpretations of the other's responses to his own behavior. What has happened is not merely a matter of release, not merely a matter of awareness of self; it is a removal of barriers to full communication. (I shall revert to the significance of the transference relationship in discussing other therapists.)

Among more recent psychiatrists, none has dealt so directly with problems of hostility as Karen Horney. "Hostile impulses," she concludes, "form the main source from which neurotic anxiety springs" (10). Though she allows for the possibility of "conscious control" of hostility, she is chiefly concerned with its repression, which she defines as "pretending that everything is all right and thus refraining from fighting when we ought to fight, or at least when we wish to fight." Unambiguously she declares that "if hostility is repressed the person has not the remotest idea that he is hostile."

The tasks of understanding and alleviating conscious hostilities are so great, and my own psychiatric sophistication so small, that I prefer only to gaze beyond the great divide, and not to cross it. I believe it is not necessary to exclude unconscious hostilities from the general thesis. I suspect, in fact, that the important differences between conscious and unconscious hostilities lie rather in the means of removing them than in the psychological principles by which they are acquired and perpetuated.

In her most recent work (12), Horney develops much further the theory of how hostility functions in the interpersonal relations of adults. An individual, she finds, tends to develop along one of three lines: moving toward people, against them, or away from them. The one "predominant attitude" does not exclude the other two entirely, but "most strongly determines actual conduct. It represents those ways and means of coping with others in which the particular person feels most at home." The neurotic is simply the person for whom the three attitudes are incompatible; conflict leads to hypertrophy of one of the three, manifested in compulsive ways, and to relative atrophy of the other two.

For Horney, there are three interdependent components of "basic anxiety": helplessness (prominent in "moving toward" people), hostility ("moving against"), and isolation ("moving away"). Hostility, she insists, is a necessary ingredient in this neurotic brew. But for Horney it is primarily a matter of hostile impulses directed against others—i.e., overt hostility—and it is these impulses which are subject to repression. She is much less explicit concerning what I have called covert hostility—i.e., hostile interpretations of others' behavior. Nevertheless, she does record the presence of such interpretations for all three "types" of neurotic. Such "covert" hostility is most obvious among those who follow the main line of "moving against" people; "the aggressive type takes it for granted that everyone is hostile," she reports. The "moving away" type she describes as hyper-sensitive "to everything in any way resembling coercion, influence, obligation, and so on." Resentment of constraint is the constant earmark, and others are constantly viewed as threats to privacy and loss of freedom or independence.

Similar tendencies are reported for the "moving toward" type—though thoroughly repressed. Beneath the outward compliance of such persons she finds, not surprisingly, resentment at being taken advantage of. Horney verbalizes their feelings, largely unconscious, she believes, as follows: "I am weak and helpless . . . alone in this hostile world."

Horney thus finds that both covert and overt hostility are invariably found among neurotics, and that the latter as well as the former is repressed. She is, in fact, quite specific on this point: "if he represses his hostility it means that he is no longer aware that some individual represents a menace to him" (11).

What happens in successful therapy? Like Freud, Horney considers the transference of central importance. "Were someone to ask me which of Freud's discoveries I value most highly," she writes, "I should say without any hesitation: it is his finding that one can utilize for therapy the patient's emotional reactions to the analyst and to the analytic situation. I differ from Freud," she continues, "in that, after recognition of the neurotic trends, while he primarily investigates their genesis I primarily investigate their actual functions and consequences . . . by working through the consequences, the patient's anxiety is so much lessened, and his relation to self and others so much improved, that he can dispense with his neurotic trends."

I believe the following rephrasing of Horney's version of what happens during psychoanalysis would not be a distortion of her position, though it is obviously incomplete. The role of the therapist, as an objective and non-blaming communicant, is a unique one in our society. To such a person the patient finds it possible to communicate feelings of helplessness, hostility, and isolation which, for reasons of self-defense, he had been unable to communicate to those in relation to whom he feels helpless, hostile, alone. And it is more than a one-way communication which he is enabled to develop. Not only does he express himself (and incidentally gain relief); he also discovers meanings that he is unwittingly conveying to others, and thereby "understands" the responses of others to his own behavior. He has been, to a greater or less degree, restored from a world of private meanings to a world of "realistic"—i.e., communicable —meanings.

If this represents a somewhat venturesome interpretation of another's position I should like, for a parenthetical moment, to become even bolder. Most psychoanalysts (not including Horney, as far as I can discover) have made much of such concepts as catharsis, abreaction, release. There can be no doubt that tension is commonly relieved during psychonanalysis—or in any other therapy that is successful, for that matter. But what I should like to point out is that it is not only the expression of impulses which have been restrained; it is their expression *in a social situation*—they are communicated to the therapist. What has been "kept in," I suspect, is the exposure of one's self to another, quite as much as admission to oneself. What has been gained by the release, if so, is simply the freedom from having to guard oneself against exposure. Being restored to a world of communication (even though it is only a two-person world) makes it less necessary to man the barricades.

If I seem to have departed from my special thesis concerning hostility, it has been only because I have been eager to follow whatever clues are offered by the practice of psychotherapy, which represents a designed attempt to alter personality. So far, I have borrowed chiefly from a single psychotherapist, having chosen Horney not only because of the primary emphasis she gives to interpersonal relationships, but also because of her insistence that hostile attitudes toward others are always involved in interpersonal disturbances. Now, however, I want to turn to another practitioner, who has comparatively little in common with the psychoanalytic school.

The work of Carl Rogers does not particularly emphasize hostile atttitudes, nor does he stress the importance of interpersonal relations as clearly as does Horney. Nevertheless, there are two reasons for citing his work: in at least one instance he has specifically reported upon the treatment of interpersonal conflicts; and the problems presented by his patients commonly fall short of full-blown neurosis and thus illustrate those everyday situations in which I am interested.

In a recent summary statement of his methods (28), Rogers outlines the following stages in the therapeutic process: release, exploration, widening awareness (particularly of the denied elements in conflict), an altered frame of reference (particularly as to self-other relations) and, finally, increased conscious control. The technique *par excellence* by which these changes are made possible is that of a "permissive" counselor-client relationship. Rogers' writing is studied with such phrases as "warmth and responsiveness . . . permissiveness in regard to expression of feeling . . . complete lack of any moralistic or judgmental attitude . . . understanding attitude . . . freedom from any type of pressure or coercion . . ." "In this respect," he stresses, "the therapeutic situation differs markedly from the other relationships of ordinary life" (27).

Rogers is very explicit concerning the matter of "expression." "Hatred for a father, feelings of conflict over sexual urges, remorse over past acts, dislike of coming for help, antagonism and resentment toward the therapist, all may be expressed . . . The client may bring into the situation, as rapidly as his inhibitions will allow him, all the forbidden impulses and unspoken attitudes which complicate his life" (27). He is also explicit concerning the nature of the barriers which prevent such expression in other relationships. "Amid the pressures of real life situations . . . some sort of defensive 'front' must be maintained in every situation, but in the counseling relationship (he is) freed from any necessity of being defensive" (27).

Concerning communication in the other direction, however— i.e., the interpretation of meanings in others' behavior—Rogers has little to say. Nevertheless, this aspect of the matter is implicit in his treatment of "insight" of the discovery of "denied elements" and "altered frames of reference." In a report dealing with the implications of his therapeutic methods for the handling of social conflicts (28), he cites six cases of interpersonal conflict, obtained from clients individually treated. All of them involve rather intense hostilities. In the case of the six, as treatment proceeds, there is marked change in the degree of reading hostility into the behavior of the other person involved in the conflict. For example, a man suspects his wife's fidelity and has "plenty of evidence to prove it." Gradually he arrives at a point where he can say, "Those things I've thought of her . . . were really in me . . . I'm the one at fault." A good relationship is restored, and has persisted for several years.

Rogers points out that the patient invariably finds his problem insoluble, and that from his initial perspective it *is* insoluble. Hence the problem is to change the perspective—or, in Rogers' language, to reach "a new frame of reference in which the whole nature of the problem is radically altered . . . As the denied elements are admitted into consideration, the whole picture of the relationship between the self and the others is changed. The problem that seemed insoluble now appears to be a mutual problem and a soluble one" (28).

The nature of this change in frame of reference is of the utmost importance. In every one of the six cases cited the patient has been enabled to view himself through the eyes of the person with whom he is in conflict. Now I am less interested in this confirmation of the old adage about seeing ourselves as others see us than I am in understanding what it is about the therapeutic situation which permits the change. I think Rogers' answer is correct. Defenses which are necessary in the presence of the person with whom there is conflict are not necessary with the therapist. Hence, "normal" two-way communication takes place. It is not so much that he expresses his hostilities in the presence of the therapist; this kind of overt hostility is as likely as not also expressed in the conflict situation itself. But rather, when no defenses are needed, he can, so to speak, complete the communicative process. He can, to use G. H. Mead's memorable phrase, go on to "take the role of the other."

This, of course, is precisely the opposite of autism. The consequence of taking the role of the other is that the other comes to be seen as reasonable rather than as hostile. (I do not mean to imply an all-or-none shift, but merely to indicate the direction of the shift.) His behavior is seen as response to my behavior—as determined by a set of conditions rather than as arbitrary or wilful antagonism. The interpersonal conflict becomes a situation in which he is involved rather than a hostile force with which he is confronted. Autistic interpretations of others' behavior are subject to correction by two-way communication.

In most of the cases cited by Rogers, we find that the patient, once having taken the role of the other in the presence of the therapist, is then able to do so also in the presence of the person toward whom he has been hostile, with resulting improvement in relationship. Usually the patient "does something about it"; the hostile mother makes a calculated attempt to be less nagging and more affectionate; the daughter of the overbearing father takes her courage in both hands as she makes a gesture of independence. The significant change, however, is that hostile expression in the patient's behavior becomes less necessary as hostile impressions from others' behavior disappear.

In short, individual therapy, when successful, brings the patient back to social reality, which I shall define as that kind of relationship with other individuals which makes it possible both to express and to accept meanings concerning one's own status relationship without distortion.

## AUTISTIC HOSTILITY TO OTHERS AS MEMBERS OF GROUPS

These, I believe, are some of the things to be learned from attempts to change private attitudes of hostility by means of individual therapy. To what degree do the same principles apply to hostile attitudes which are shared by other members of one's own group, such as those which are directed toward members of national, racial, class, and other groups?

I believe that the same principles do apply, that the shared defensiveness of hostility to others as members of groups is essentially like the private defensiveness of interpersonal hostility. I believe, furthermore, that it is the very shared nature of the defensiveness which provides us with the necessary instruments for the reduction of group hostilities.

I shall take as my point of departure Gardner Murphy's phrase, "socially shared autisms." He points out that "Autistic responses (do not) necessarily separate a man from his fellows . . . It is characteristic of every social group to develop its own socially shared autisms. There are very clear, consistent and well organized pictures of Christian Scientists in the minds of good Roman Catholics, and of Mormons in the minds of good Presbyterians. These pictures have been built up through a great deal of consistent social sharing" (22).

Autism is here defined not in terms of individual privacy, but as a shared insulation. To quote Murphy again, a shared autism "springs not from contact with reality but from the need for protection from surprises and ego injuries." This seems to me strictly congruent with Bleuler's original definition of the term (4) which (though in the context of individual symptomatology) had to do with the patient's contact with reality. And the term "reality," as I have been using it, refers not to abstract metaphysics but to social give-and-take.

The one great difference between a private and shared hostility is, of course, the social reinforcement which accompanies the shared but not the private attitude. It is not only that one finds oneself in agreement with the expressed opinions of one's associates; it is more important that one's own meanings (with reference to the out-group) square with the meanings of one's associates. The normal processes of communication go on, unimpeded, and thus a shared hostility passes all the tests of social reality, within one's own group.

The individual whose hostility is a private one, however, must muster his own defenses. As we have seen, this commonly involves some degree of distortion, either of his understanding of those toward whom he feels hostile, or of what he intends to communicate to them, or of both. His perceived self-other relationship is not socially reinforced, and does not represent social reality, even within his own circle.

In respect to the objects of hostility, however, the private and the shared attitudes are alike. In both cases there is a more or less fixed perception of self-other relationships, usually in terms of threat, and defense against threat. In both cases this frame of reference is maintained by barriers to communication with the objects of hostility. And the result, in both cases, is a distortion of communicated meanings and hence a distortion of social reality.

There are two characteristics of group barriers to communication which I want to note. The first has to do with the individual origins of habits of non-communication. Whereas hostility toward individuals, *qua* individuals, is likely to follow a changed perception of interpersonal status, hostilities toward others as members of groups are commonly a part of the original perception of status relationship, so that no change has been introduced. That is, the beginning of hostility toward Negroes or Catholics or people on the other side of the tracks coincides with the first distinguishing of Negroes, Catholics, etc., as constituting a group. Hostility dates not from an interpersonal experience which changes the status relationship, in most cases, but from the moment when all individuals of a given kind are classified together as a group. From that moment the status relationship is perceived as involving threat.

In the area of race attitudes, if in no other, present evidence seems to justify such a conclusion. Lasker's conclusion in 1929 (15) was that race prejudice in children is due chiefly to "the absorption of adult attitudes." Horowitz, in 1936 (13), concluded that "attitudes toward Negroes are now chiefly determined not by contact with Negroes, but by contact with the prevalent attitude toward Negroes." Murphy and Likert, two years later (23), make the same point, drawing their data from altogether different sources and by quite different methods: "The individual usually acquires his prejudices against a minority group not primarily from contact with this minority group, but chiefly from contact with the prevailing attitude toward this minority group."

Two bits of more recently published evidence may be offered in which hostile attitudes are studied *in statu nascendi*. Hartley, in an analysis of prejudice (9) included, among 35 racial and national groups toward whom his subjects expressed attitudes, three non-existing groups—Danireans, Pireneans, and Wallonians. Correlations of scores of social distance toward these three groups correlated consistently about .8 with social distance toward the other 32 groups, among five sets of subjects. Examination of these regression lines, moreover, shows uniformly that those extremely hostile to the non-existing groups were also extremely hostile in total score of attitude toward the other 32 groups, and *vice-versa;* apparently there were no exceptions at all. For these hostile individuals, in short, to know that a strange group existed (or so they supposed) was to take a hostile attitude toward members of that group. As one such respondent noted on the margin of his questionnaire, "I don't know anything about (the Danireans); therefore I would exclude them from my country." Another respondent, however, whose total social distance score is low, wrote in the following note: "I don't know anything about them; therefore I have no prejudices against them."

In my own study of changing social attitudes in a student community (24) an instance of the sudden emergence of a new attitude is recorded. The Spanish Civil War broke out in July, 1936, and three months later nearly all students expressed well defined attitudes toward General Franco's regime—nearly all of them hostile. Practically none of them had even suspected that a war was brewing, three months earlier; much less had they heard of a general named Franco. Yet once the issue was defined, once the group of Spanish nationalists had been identified (in most cases by the label of "fascist"), hostility to members of the group emerged, almost full-blown.

A second characteristic of group barriers to communication is that they are commonly institutionalized, as by segregation or other forms of discrimination. Perhaps the acme of such formalization was achieved by the Jews of old, who prescribed such rigid eating codes that it became almost literally impossible for any repast to be shared with a non-Jew.

The effects of racial segregation and discrimination upon attitudes have been noted with particular cogency by Carey McWilliams (19). Those who object to the outlawing of discrimination—for example, by Fair Employment Practices legislation—often point out that attitudes are neither created nor changed by such compulsory enforcement. To this McWilliams replies that it is necessary to distinguish between prejudice and discrimination. The Fair Employment Practice Committee is designed to alter not attitudes but behaviors, which can be modified by law enforcement. But it is also true that discriminatory behaviors serve to create attitudes. Group prejudices are acquired by contact with prejudice rather than by contact with its victims, and there is no surer way to bring a child into contact with prejudice than to allow him to observe and to participate in segregation and other forms of discrimination. While the prevention of discrimination is thus not likely to reduce prejudice very markedly, it can to a certain degree prevent the assimilation of prejudice by the young.

Among contemporary investigators of group barriers, the work of Allison Davis (6) is outstanding. He points out, first, that lower-class Negroes differ pretty consistently from middle-class Negroes with regard to such matters as church membership, sex habits, the use of aggression, and supervision of their children. He then goes on to show that it is these very behavior differences which serve as barriers to fraternization between the classes. Middle-class parents, who are upward-mobile but not too secure, seize upon these behavior differences as ear-marks of their hard-won and still precarious status. By creating attitudes of restraint and inhibition on the part of children, and by attempts to prevent their associating with lower-class children, they seek to make it impossible for their own children to acquire lower-class habits. Thus lower-class Negroes find it impossible to acquire middle-class ways, because they are excluded from intimate companionship; and middle-class Negroes do not allow themselves to associate with those by whom they might be "contaminated," and thereby decline in class status.

In two ways, then, group-shared hostilities toward members of other groups are protectively barricaded—both by the manner in which the individual originally acquires his perception of the status relationship, and by the segregational devices which serve to perpetuate the status differentiation. Both serve to prevent communication between members of hostile groups, except under conditions in which meanings are fixed in advance. (E.g., a Negro must address a white man by his last name, and a white man must address a Negro by his first name.) The conditions of social reality are not met; what is conveyed through communication is the meaning of the prescribed situation, as determined by standard frames of reference, and not actually felt meanings of the present interpersonal relationship.

We have seen that in the case of private hostilities, individually treated, the process of restoring social reality begins with the non-defensive atmosphere provided by the therapist. How is it possible to obtain a similarly non-defensive atmosphere in the case of shared hostilities? The necessary conditions are easily described; to create them is difficult but not impossible: group-shared defensive frames of reference are most likely to give way to non-defensive ones when individuals discover that other members of their own group are acting non-defensively. Since the defensiveness is group-supported in the first place, it can best be changed by providing group support for non-defensiveness.

There are two levels at which intra-group communication commonly supports the defensiveness associated with hostility toward other groups: at the face-to-face level and through the media of mass communication. Hence I shall make brief suggestions regarding the creation of the necessary conditions of non-defensiveness at each level.

At the face-to-face level, the recent work of Kurt Lewin and his associates on "group decision" is directly applicable. He finds, for example, that groups of women who were faced with the common problem of changing their habits of meat-eating, when confronted with each other's decisions to try new dishes, actually proceeded to do so, in spite of long-standing aversions (16). More relevant to the present problem is a successful attempt, by similar methods, to change supervisors' attitudes of hostility toward older women workers in a garment factory (18). Lewin's conclusion seems warranted that under certain conditions it is easier to change several individuals together than one alone. In short, that same social reinforcement which serves to maintain a group autism may also serve to modify it, and to support the changed frame of reference. This provides a working hypothesis of the first importance, at the face-to-face level. As applied to Negro-white relations, for example, the hypothesis would be as follows: individual hostility is most likely to be reduced when institutionalized barriers to communication with members of the other group are crossed, with the shared support of members of one's own group.

Much more experimental work is needed, obviously. It would be fascinating, for example, to see whether a group composed of Negroes and whites could be used to confirm the hypothesis. Group decision could take the form of agreeing to break down some particular racial barrier, such as eating together. Even more significantly, it could take the additional form of agreeing to arrange further group meetings, bringing in new individuals who would be stimulated to similar group decision, perhaps beginning a "chain reaction."

I think it noteworthy that, in one of the few experiments in which Negro prejudice has been sharply reduced, namely that by F. T. Smith (32), the experimental conditions were such as to make possible both of these major conditions for reducing group hostility. That is, ordinary Negro-white barriers were crossed, as white subjects were entertained in the homes of Negroes, for example; and (presumably) the white subjects provided considerable social reinforcement for each other's changing attitudes. Unfortunately we are told little about the interactions among the white subjects and, also unfortunately, we know nothing of the effects of the experimental procedures upon the Negroes involved.

There are also barriers to communication at the level of the public, as distinguished from the face-to-face level, which tend to result in defensiveness, group autisms, and hostility. Have we any evidence as to how attitudes of non-defensiveness can be created, so that it becomes more possible for individuals to "take the role of the other" even when that other is only an anonymous member of a distant group?

It is not difficult to describe the nature of the barriers. Distance and strangeness themselves make communication difficult. And yet, as we all know, and as Hartley's subjects so pointedly indicated, strangeness may be a reason for taking either an exclusive or an inclusive attitude. Mikhailovitch's Chetniks were just as strange in the days when most Americans considered them heroes as when they came to be considered German collaborators. Turks, who for so many years appeared at the bottom of our social distance scales, were strange and distant, but Negroes, who shared bottom position with them, were not.

Such evidence as we have, moreover, seems to indicate that the mere supplying of additional information concerning distant peoples toward whom an attitude is already held is not likely to change that attitude markedly. Bennington students, pro-Loyalist in attitude toward the Spanish Civil War, were well armed with facts supporting their own position. Catholic University students, anti-Loyalist in attitude, were equally well supplied with a different set of facts. At both institutions those whose attitudes were most intense were best informed, even concerning such neutral facts as names and dates (25). There is much documentation for the conclusion that people who have attitudes tend to acquire and retain information in their service.

Press and radio, as media of communication, obviously have much to do with the context within which information concerning distant groups is supplied. Sargent (29), for example, has shown how the same labor union may be referred to by one newspaper as "agitator" and by another as "leader." By such means, often, are "pictures in our heads" created. And yet we know that individuals' attitudes concerning remote events and groups are not just passively molded by the context in which their information happens to reach them. People also develop attitudes toward sources of information, and better educated people even become critical of clichés and stereotypes (34). The crucial questions thus become: What influences do determine the context into which information concerning remote groups is fitted? What determines whether or not a "biased" context, as in a newspaper account, will be accepted? What determines the nature of the bias to which one subjects one's self, as in the selection of a newspaper?

I think the evidence is overwhelming to the effect that the determinants are similar to those by which race prejudice is acquired. Individuals acquire hostile attitudes toward remote groups by contact with the attitudes of those who are not remote. As Sherif and Cantril put it, "major events are judged in terms of frames of reference which enable people to relate those events to their own self-interest" (31). And "own self-interest" is judged in terms of groups to which one feels that one belongs—in terms of one's own microcosm. Specifically, if remote peoples are referred to in terms of threat by leaders of one's own group, or by newspapers or radio commentators in whom one has confidence, one will develop a hostile attitude toward that remote group.

Much is to be learned concerning the process by which information concerning groups comes to function in the lives of individuals, I believe, from the study of rumor. Knapp (14) has shown that "rumors become harmonized with the cultural traditions of the group in which they circulate." The hostilities with which rumors so commonly deal are made over by each group into which a rumor penetrates. The same tale may be variously used against Jews, Negroes, or Irish, even though the original source from which it grew may have referred to none of these.

There can be no doubt that public forms of communication provide additional opportunities for the development of group autisms toward distant peoples. Nevertheless, it is the existing group autisms which are responsible for the use which is made of the mass-communicated information. I should not like to have anyone conclude that I am defending the *status quo* in respect to press and radio. I am simply suggesting that, as psychologically-minded social scientists, it will not do simply to point the finger of blame at the mass media of communication. Our tasks are primarily those of understanding the barriers which reside in the interaction patterns within groups, and of removing them.

I should like to make a further observation concerning group-supported attitudes; it is applicable both at the face-to-face level and at the level of mass communication. Sometimes assumed group support is illusory. Nearly fifteen years ago Schanck showed how a widespread illusion could be maintained by restricted communication in a rural village (30). For example, each of a group of Methodists who indulged in card-playing assumed that each of the others disapproved of the practice. Schanck did not make the experiment of releasing this information to the community, but the persistence of the taboo would almost certainly have been reduced if he had.

Many social norms upon which hostilities depend are, I suspect, equally illusory. It might be said, perhaps, that they are maintained by autistic communication. Some indication of what happens when the illusion is uncovered is to be found in my own study of the Bennington community (24). As entering freshmen, students took for granted the norms familiar to them; "our kind of people," naturally, would look with disapproval upon labor unions, the New Deal and all its works. Within a year or two most of them had discovered that nearly all of the individuals whom they most respected, whether students or faculty, shared quite different norms. Following the discovery that, in this community, the social basis of their norms was illusory, the minority persisted in their previous attitudes by insisting that their political frames of reference had nothing to do with the college community. The majority, however, modi-fied their attitudes in accordance with the local norms—including their previous attitudes of hostility to labor unions, New Dealers, etc.

At another nearby women's college there was a much lesser degree of shift to non-conservative attitudes on the part of seniors. At this college, moreover, there was almost no awareness that there was any trend whatever away from freshman conservatism. Those who had acquired liberal attitudes had a good deal more local support than they realized, whereas at Bennington there was full awareness—in fact, some over-awareness—of the freshman-to-senior trend. The difference between the two communities lay not only in the degree of freshman-to-senior attitude shift. At Bennington the shift was accompanied, and in part caused, by overt expression on the part of those whose attitudes had changed. Few students were permitted to have illusions about locally dominant attitudes.

The recent development of public opinion surveys ought, of course, to reduce public illusions as to attitudes which are or are not widely shared. And yet I am not sure that they have been very effective in this way. Bruner has shown (5) that during the early years of the recent war Congressional action rather consistently lagged behind "public opinion," as shown by the polls. We have no way of knowing, so far, how many individuals were aware that their own opinions, which were actually those of the majority, were being treated as if they were still minority opinions. Nor, conversely, do we know how many in the minority camp still supposed themselves in the majority. Still more unfortunately, we do not know what effects, if any, such knowledge would have had upon attitudes.

The important questions go much deeper, of course, than mere assumptions concerning majority and minority position. We need to know not only how much support people believe they have in various opinions, but from what sources they believe it comes. What difference would it make to them if they had more, or less, or a different kind of support? How well informed are people concerning actual distributions of opinion? Would their attitudes be changed if they were better informed about others' opinions? Such questions are not beyond our research capacities. And in an era of rapid social change it is a likely hypothesis that popular illusions concerning attitudinal adaptation to change serve as a brake to the kinds of adaptation that are necessary.

One final point. Most of my suggestions presuppose a certain amount of what Gordon Allport has called "participation" (2); i.e., they involve activity rather than passivity, and under conditions of social relationship such that the individual's ego becomes engaged, as well as his muscles. If I may pursue Professor Allport's inquiry a step further, I should like to ask why it is that so many psychologists stop short of participation, in his sense, in activities toward which their attitudes are favorable. We believe in fairness and non-discrimination; we know that discrimination tends to perpetuate prejudice, and that only organized action can reduce discrimination. Nevertheless, most of us stop short of organized action.

Now the "normal" thing is to be active in getting what one wants. Most of us are perfectly sincere in wanting to reduce discrimination (for example); why are we not more active participants in the attempt to minimize it? Could it be, I wonder, the result of certain assumptions we make concerning conformity among social scientists? Perhaps we are all just a little like the Methodists of Elm Hollow, who do their card-playing in secret.

We of this Society have a ready means of ascertaining whether our non-active conformity is based upon an illusion, and if so, of dispelling it. We have only to develop hypotheses concerning the means of reducing hostilities, and to test them out in flesh-and-blood situations.

Medical research is not hampered by the assumption that pain and disease are bad. Prejudice and discrimination are also bad.

By directing our research to the practical end of eliminating them I think we may find not only that our research is better, but also that we have moved from illusion toward social reality.

## REFERENCES

1. Ackerman, N. W. Some theoretical aspects of group therapy. In *Group psychotherapy: a symposium.* New York: Beacon House, 1945. Pp. 117–124.

2. Allport, G. W. The psychology of participation. *Psychol. Rev.,* 1945, **52,** 117–132.

3. Bales, R. F. Social therapy for a social disorder—compulsive drinking. *J. soc. Issues,* 1945, **1,** No. 3, 14–22.

4. Bleuler, E. *Textbook of psychiatry.* New York: Macmillan, 1924.

5. Bruner, J. S. *Mandate from the people.* New York: Duell, Sloan & Pearce, 1944.

6. Davis, A. Child training and social class. In R. G. Barker, J. S. Kounin, & H. F. Wright (Eds.), *Child behavior and development.* New York: McGraw-Hill, 1943. Pp. 607–619.

7. Dollard, J., Doob, L. W., *et al. Frustration and aggression.* New Haven: Yale Univ. Press, 1939.

8. Fromm, E. *Escape from freedom.* New York: Rinehart, 1941.

9. Hartley, E. L. *Problems in prejudice.* New York: King's Crown Press, 1946.

10. Horney, K. *The neurotic personality of our time.* New York: Norton, 1937.

11. Horney, K. *New ways in psychoanalysis.* New York: Norton, 1939.

12. Horney, K. *Our inner conflicts.* New York: Norton, 1945.

13. Horowitz, E. L. The development of attitude toward the Negro. *Arch. Psychol.,* 1936, No. 194.

14. Knapp, R. A psychology of rumor. *Pub. Opin. Quart.,* 1944, **8,** 22–37.

15. Lasker, B. *Race attitudes in children.* New York: Holt, 1929.

16. Lewin, K. *The relative effectiveness of a lecture method and a method of group decision for changing food habits.* Nat'l Research Council, 1942.

17. Low, A. The combined system of group psychotherapy and self-help as practiced by Recovery, Inc. In *Group psychotherapy: a symposium.* New York: Beacon House, 1945. Pp. 94–99.

18. Marrow, A. J., & French, J. R. P., Jr. Changing a stereotype in industry. *J. soc. Issues,* 1945, **1,** No. 3, 33–37.

19. McWilliams, C. Race discrimination and the law. *Science and Society,* 1945, **9,** 1–22.

20. Moreno, J. L. Scientific foundations of group psychotherapy. In *Group psychotherapy: a symposium.* New York: Beacon House, 1945. Pp. 77–84.

21. Muenzinger, K. F. *Psychology: the science of behavior.* New York: Harper, 1942.

22. Murphy, G. The freeing of intelligence. *Psychol. Bull.,* 1945, **42,** 1–19.

23. Murphy, G., & Likert, R. *Public opinion and the individual.* New York: Harper, 1938.

24. Newcomb, T. M. *Personality and social change.* New York: Dryden, 1943.

25. Newcomb, T. M. The influence of attitude climate upon some determinants of opinion. *J. abnorm. soc. Psychol.,* 1946, **41,** 291–302.

26. Rank, O. *Will therapy and truth and reality.* New York: Knopf, 1945.

27. Rogers, C. R. *Counseling and psychotherapy.* Boston: Houghton Mifflin, 1942.

28. Rogers, C. R. Implications of non-directive therapy for the handling of social conflicts. Unpublished manuscript, 1946.

29. Sargent, S. S. Emotional stereotypes in the Chicago Tribune. *Sociometry,* 1939, **2,** 69–75.

30. Schanck, R. L. A study of a community and its groups and institutions conceived of as behaviors of individuals. *Psychol. monog.,* 1932, **43,** No. 195.

31. Sherif, M., & Cantril, H. The psychology of "attitudes." *Psychol. Rev.*, 1945, **52**, 295–319; 1946, **53**, 1–24.

32. Smith, F. T. An experiment in modifying attitudes toward the Negro. *Teach. Coll. Contr. Educ.*, 1943, No. 887.

33. Sullivan, H. S. Conceptions of modern psychiatry. *Psychiatry*, 1940, **3**, No. 1.

34. Williams, F. W. Information as a determinant of opinion. In H. Cantril (Ed.), *Gauging public opinion*. Princeton: Princeton Univ. Press, 1944. Ch. 14.

# CHAPTER 10

....................................................................

# Communication: Its Blocking and Facilitation

# BY CARL R. ROGERS

It may seem curious that a person whose whole professional effort is devoted to psychotherapy should be interested in problems of communication. What relationship is there between providing therapeutic help to individuals with emotional maladjustments and the concern of this conference with obstacles to communication? Actually the relationship is very close indeed. The whole task of psychotherapy is the task of dealing with a failure in communication. The emotionally maladjusted person, the "neurotic," is in difficulty first because communication within himself has broken down, and second because as a result of this his communication with others has been damaged. If this sounds somewhat strange, then let me put it in other terms. In the "neurotic" individual, parts of himself

From *Etc.: A Review of General Semantics*, 1952, **9**, 83–88. Reprinted by permission of the author and the publisher. Presented at the Northwestern University Centennial Conference on Communications in 1951.

which have been termed unconscious, or repressed, or denied to awareness, become blocked off so that they no longer communicate themselves to the conscious or managing part of himself. As long as this is true, there are distortions in the way he communicates himself to others, and so he suffers both within himself, and in his interpersonal relations. The task of psychotherapy is to help the person achieve, through a special relationship with a therapist, good communication within himself. Once this is achieved he can communicate more freely and more effectively with others. We may say then that psychotherapy is good communication, within and between men. We may also turn that statement around and it will still be true. Good communication, free communication, within or between men, is always therapeutic.

It is, then, from a background of experience with communication in counseling and psychotherapy that I want to present here two ideas. I wish to state what I believe is one of the major factors in blocking or impeding communication, and then I wish to present what in our experience has proven to be a very important way of improving or facilitating communication.

I would like to propose, as an hypothesis for consideration, that the major barrier to mutual interpersonal communication is our very natural tendency to judge, to evaluate, to approve or disapprove, the statement of the other person, or the other group. Let me illustrate my meaning with some very simple examples. As you leave the meeting tonight, one of the statements you are likely to hear is, "I didn't like that man's talk." Now what do you respond? Almost invariably your reply will be either approval or disapproval of the attitude expressed. Either you respond, "I didn't either. I thought it was terrible," or else you tend to reply, "Oh, I thought it was really good." In other words, your primary reaction is to evaluate what has just been said to you, to evaluate it from *your* point of view, your own frame of reference.

Or take another example. Suppose I say with some feeling, "I think the Republicans are behaving in ways that show a lot of good sound sense these days," what is the response that arises in your mind as you listen? The overwhelming likelihood is that it will be evaluative. You will find yourself agreeing, or disagreeing, or making some judgment about me such as "He must be a conservative," or "He seems solid in his thinking." Or let us take an illustration from the international scene. Russia says vehemently, "The treaty with Japan is a war plot on the part of the United States." We rise as one person to say "That's a lie!"

This last illustration brings in another element connected with my hypothesis. Although the tendency to make evaluations is common in almost all interchange of language, it is very much heightened in those situations where feelings and emotions are deeply involved. So the stronger our feelings, the more likely it is that there will be no mutual element in the communication. There will be just two ideas, two feelings, two judgments, missing each other in psychological space. I'm sure you recognize this from your own experience. When you have not been emotionally involved yourself, and have listened to a heated discussion, you often go away thinking, "Well, they actually weren't talking about the same thing." And they were not. Each was making a judgment, an evaluation, from his own frame of reference. There was really nothing which could be called communication in any genuine sense. This tendency to react to any emotionally meaningful statement by forming an evaluation of it from our own point of view is, I repeat, the major barrier to interpersonal communication.

But is there any way of solving this problem, of avoiding this barrier? I feel that we are making exciting progress toward this goal and I would like to present it as simply as I can. Real communication occurs, and this evaluative tendency is avoided, when we listen with understanding. What does that mean? It means *to see the expressed idea and attitude from the other person's point of view, to sense how it feels to him, to achieve his frame of reference in regard to the thing he is talking about.*

Stated so briefly, this may sound absurdly simple, but it is not. It is an approach which we have found extremely potent in the field of psychotherapy. It is the most effective agent we know for altering the basic personality structure of an individual, and improving his relationships and his communications with others. If I can listen to what he can tell me, if I can understand how it seems to him, if I can see its personal meaning for him, if I can sense the emotional flavor which it has for him, then I will be releasing potent forces of change in him. If I can really understand how he hates his father, or hates the university, or hates communists—if I can catch the flavor of his fear of insanity, or his fear of atom bombs, or of Russia—it will be of the greatest help to him in altering those very hatreds and fears, and in establishing realistic and harmonious relationships with the very people and situations toward which he has felt hatred and fear. We know from our research that such empathic understanding—understanding *with* a person, not *about* him—is such an effective approach that it can bring about major changes in personality.

Some of you may be feeling that you listen well to people, and that you have never seen such results. The chances are very great indeed that your listening has not been of the type I have described. Fortunately I can suggest a little laboratory experiment which you can try to test the quality of your understanding. The next time you get into an argument with your wife, or your friend, or with a small group of friends, just stop the discussion for a moment and for an experiment, institute this rule. "Each person can speak up for himself only *after* he has first restated the ideas and feelings of the previous speaker accurately, and to that speaker's satisfaction." You see what this would mean. It would simply mean that before presenting your own point of view, it would be necessary for you to really achieve the other speaker's frame of reference—to understand his thoughts and feelings so well that you could summarize them for him. Sounds simple doesn't it? But if you try it you will discover it one of the most difficult things you have ever tried to do. However, once you have been able to see the other's point of view, your own comments will have to be drastically revised. You will also find the emotion going out of the discussion, the differences being reduced, and those differences which remain being of a rational and understandable sort.

Can you imagine what this kind of an approach would mean if it were projected into larger areas? What would happen to a labor-management dispute if it was conducted in such a way that labor, without necessarily agreeing, could accurately state management's point of view in a way that management could accept; and management, without approving labor's stand, could state labor's case in a way that labor agreed was accurate? It would mean that real communication was established, and one could practically guarantee that some reasonable solution would be reached.

If then this way of approach is an effective avenue to good communication and good relationships, as I am quite sure you will agree if you try the experiment I have mentioned, why is it not more widely tried and used? I will try to list the difficulties which keep it from being utilized.

In the first place it takes courage, a quality which is not too widespread. I am indebted to Dr. S. I. Hayakawa, the semanticist, for pointing out that to carry on psychotherapy in this fashion is to take a very real risk, and that courage is required. If you really understand another person in this way, if you are willing to enter his private world and see the way life appears to him, without any attempt to make evaluative judgments, you run the risk of being changed yourself. You might see it his way, you might find yourself influenced in your attitudes or your personality. This risk of being changed is one of the most frightening prospects most of us can face. If I enter, as fully as I am able, into the private world of a neurotic or psychotic individual, isn't there a risk that I might become lost in that world? Most of us are afraid to take that risk. Or if we had a Russian communist speaker here tonight, or Senator Joe McCarthy, how many of us would dare to try to see the world from each of these points of view? The great majority of us could not *listen;* we would find ourselves compelled to *evaluate,* because listening would seem too dangerous. So the first requirement is courage, and we do not always have it.

But there is a second obstacle. It is just when emotions are strongest that it is most difficult to achieve the frame of reference of the other person or group. Yet it is the time the attitude is most needed, if communication is to be established. We have not found this to be an insuperable obstacle in our experience in psychotherapy. A third party, who is able to lay aside his own feelings and evaluations, can assist greatly by listening with understanding to each person or group and clarifying the views and attitudes each holds. We have found this very effective in small groups in which contradictory or antagonistic attitudes exist. When the parties to a dispute realize that they are being understood, that someone sees how the situation seems to them, the statements grow less exaggerated and less defensive, and it is no longer necessary to maintain the attitude, "I am 100% right and you are 100% wrong." The influence of such an understanding catalyst in the group permits the members to come closer and closer to the objective truth involved in the relationship. In this way mutual communication is established and some type of agreement becomes much more possible. So we may say that though heightened emotions make it much more difficult to understand *with* an opponent, our experience makes it clear that a neutral, understanding, catalyst type of leader or therapist can overcome this obstacle in a small group.

This last phase, however, suggests another obstacle to utilizing the approach I have described. Thus far all our experience has been with small face-to-face groups—groups exhibiting industrial tensions, religious tensions, racial tensions, and therapy groups in which many personal tensions are present. In these small groups our experience, confirmed by a limited amount of research, shows that this basic approach leads to improved communication, to greater acceptance of others and by others, and to attitudes which are more positive and more problem-solving in nature. There is a decrease in defensiveness, in exaggerated statements, in evaluative and critical behavior. But these findings are from small groups. What about trying to achieve understanding between larger groups that are geographically remote? Or between face-to-face groups who are not speaking for themselves, but simply as representatives of others, like the delegates at Kaesong? Frankly we do not know the answers to these questions. I believe the situation might be put this way. As social scientists we have a tentative test-tube solution of the problem of breakdown in communication. But to confirm the validity of this test-tube solution, and to adapt it to the enormous problems of communication-breakdown between classes, groups, and nations, would involve additional funds, much more research, and creative thinking of a high order.

Even with our present limited knowledge we can see some steps which might be taken, even in large groups, to increase the amount of listening *with,* and to decrease the amount of evaluation *about.* To be imaginative for a moment, let us suppose that a therapeutically oriented international group went to the Russian leaders and said, "We want to achieve a genuine understanding of your views and even more important, of your attitudes and feelings, toward the United States. We will summarize and resummarize these views and feelings if necessary, until you agree that our description represents the situation as it seems to you." Then suppose they did the same thing with the leaders in our own country. If they then gave the widest possible distribution to these two views, with the feelings clearly described but not expressed in name-calling, might not the effect be very great? It would not guarantee the type of understanding I have been describing, but it would make it much more possible. We can understand the feelings of a person who hates us much more readily when his attitudes are accurately described to us by a neutral third party than we can when he is shaking his fist at us.

But even to describe such a first step is to suggest another obstacle to this approach of understanding. Our civilization does not yet have enough faith in the social sciences to utilize their findings. The opposite is true of the physical sciences. During the war when a test-tube solution was found to the problem of synthetic rubber, millions of dollars and an army of talent was turned loose on the problem of using that finding. If synthetic rubber could be made in milligrams, it could and would be made in the thousands of tons. And it was. But in the social science realm, if a way is found of facilitating communication and mutual understanding in small groups, there is no guarantee that the finding will be utilized. It may be a generation or more before the money and the brains will be turned loose to exploit that finding.

In closing, I would like to summarize this small-scale solution to the problem of barriers in communication, and to point out certain of its characteristics. I have said that our research and experience to date would make it appear that breakdowns in communication, and the evaluative tendency which is the major barrier to communication, can be avoided. The solution is provided by creating a situation in which each of the different parties come to understand the other from the *other's* point of view. This has been achieved, in practice, even when feelings run high, by the influence of a person who is willing to understand each point of view empathically, and who thus acts as a catalyst to precipitate further understanding.

This procedure has important characteristics. It can be initiated by one party, without waiting for the other to be ready. It can even be initiated by a neutral third person, providing he can gain a minimum of cooperation from one of the parties.

This procedure can deal with the insincerities, the defensive exaggerations, the lies, the "false fronts" which characterize almost every failure in communication. These defensive distortions drop away with astonishing speed as people find that the only intent is to understand, not judge.

This approach leads steadily and rapidly toward the discovery of the truth, toward a realistic appraisal of the objective barriers to communication. The dropping of some defensiveness by one party leads to further dropping of defensiveness by the other party, and truth is thus approached.

This procedure gradually achieves mutual communication. Mutual communication tends to be pointed toward solving a problem rather than toward attacking a person or group. It leads to a situation in which I see how the problem appears to you, as well as to me, and you see how it appears to me, as well as to you. Thus accurately and realistically defined, the problem is almost certain to yield to intelligent attack, or if it is in part insoluble, it will be comfortably accepted as such.

This then appears to be a test-tube solution to the breakdown of communication as it occurs in small groups. Can we take this small-scale answer, investigate it further, refine it, develop it and apply it to the tragic and well-nigh fatal failures of communication which threaten the very existence of our modern world? It seems to me that this is a possibility and a challenge which we should explore.

# CHAPTER 11

.......................................................................................................

# A Variational Approach to Empathy

## BY ABRAHAM S. LUCHINS

Consideration of the status of the construct of empathy first requires stipulation of its meaning. Empathy has been used to denote one's understanding of another person's feelings and thoughts. It has also been applied to the awareness of emotional qualities of objects and events. Furthermore, it has been used as the name of a theory of how this understanding or awareness comes about. In the early 1900's, Lipps (10) used the term for a theory in which motor mimicry or imitation was considered essential to the understanding of other people. But other theories attempting to account for such understanding have been promulgated. Among them are McDougall's concept of sympathy or active sympathy (14), Wundt's rethinking of one's own personality in terms of others (20), Mead's assuming the role of the other (15), Sullivan's emotional contagion or communion (17), the Gestalt psychologists' theory of direct

From *The Journal of Social Psychology,* 1957, **114,** 11–18. Reprinted by permission of the author and the publisher. Presented at the annual convention of the American Psychological Association in 1953.

perception of emotions as presented by Köhler (7, 8) and Koffka (9), and the doctrine of *Verstehen* represented in the writings of Dilthey (2) and Spranger (16). Some, but not all, of these theorists utilize the term empathy. For example, Sullivan (17) labels as empathy his conception of emotional linkage of infant and mother. Freud (4, p. 61) suggests that our understanding of a person who has little emotional significance for us is brought about by a process of empathy which involves inference and mimicry; but when the person has emotional significance for us or is very similar to us, the understanding is brought about by another process which is emotional, unconscious, and involves no mimicry. Freud labels this other process as identification. However, some psychologists use identification as synonymous with empathy.

Thus we see a need for explicit denoting of the referent of the word empathy, to indicate whether it is the phenomenon of understanding others, or the awareness of emotional properties of people, objects, or events, or one of the many theories of how this understanding or awareness comes about.

## THE ASSUMPTION OF IDENTIFICATION AND PROJECTION

A survey of definitions of empathy used in contemporary research reveals that many of them revolve around the idea that the empathizer somehow identifies, puts himself in the place of, or assumes the role of the object of empathy (3, 6, 18).

This assumption has been criticized on various grounds (1, pp. 526–530; 7, pp. 235–241; 9, pp. 655–656). Firstly, it is possible to be aware of others' emotions and thoughts when one's own emotions and thoughts are not at all identical with them, and perhaps, are even in sharp contrast with them. You may perceive the man before you as sad, although you yourself may not be sad. You may be only too well aware of the gaiety of others when you are immersed in woe. Or you may be aware of emotions and thoughts in others which you yourself perhaps never experienced.

The assumption of identification seems to me to be particularly untenable when the object of empathy is a social situation or a group of people. With whom is an individual identifying when he is aware of the fury of a lynch mob? Does he identify with the victim, with the leader, with the "mob spirit"? Does he identify with the "average" member of the mob? If so, on what basis does he determine this "average" member? Does he identify with everyone or with a sample and then by some sort of rapid calculation arrive at the average of his identifications? This explanation is contrary to common experiences. We often form an impression as soon as we step into a room. Before we are aware of individual members of the group, we may be aware of the group's tenseness, freeness, pugnacity, coldness, warmness, etc. Our thresholds for recognition of feeling tones and moods may be lower than our thresholds for recognition of specific stimuli which give rise to the mood.

A process of identification also seems inadequate when the object of empathy is not human. It cannot readily account for our perception of gloominess in the landscape or stateliness in the tall cedar tree. Do we identify with the landscape or the tree?

Related to the assumption of identification is that of projection. Empathy is often defined as an ability to feel into or to project, in a "non-Freudian sense," into people, objects, or events. (A distinction between empathy and projection has recently been drawn by Hastorf and Bender, 5.) Suppose that John reports that he sees before him, seated in a chair, a sad man who will probably burst into tears. And the man does begin weeping and admits that he feels sad. Some psychologists would say that while John perceived the man and the chair, he did not really perceive the sadness. Rather, he projected the quality of sadness into the man. Projection by itself, however, would not be able to account for the accuracy of the prediction. Why did John happen to project sadness and to predict tears rather than to project gladness and to predict laughter? One answer would be that in the past John learned to associate certain facial and postural expressions with his own feeling of sadness. At the sight of these in a man, the associated feeling was aroused and projected. Our emotions are considered to be associated with certain visual expressions and to be aroused at the sight of these expressions in others. Among the criticisms leveled against this explanation is that it presupposes our going around with mirrors and studying our visual expressions whenever we experience emotions.

The projective hypothesis also seems inadequate when the object of empathy is a group or an inanimate object. Why is gloominess projected into a certain landscape and gleefulness into the daffodil and not the other way around? How can an observer project group structures and moods when he himself may never have experienced them?

Fundamental to both the identification and projection assumptions is the implicit doctrine that emotions and thoughts are purely "subjective." They exist only in the ego of the observer or of the observed. Thus the sadness which John reports is not considered to be objectively given in the same sense as is the chair or the body of the man. In short, implicit or explicit in many current conceptions of empathy are the assumptions that emotions are always centered in the ego and that identification or projection or both are needed to account for reports of the emotional qualities one seems to perceive in people, objects, and events.

## AN ALTERNATIVE INTERPRETATION

These assumptions are not accepted by all theories. One interpretation which does not posit these assumptions is that of the Gestalt psychologists (7, 8, 9, 19). They maintain that emotional qualities may be the *objective* side of the phenomenal perceptual field, that emotions may be carried by objects other than the self. The objects referred to are not the geographical but the *behavioral* objects. The sadness of the man is considered to be as much an objective part of John's perceptual field as is the body of the man or his chair. Moreover, facial and bodily events are considered to correspond, to some extent, to the concomitant mental events. Finally, some characteristics of the overt behavior are regarded as mirrored in or mapped by the psychophysical perceptual organization which is set up in the observer. In short, isomorphic relationships may hold between the mental and concomitant bodily events as well as between the latter and the corresponding psychophysical organization in the observer. In this manner, Gestalt theory would account for our direct perception and understanding of other people's emotions and thoughts. The processes which account for perception of the form qualities of the man and the chair would be considered adequate to account for perception of his mood or emotional qualities. The same interpretation is offered for perception of emotional qualities of non-human objects and events, for what has been called the physiognomic or tertiary qualities of experience (8, pp. 78–83; 9, pp. 654–658). Non-human objects, as *behavioral* objects, are considered to be charged with emotions, with the emotional properties extending from the object to the observer and not always the other way around.

The Gestalt interpretation may also be criticized. But rather than getting involved with the relative merits of existing theories, let us recognize that there are interpretations which do not presuppose identification or projection, or that emotional properties stem solely from the ego. Hence, in defining empathy, it would be well if we did not make a definition hinge on these assumptions or on any one interpretation of the underlying process. In the early stages of investigation, it might be best to define empathy operationally and to leave open the question of the kind of process which brings it about.

## CONCERN WITH EMPATHIC ABILITY

Research on empathy seems to have been influenced by the assumption that emotional qualities are not objective and by the assumption that identification or projection are essential to empathic behavior. These influences are manifested, for example, in the concern with the empathizer and his empathic ability. While psychologists recognize that conditions may influence empathic behavior, they pay relatively little attention to the study of empathic-fostering or empathic-hindering properties of conditions. Everyday observations and even experimental findings (**1**, p. 507) suggest that some people may be easier or harder to empathize with than others, yet there has been little study of the empathic-arousing property of people, objects, or events.

The chief goal seems to be the development of tests which will measure empathic ability, a test which will separate successful from unsuccessful empathizers. Such tests may be of practical value but they do not lead to the discovery of the crucial variables involved in any given act of empathy. Moreover, although the tests are presumably concerned with the individual, they do not reveal the contribution of his personality to the act of empathy. Nor does the correlation of his score on the empathy tests with his scores on personality tests reveal this contribution or the personality dynamics involved in a given act of empathy.

## IMPLICATIONS FOR RESEARCH

There is a need for research aimed at discovering the conditions under which an individual manifests a given kind and degree of empathy. Research is also needed to discover factors which increase or decrease an individual's empathic behavior. This does not rule out the study of individual differences or the role of personality factors. An individual may be characterized in terms of the conditions under which he manifests certain empathic behavior and in terms of the relationship between the factors introduced into a situation and the influence of these factors on his behavior. In short, the individual's empathic behavior in a given situation can serve as a baseline for comparisons with his behavior in experimental variations of this situation. This seems to me to constitute a more intrinsic characterization of empathic behavior than one which uses other individuals' scores as the baseline for comparisons.

Systematic research along some such lines as the following would seem to be called for:

*a.* For a given individual and a given object of empathy, study the influence of different attitudinal and situational factors.

*b.* For a given individual, employ different people as objects of empathy. Vary their relations to the empathizer and allow their bodily movements and other overt actions to differ in the manner in which they adequately express—or are isomorphic to—the concomitant emotions and thoughts.

*c.* For a given individual, compare objects of empathy which consist of a person, a group, an event, or non-human object, as well as descriptions of people, objects, or events.

*d.* Study mutual empathy—that is, when two people or two groups understand each other—an important but neglected area of research!

*e.* Determine the conditions under which the most or the least empathy has occurred for a given individual or a given group of people.

*f.* Attempt to minimize or maximize empathy for a given individual or a given group of people.

The above may be described as a *variational approach* to empathy, an approach which would vary methods and conditions in an effort to alter manifestations of empathy. As examples of preliminary variational approaches to empathy, I shall briefly describe three research projects, one already completed, one in progress, and a third contemplated.

## VARIATIONAL APPROACHES TO EMPATHY

The first project stems from work on group psychotherapy (12) and on training of therapists (13). The objectives were to create awareness in both patients and therapists of the character of the group's structures and processes and also to help them to see themselves as others see them, as well as to see others as others see themselves. Among the techniques used were the following. Each member of the group was asked to give his impressions of what had occurred in the present group session. At other times, members were also asked to describe what had taken place in a recording made of one of their own sessions, or of another group's sessions. The various descriptions were then discussed with emphasis on why there was agreement or disagreement. Also, in some group meetings, each member was asked for his impression of every other member as well as what he believed each member thought of him. Similarly, they were questioned concerning the momentary thoughts and feelings of other members of the group.

Analysis of the findings suggested that certain factors tended to interfere with an individual's understanding of another individual or of the nature and direction of group activities. These factors include: centering on one's own needs, emotions, or purposes; focusing on only one feature of an individual's behavior; focusing on only isolated individuals in the group or on only one event or on one emotional nuance of the group session; stereotypes concerning the relationship between physical features and personality traits; prejudices regarding an individual's race, religion, or nationality; lack of information concerning what had happened in previous sessions; lack of knowledge of group standards; viewing a patient or the group in terms of psychiatric information picked up in popular books or in various therapeutic experiences; keeping a distance between oneself and the others because of reluctance to become involved in group activity.

Two conclusions may be drawn from these studies. (a) A person's understanding of others seems to depend on himself, on the others, and on field conditions. (b) The so-called empathic ability is amenable to training. These findings suggest that instead of only measuring empathic ability, psychologists should also be concerned with creating or increasing this ability.

These findings corroborate some of the work on factors influencing the formations of impressions of personality (11). Recent experimentation, done under contract with the communication and attitude-change project of Yale University, in cooperation with Carl Hovland, indicates that one's impression of an individual is related to the *order* in which he receives information about this individual. For example, under certain conditions of presentation, a *primacy effect* has been found— that is, the impression tends to be based on the *earlier* part of the message. Subjects do not assimilate the later part of the message which contains information rather contradictory to the earlier part. Under other conditions of presentation, a *recency* effect prevails—that is, the impression tends to be based on the later part of the same message. This would suggest that our understanding or empathy with others may depend on the *order* in which we obtain information about them. Research is still in progress, the aim now being to see what can be done to increase or to decrease the primacy and the recency effects.

Let us now turn to the contemplated research. It is proposed to use a motion picture, perhaps a newsreel, which portrays a vivid dramatic social scene and another motion picture of a less dramatic scene. It is planned to vary the audience, by showing films to people of different ages, socioeconomic backgrounds, and cultural backgrounds. We are interested in whether the subjects' impressions will reveal that certain aspects are invariant for all people or for all who belong to a certain group. One problem will be to see what conditions have to be created in order to make a person recognize what is actually depicted in the film. Another problem will be to see what can be done to make one individual or group of individuals gain the same impression from the film as did some other individual or group.

It is also planned to vary attitudes and assumptions toward the film, by giving certain information prior to its showing or by seeking to create a certain social atmosphere before or during its presentation.

Finally, it is planned to vary the presentation of the film, by omitting certain scenes or certain objects in a scene, by altering the order of scenes or by running the reel backwards, by introducing different background music or other sound effects, and by using different colors of spotlights. To see the influence of motion, it would also be of interest to compare slides with slow as well as rapid motion pictures of the scenes.

It is hoped that intensive investigation of this sort, which systematically varies the empathizers, the objects of empathy, and the conditions under which the behavior occurs, will throw light on some of the theoretical and practical problems concerning empathy which have been raised today.

## REFERENCES

1.   Allport, G. W. *Personality.* New York: Holt, 1937.
2.   Dilthey, W. Ideen über eine beschreibende und zergliedernde Psychologie. *Gesammelte Schriften.* Leipzig: Teubner, 1924. (Vol. 1, pp. 139–240.)

3. Dymond, R. F. A scale for the measurement of empathic ability. *J. consult. Psychol.*, 1949, 13, 127–133.

4. Freud, S. *Group psychology and the analysis of the ego.* London: Hogarth Press, 1921.

5. Hastorf, A. H., & Bender, I. E. A caution respecting the measurement of empathic ability. *J. abnorm. soc. Psychol.*, 1952, 47, 574–576.

6. Kerr, W. A., & Speroff, B. J. *The measurement of empathy.* Chicago: Psychometric Affiliates, 1951.

7. Köhler, W. *Gestalt psychology.* New York: Liveright, 1929.

8. Köhler, W. *The place of value in a world of facts.* New York: Liveright, 1938.

9. Koffka, K. *Principles of Gestalt psychology.* New York: Harcourt, Brace, 1935.

10. Lipps, T. Das Wisen von Fremden Ichen. *Psychol. Untersuchungen,* 1907, 1, 694–722.

11. Luchins, A. S. Forming impressions of personality: a critique. *J. abnorm. soc. Psychol.,* 1948, 43, 318–325.

12. Luchins, A. S. Restructuring social perceptions: a group psychotherapy technique. *J. consult. Psychol.,* 1950, 14, 446–450.

13. Luchins, A. S. Patients view the therapist: a training and research device. *J. consult. Psychol.,* 1951, 15, 24–31.

14. McDougall, W. *An introduction to social psychology.* (13th ed.) Boston: Luce, 1918.

15. Mead, G. H. *Mind, self and society.* Chicago: Univ. Chicago Press, 1934.

16. Spranger, E. Verstehen und erklären. Groningen: Proceed. Eighth Internat. Congress of Psychol., 1927, 147–158.

17. Sullivan, H. S. *Conceptions of modern psychiatry.* Washington, D. C.: William Alanson White Psychiatric Foundation, 1947.

18. Warren, H. C. *Dictionary of psychology.* Boston: Houghton Mifflin, 1934.

19. Wertheimer, M. *Productive thinking.* New York: Harper, 1945.

20. Wundt, W. *Logik.* Stuttgart: F. Enke, 1895. (Vol. III, Chap. ii, Sec. 5.)

# Part IV

---

DISCUSSION

# CHAPTER 12

••••••••••••••••••••••••••••••••••••••••••••••••••••••••••••••••••••••••••••

# The Phenomenological Approach in Personality Theory: Some Critical Remarks

## BY M. BREWSTER SMITH

The "phenomenological approach" has recently come to be something of a rallying cry to a number of psychologists who share the "tender-minded" bias that psychology must, after all, come to terms with human experience, and who go so far as to believe that careful attention to this experience will leave the science of psychology not merely more satisfying to like-minded people, but also better science. Sharing this point of view and agreeing heartily with the program recommended by MacLeod (7) in his article on "The Phenomenological Approach to Social Psychology," the present writer has been dismayed by some recent publications which, it seems to him, misconstrue the appropriate role of a phenomenological approach in a way that invites the critical to reject humanized psychology lock, stock, and barrel. Since the writer would regard such an outcome as

From *The Journal of Abnormal and Social Psychology,* 1950, **45,** 516–522.
Reprinted by permission of the author and the publisher.

highly unfortunate, he feels that a clarification of the issues is badly needed, and herewith makes an atttempt in this direction.

The position with which he would take particular issue is that of Snygg and Combs (3, 11) whose point of view has also been espoused by Rogers (9). These authors contrast the objective or external frame of reference in psychology with the phenomenological, or internal frame of reference, and, declaring their stand firmly with phenomenology, proceed to muster on their side the names of Lewin, Lecky, Allport, Murphy, and Angyal, among others, even including the seemingly less tractable father-figure of Freud. In essence, their contention is that the locus of psychological causation lies entirely within the phenomenal field of conscious experience, and that it therefore behooves the psychological theorist—and therapist—to formulate his problems and concepts accordingly. Snygg and Combs give much attention to the individual's perceptual-cognitive field, particularly to the *self,* as its most salient feature. Written from this standpoint, psychology comes close to a rapprochement with common sense.

While applauding their emphasis on perception and the self, the present writer proposes that they are confusing phenomenology with what may be termed the subjective frame of reference. Sharply maintained, this distinction further helps to clarify certain persistent ambiguities in the theory of ego and self.

## PHENOMENOLOGY AND COMMON SENSE

One of the genuine merits of the phenomenological approach is that it brings psychology somewhat closer to the world of common sense. There is always the danger that psychology, in its concern for rigor and neatness, may divorce itself too completely from this source of problems and partial insights. Focusing scientific attention on the phenomenal world as it is presented to us, the world from which common sense also takes its start, the phenomenological approach can bring into the ken of the psychologist data and problems too often left to common sense by default. Like common sense, and unlike some current varieties of psychological theory, it does deal with experience, and thus presents itself as an attractive alternative to those who find a behavioristic psychology uncongenial.

But phenomenology is not common sense, nor can it rightly be called upon to justify a common-sense psychology. In MacLeod's phrase, the phenomenological approach "involves the adoption of what might be called an attitude of disciplined naivete" (7, p. 194). In many respects, its results may run exactly counter to common-sense conclusions. Common sense, with its preconceived categories and stock explanations, neither disciplined nor naive, is full of pseudo-scientific theory, while phenomenology limits its concern to the unprejudiced *description* of the world of phenomena. To take the phenomenal world presented in conscious experience as completely explanatory of behavior is closer to common sense than to phenomenology or adequate science.

Yet this is essentially what Snygg and Combs have done in their attempt to rewrite psychology in a "phenomenological frame of reference." *"All behavior, without exception,"* they say, *"is completely determined by and pertinent to the phenomenal field of the behaving organism"* (11, p. 15, italics theirs). And they go on to explain that

by the phenomenal field we mean the entire universe, including himself, as it is experienced by the individual at the instant of action. . . . Unlike the "objective" physical field, the phenomenal field is not an abstraction or an artificial construction. It is simply the universe of naive experience in which each individual lives, the everyday situation of self and surroundings which each person takes to be reality (11, p. 15).

While they bow unnecessarily to current prejudice in avoiding the word *consciousness,* their meaning is clear, and their index spells it out: "Consciousness, *see* Phenomenal field."

It is one variant of common sense that consciousness completely explains behavior, but at this juncture, it is hard to see how such a view can be regarded as an acceptable scientific postulate. Quite apart from the metaphysical controversy about the status of consciousness as "real" or respectable, we have behind us Würzburg and we have behind us Freud, to mention but two major sources of evidence that a psychology of experience or consciousness has distinct explanatory limits. Where is the determining tendency represented in the phenomenal field? What of the inacceptable strivings that warp our behavior, what of our defensive techniques of adjustment that so often prove most effective precisely when we are least aware of them? It is no satisfactory solution to speak, as Snygg and Combs do, of a "unified field of figure-ground phenomena of which the individual is more or less conscious . . . (in which) the vague and fuzzy aspects of behavior correspond to and are parts of the vague and incompletely differentiated aspects of the field" (**11,** p. 17). The clinical literature abounds with instances of unconsciously determined behavior which, far from being "vague and fuzzy," is on the contrary highly differentiated.

One suspects that such a psychology of consciousness has an element of common-sense appeal not unlike the attraction of allied forms of psychotherapy. It does make sense to the layman: it accords with what he is ready and able to recognize in himself. And it has distinct value within limits that it refuses to recognize. Because it over-states its claims, however, it may tend to promote the state of affairs away from which we have been striving—every man his own psychologist.

But MacLeod has already made the relevant point succinctly: "The phenomenological method, in social psychology as in the psychology of perception (and we would add, psychology generally) can never be more than an approach to a scientific inquiry" (**7,** p. 207). It provides certain kinds of data, not *all* the data. It furnishes the basis for certain valuable theoretical constructs;

it does not give birth to them in full concretene[
problems and provides some clues; the psycholo[
clinical must *infer* the answers.

## SUBJECTIVE CONSTRUCTS AND THE O~~BJERVER~~  
## FRAME OF REFERENCE

Here we reach the crux of the matter. If a psychology of consciousness is necessarily incomplete yet we do not abandon our
hope for a psychology that comes to terms with human experience, what is the solution? A discussion of two lesser questions may indicate the nature of the answer. In the first place,
does the decision to frame our psychological concepts and
theories in terms appropriate to the "private world" of the behaving person commit us to the exclusive use of phenomenal
concepts? Secondly, what is the appropriate role of the phenomenological approach in the service of this kind of theory-
building?

Lewin, whose psychological life space Snygg and Combs
equate to their phenomenal field (**11,** p. 15), was entirely clear
in maintaining a sharp distinction between the two concepts.
He said:

It is likewise doubtful whether one can use consciousness as the
sole criterion of what belongs to the psychological life space at a
given moment in regard to social facts and relationships. The mother,
the father, the brothers and sisters are not to be included as real facts
in the psychological situation of the child only when they are immediately present. For example, the little child playing in the garden
behaves differently when he knows his mother is at home than
when he knows she is out. One cannot assume that this fact is continually in the child's consciousness. Also a prohibition or a goal can
play an essential role in the psychological situation without being
clearly present in consciousness. . . . Here, as in many other cases it
is clear that one must distinguish between "appearance" and the
"underlying reality" in a dynamic sense. In other words, the phe-

nomenal properties are to be distinguished from the conditional-genetic characteristics of objects and events, that is, from the properties which determine their causal relationships. . . . As far as the conceptual derivation is concerned, one may use effectiveness as the criterion for existence: *"What is real is what has effects"* (6, p. 19).

Lewin's life space, then, is *not* merely the phenomenal field. And he adds to our previous considerations cogent reasons for thinking that a psychology of the phenomenal field cannot be adequately explanatory. His life space is not immediately given in the concreteness of experience; it is an abstract, hypothetical construct, inferred by the psychologist-observer to account for the individual's behavior.

It is, however, a construct of a type that differs from constructs of behavioristic psychology. It is formulated in terms of what is behaviorally real to the acting individual, not primarily in terms of what is physically observable to the scientist. Hence it is legitimate to speak of theories like Lewin's as anchored in a *subjective* (not phenomenological) *frame of reference.* Lewin's concepts and many of Freud's are in this sense *subjective constructs,* not because they are built of the stuff of conscious experience, but because they attempt to deal with what is effectively real to the individual, even when it is real to the scientific observer only in this secondary, indirect way.

The subjective frame of reference in theory construction is to be contrasted with the *objective frame of reference,* wherein concepts are chosen so as to be rooted as closely as possible in effective realities shared by any qualified observer. This is the distinction which Snygg and Combs seek, which makes them see both Freud and Lewin as precursors. There is no absolute difference between the two frames of reference; it is rather a question of which criteria are weighted most strongly in the selection of constructs.

Both the subjective and objective frames of reference pertain to the choice of constructs and the theoretical context in which they are embedded. They in no sense conflict with what has been called the *observer's frame of reference,* which, indeed, lies at the foundation of all science. The problem establishing a bridge between the point of view of the observer and *either* subjective or objective inferential constructs is the familiar one of operational definition. It cannot, in the last analysis, be avoided unless one chooses the alternative of claiming *direct* access to the point of view of the observed. This is the point of view of intuitionism, which asserts that the observer's and subject's points of view can be merged. But is this science? Not in the sense of a systematic search for understanding that can withstand the equally systematic doubt of the man from Missouri.

Subjective constructs framed in terms of the "private world" of the behaving individual remain constructs, and as such must ultimately be rooted in data accessible to the observer's frame of reference. There is no reason at all why their source should be restricted to the data of communicated conscious experience, in answer to our first question. But the phenomenological approach, or, more generally, any means of access to the experience of the subject, is of course crucial to the formulation of subjective constructs and the investigation of their relationships. Perhaps the point has been labored, but it is an essential one: the phenomenological approach, the clinical interview, the projective protocol, the behavioral observation—none of these yield direct knowledge of psychological constructs, subjective or objective, while all of them can provide the basis for inferring explanatory constructs and their relationships. If the canons of inference can be made sufficiently explicit, they provide the operational definitions that secure the constructs in the scientific home base of the observer's frame of reference.

Methods that get the subject to reveal his private world as he sees it need to be supplemented by others which permit the observer to infer effective factors that are distorted or disguised in the subject's awareness. But the broadly phenomenological methods remain a signally important source of data. Certain important subjective constructs such as the *self,* moreover, are anchored fairly directly in the data of phenomenological report.

## EGO, SELF, AND PHENOMENOLOGY

Although there is still considerable confusion in usage, a degree of consensus seems to be emerging to employ the term *self* for the phenomenal content of the experience of personal identity. A salient feature of the phenomenal field that has figured largely in personality theory, the self in this sense has the conceptual properties of a phenomenal object. Murphy (8) and Chein (2) use it with this meaning. Snygg and Combs agree, writing with somewhat franker circularity:

Of particular importance in the motivation of behavior will be those parts of the phenomenal field perceived by him to be part or characteristic of himself. To refer to this important aspect of the total field we have used the term *phenomenal self* (11, p. 111).

Within the phenomenal self, they distinguish as a stable core the *self concept:* "Those parts of the phenomenal field which the individual has differentiated as definite and fairly stable characteristics of himself" (11, p. 112).

Sharing with Murphy a strong emphasis on responses to the self as fundamental to motivational theory, Snygg and Combs go so far as to state that the basic human need is "the preservation and enhancement of the phenomenal self" (11, p. 58). Changes in the perception of the self play a major role in the theory of the therapeutic process that they share with Rogers (9).

Let us look more closely, however, at how these writers actually use the term. Passages like the following can readily be found:

. . . when the self is free from any threat of attack or likelihood of

attack, then it is possible for the self to consider these hitherto rejected perceptions, to make new differentiations, and to reintegrate
the self in such a way as to include them (9, p. 365).

A self threatened by its perceptions, may deny the perception by
simply refusing to enter the situation where such a perception is
forced upon him (11, p. 148).

Can a phenomenal self consider perceptions and reintegrate
itself; can a threatened phenomenal self deny perceptions; or is
this rather double-talk resulting from the attempt to make one
good concept do the work of two? If, as this writer suspects, the
latter is the case, what is the nature of the hidden second concept, which evidently is not merely a percept or phenomenal
entity? To give it a name he would suggest the conventional
term *ego,* realizing that usage in this respect is even more ambiguous than with the term *self.* The important point is that the
concept, implicit in the writings of Rogers and of Snygg and
Combs, is a subjective construct but does not refer to a phenomenal entity, whereas the self, on the other hand, is a coordinate subjective construct that does. The relation between the
two will bear closer examination.

It is not necessary, at this juncture, to propose a definitive
theory of the ego, nor to enter into an involved discussion of
alternative views about its nature. What is relevant is that starting from an attempt to write a psychology in phenomenal terms,
our authors in spite of themselves give implicit recognition to
organizing, selective processes in the personality which are somehow guided by the nature and status of the self (among other
things) and somehow, in turn, have an influence in its nature
and status. So conceived, the relation of ego and self is highly
interdependent[1] but by no means an identity. The distinction is

---

[1] The writer doubts that it is advisable to construct the ego as narrowly
around the self as do Chein (2) and Murphy (8).

that between a dynamic configuration of on-going processes, inferred from many facts of biography and behavior, and a phenomenal entity resulting from these processes and affecting them in turn, inferred primarily (but not exclusively) from phenomenological report.

Approaching the problem on a slightly different tack, we may find it rewarding to consider three of the eight conceptions of the ego listed by Allport (1, p. 459) in the light of the distinction just made: the ego "as one segregated behavioral system among others," "as knower," and "as object of knowledge." The fundamental conception advanced here is not unlike the first of these senses, if one reads into it a dynamic quality not expressed in Allport's formulation. As an on-going system or organizing and selective processes mediating the individual's intercourse with reality, it includes a variety of processes without being coterminous with the total personality.[2] Among these processes or functions is that of the ego as "knower," which the writer would take in a less metaphysical sense than Allport's to embrace the cognitive-perceptual functions of personality. These have been described with reason in psychoanalytic theory (5, pp. 105–106) as an integral aspect of the ego system. Among the phenomena that the ego "knows" is the *self*, Allport's "ego as object of knowledge." Like any cognitive-perceptual object, the self only imperfectly mirrors the physical, psychological, and social facts that underlie the perception. And also like similar phenomenal objects it serves as a guide to appropriate behavior. But the relation of self to ego-processes is no more and no less obscure than the relation of cognitive structures to behavior generally.

[2] How to distinguish within the personality between *ego* and *non-ego* is, of course, an important problem, though it will not be attempted here. The distinction, however, is not the same as the phenomenal one between the *self* and *not-self* (often described, confusingly, as *ego-alien*).

## "EGO-INVOLVEMENTS" AND "EGO DEFENSE"

We have sought to reinstate the ego as a subjective but non-phenomenal construct mainly through an examination of the pitfalls encountered by the attempt to avoid such a concept. If the ego-self distinction as outlined above is worth making, however, it should make a difference in the formulation of other knotty problems. Does it? Two such problems—the nature of "ego-involvements" and of the "mechanisms of defense" will be examined briefly as test cases.

As it emerges in the work of Sherif and Cantril (10), the concept of ego-involvement lacks clarity and focus. Widely divergent sorts of psychological facts turn out to be embraced by the term, which like so many in popular psychological currency rather identifies a disparate group of problems than clarifies them. More often than not, ego-involvement means the involvement of a person's pride and self-esteem in a task; he feels put to the test and ready to be ashamed of a poor performance. In other instances, the term is invoked to cover immersion in a cause, or falling in love—cases in which the person, to be sure, cares as deeply about outcomes as in the first type, but may be engrossed to the point of losing self-awareness.

Now the present self-ego distinction makes excellent sense when applied here. Since the distinctive character of the first sort of examples lies in the fact that the individual's conception of his self and its worth is at stake, these can aptly be described as *self-involvement*. The second type of case can often still be called ego-involvement without inconsistency. The situation in the latter instances touches on the person's central system of on-going psychological processes so closely that he may lose himself in it. Similar engrossment can, to be sure, result from the involvement of equally imperative non-ego processes: who is to say, without intimate acquaintance with the principals, whether being in love should be called ego-involvement or "id-involvement"! However that may be, note that self-involvement and ego-involvement thus conceived may vary independently. A person may care about a task both because of its intrinsic meaning for him and with after-thought for its bearing on his prestige and self-esteem. Or either or neither may be the case. The behavioral conditions and consequences of ego- and self-involvement should furthermore be quite distinct.

The situation is somewhat different in regard to the theoretical status of the mechanisms of defense. Here the classical formulation by Anna Freud (4) regards the defense mechanisms as employed by the ego (the term is used essentially in our sense) to protect itself, primarily from disruption by strong unassimilated urges, but also from threats from the external world. As a more or less precariously balanced system mediating between inner strivings and outer reality, the ego, in this view, has recourse to these sometimes drastic techniques in order to preserve its balance, and maintain the course of behavior at a lower level of adjustment if need be rather than run the risk of its catastrophic disruption. Murphy (8), and later Snygg and Combs (11), on the other hand, say in effect that it is rather the self that is defended. Under conditions of threat, enhancement and preservation of the self may be achieved by the classical defense mechanisms. Is it necessary to choose between these divergent formulations, or can the conflict be resolved?

The present writer would maintain that the mechanisms of defense can ultimately all be conceived as defenses of the ego, since they serve to bolster up the ego's adjustive compromise. As contributors to this compromise, they can also best be regarded as a part of the activity included in the ego system. But in a more immediate sense, any particular one of an individual's defenses may or may *not* be a *self*-defense mechanism. Since the maintenance of a favorable self-image is important to sound ego functioning, though not its only requisite, the end of ego defense can often be served most efficiently by self-defense mechanisms. Certain mechanisms, like identification, may, indeed, always take effect through the defense of the self. There are, however, instances of ego-defense mechanisms which involve the self only indirectly if at all. In regression, for example, one can hardly suppose that the self is enhanced in any way. What is more likely is that by retreating to an earlier, more deeply established, or simpler level of ego organization, the person seeks, perhaps ineptly, to cope with disturbing experiences that, by reason of circumstance, constitution, or previous learning, he has not the strength to meet maturely. In most cases, the relative significance of the self in the defensive process probably cannot be assessed in any simple way, since changes in the self for better or worse may be the *consequence* of the fortunes of the ego and its defenses, as well as the focus of defensive techniques.

A formuation of this sort, which seems to agree with present clinical experience, again suggests the usefulness of a distinction between phenomenal and non-phenomenal (shall we say *functional?*) subjective constructs, with both employed in proper coordination. A purely phenomenological psychology, on the other hand, cannot adequately describe *all* the defensive processes, since neither all the effective threats to the ego nor all the defenses against them are registered accurately in conscious awareness. Indeed, it is largely the consequence of "silent" defensive processes that phenomenological reports must be viewed with so much circumspection in personality research.

## CONCLUSIONS

Starting from a discussion of Snygg and Combs' proposal of a phenomenological frame of reference for psychology (11) the writer has sought to establish the following major points:

1. While common sense may favor an explanatory psychology framed entirely in terms of conscious experience, such a psychological system does violence to currently available knowledge.

2. Phenomenology, as distinct from common sense, is descriptive, not explanatory. It is an approach or method ancillary to the formulation of problems and derivation of constructs, and does not give birth to these constructs full blown.

3. The subjective and objective frames of reference, which denote relatively different alternative contexts within which constructs may be selected, are both entirely compatible with the observer's frame of reference. Subjective constructs to be scientifically admissible must ultimately be anchored in the data of observation.

4. The phenomenological approach provides one method of deriving subjective constructs. But not all subjective constructs need represent phenomenal entities. They may, thus, denote functional entities that are either absent from the phenomenal field or inaccurately presented in it.

5. The coordinate use of phenomenal and non-phenomenal subjective constructs, maintained in clear distinction from one another, serves to clarify the theory of the ego and the self. It is proposed that an adequate theory of personality must distinguish, among other constructs: (a) the *ego*, a *non-phenomenal* subjective construct representing a configuration of on-going processes, among which is the cognitive-perceptual function. Through exercise of this function, the ego "knows," among other things, (b) the *self*, a *phenomenal* subjective construct.

6. When carried into current problems concerning the nature of "ego-involvement" and of the "mechanisms of defense," the above distinction seems productive.

## REFERENCES

1. Allport, G. W. The ego in contemporary psychology. *Psychol. Rev.*, 1943, **50**, 451–478.
2. Chein, I. The awareness of self and the structure of the ego. *Psychol. Rev.*, 1944, **51**, 304–314.
3. Combs, A. W. A phenomenological approach to adjustment theory. *J. abnorm. soc. Psychol.*, 1949, **44**, 29–35.
4. Freud, A. *The ego and the mechanisms of defense.* New York: International Universities Press, 1946.
5. Freud, S. *New introductory lectures on psychoanalysis.* New York: Norton, 1933.
6. Lewin, K. *Principles of topological psychology.* New York: McGraw-Hill, 1936.
7. MacLeod, R. B. The phenomenological approach to social psychology. *Psychol. Rev.*, 1947, **54**, 193–210.
8. Murphy, G. *Personality: a biosocial approach to origins and structure.* New York: Harper, 1947.
9. Rogers, C. R. Some observations on the organization of personality. *Amer. Psychologist*, 1947, **2**, 358–368.
10. Sherif, M., & Cantril, H. *The psychology of ego-involvements.* New York: Wiley, 1947.
11. Snygg, D., & Combs, A. W. *Individual behavior.* New York: Harper, 1949.

# CHAPTER 13

·······································································································

# The Phenomenological Approach and the Problem of "Unconscious" Behavior: A Reply to Dr. Smith

---

## BY DONALD SNYGG AND
## ARTHUR W. COMBS

We are grateful for this opportunity to comment on Dr. Smith's paper (4) and to clarify some aspects of our own position which we do not seem to have made completely clear in *Individual Behavior* (5). As we see it, Dr. Smith's major criticisms are based on the contention that many factors in behavior are unconscious and are never part of the behaver's phenomenal field. Since we seem to have skipped over this extremely important question rather rapidly in our earlier publications we are glad to have this chance to explain why we do not accept this assumption, which is so widely held that it has almost come to be "common sense."

From *The Journal of Abnormal and Social Psychology*, 1950, **45**, 523–528. Reprinted by permission of the authors and the publisher.

## IS BEHAVIOR EVER "UNCONSCIOUS"?

It seems to us that two somewhat different types of behavior have been generally ascribed to "unconscious" motives. One is the kind we described in the passage Dr. Smith has quoted (4): "the vague and fuzzy aspects of behavior (which) correspond to and are parts of the vague and incompletely differentiated aspects of the field" (5). This kind of behavior includes the postural shifts of which we are only very vaguely aware and the expressive behavior which Maslow (3) has described as being without a definite goal, "unconscious or at least not fully conscious," and correlated with "deep lying character structure," i.e., (our phraseology) with the total field rather than its differentiated parts. Dr. Smith does not seem to challenge our explanation of this type of behavior.

He does point out, however, that behavior which is much more precise and conscious is also ascribed to unconscious factors. "The clinical literature abounds with instances of unconsciously determined behavior which far from being 'vague and fuzzy,' is, on the contrary highly differentiated." (4) It is our contention that the assumption that such behavior is determined by unconscious factors is not an inevitable one and that it results from the selection of an inadequate causal field.

Does an individual ever behave with precision toward a goal he does not perceive? Or does he ever show highly differentiated behavior for reasons of which he is not aware?

It seems to us that the answers that a psychologist makes to these questions will depend on how far back in time he goes in his search for the alleged cause of the behavior. If he traces the causal chain back to a point where it is outside the behaver's present perceptual field and then designates one of these forgotten events as *the* cause then this cause has to be called unconscious. Freudian psychology, in taking the whole life span as a single causal field, has to come to this conclusion. This is a perfectly reasonable and valid observation, provided only that one understands that this observation is made from the frame of reference of the observer and *not the behaver.*

But there is no reason why the psychologist, in looking for the immediate causes of behavior, needs to go back to find an historical cause outside of the present perceptual field. If he is attempting to predict behavior with precision it is better if he does not.

Certainly, the events of an individual's life affect his behavior. But it is important for us to recognize that it is the perceptions of these events and not the physical events themselves which are the *immediate* causes of behavior. Thus an individual's behavior today may be highly precise and direct because his perceptions are precise although the reason for having that perception in the first place may no longer exist in his perceptual field at all. A psychologist, knowing of the earlier event, and perceiving that event as *the* cause of the individual's present behavior, concludes that the person is behaving for a reason of which he is not aware, i.e., of which he is unconscious. But this is only the inference of an external observer; and it is made only when the subject's behavior seems out of harmony with the situation as the observer sees it. The subject himself does not see his behavior in this way at all.

For example, a young man had a severe phobia for flying birds. A sparrow alighting on his window sill would throw him into such a panic that he would attempt to retreat by any available means. In his perceptual field a bird was an extraordinarily threatening object. What is more, his perceptions were highly differentiated and his behavior extremely precise. Now his objective psychologist, knowing that he had been most insecure as a child and knowing that his nurse had been accustomed to control him by threats of feeding him to "the wild geese in the attic" sees these events as the causes of his present behavior. Indeed, the young man himself may, at other times, ascribe his present behavior to those events because in describing his behavior he is making an external observation, just as the psychologist does. *At the instant of his panic,* however, he is not behaving in terms of unconscious causes but in terms of sharply differentiated present perceptions that birds are vicious, dangerous, and immediate threats to himself. Thus it appears that behavior described from an external point of view as unconscious, from a phenomenological point of view is not unsconscious at all but, on the contrary, may be very highly "conscious."

We believe that this explains the inadequacy of mere explanations as a means of therapy. Clients say "I can see the reasons why I feel this way, but it doesn't seem to help. I still feel this way." It is the present feelings that determine the behavior. If forgotten attitudes and events have an effect on behavior it is through the transformation they have brought about in the genesis of the present field and the effects they have thus had on its organization. The explanation of maladjustment as a function of trauma in the genetic history of the individual is so well established in psychology as to be unquestioned. It is necessary for us to remind ourselves, however, that this understanding is the psychologist's, *not* the behaver's. This principle, it seems to us, is extraordinarily important for applied psychology. It is conceivable that the applied psychologist acting in terms of his externally conceived analysis of an individual's problem may completely misfire or, even worse, complicate his client's problem by the intrusion of irrelevant data.[1] We wish to reiterate our postulate that "All behavior is determined by (and pertinent to) the phenomenological field at the moment of action" (5, p. 45).

---

[1] This seems to us a most important principle, particularly with respect to its application in psychotherapy. If present perceptions govern behavior, psychotherapy must concern itself with present perceptions rather than genetic understandings. It is the understanding and implementation of this point which probably represents the most important single difference between client-centered therapy and traditional psychoanalysis.

It seems to us that Prof. Smith's basic objection may be due to our failure to underline the imporant words in the definition of the phenomenal field which he has quoted. These words are "at the instant of action." This is important because it is only at this instant that all of the convergent lines of causation come together.[2] And they come together in the perceptual field, of which the perceived behavior is a part. At that instant the behaver cannot behave in a way inappropriate to the field because at that instant the field in a way seems to him to be reality and acts which are inappropriate to it would be self-sabotage.

The arguments against our postulate are based upon a field with a longer time-span than the one we have used. We have postulated a one to one relationship between the field and the behavior which is part of it, i.e., between the field and behavior at time x. If we tried to relate the field at an earlier time, x-y, with the behavior at time x we would, of course, expect to find no such one to one relation. As of that moment some of the causal factors which will play a part in determining the nature of the phenomenal field at time x have not yet impinged upon the field, so the phenomenal field at time x-y is not, by itself, adequate for the prediction of behavior at time x and, since all predictions of behavior have to be made before the event, i.e., at time x-y, this may lead to the erroneous conclusion that causes may operate without ever entering the perceptual field.

An observer at 11:53 watching a tavern loafer give a dozing customer the hot foot may assume that when the practical joker lights the match he is seeing a cause of behavior which is not part of the behaver's perceptual field. In this regard we should

[2] As Lewin points out (2) "the behaver's field at any given instant contains also the views of that individual about his future and past" . . . "The psychological past and the psychological future are simultaneous parts of the psychological field existing at a given time. . . ."

like to make two points: (a) The joker and his match are not acting as a cause of the customer's behavior at 11:53. (b) Whether they will affect his behavior at a future time is still uncertain. The match will not affect the potential victim's behavior unless he perceives it or its effects. If he is dead drunk or wearing an artificial foot it will burn down to his shoe and go out without having any effect on his behavior.

We are making so much of this point because if our analysis is correct the psychologist has an important new technique for the prediction of behavior. No one has ever had any trouble explaining behavior after it has occurred because in any situation there are an almost infinite number of factors which *might* have an effect on behavior. It is easy to look back *after* the behavior has occurred and construct a plausible theory about which of these might have been operating. There are so many possibilities that there can be a great many different theories, all plausible. But the prediction of behavior in advance is much more risky because predictions can be checked. And the large number of potential causal factors which make explanation after the event so easy make prediction very difficult. There are too many possibilities. The psychologist, if he is to predict with any accuracy at all, must have some principle by which he can select, from the countless potential factors physically present[3] those which will actually become determinants of the subject's behavior. If we are right in postulating that such "physical" factors can only become operative by way of the behaver's phenomenal field we have a principle capable of narrowing the behavioral possibilities to a marked degree. When we can follow this up with a reconstruction of the behaver's field at time x-y and a knowledge of the field dynamics which will enable us to predict how the factors which are at that time "external" will effect that field and be transformed

[3] Or, more accurately, from the factors in the situation which he is able to observe.

in it we shall have the basis for a genuinely predictive science of psychology. In our opinion that time has already arrived.

Step by step the process of prediction from this point of view is as follows:

1. Inference of the behaver's present field from his behavior.

2. Projection of the future field, taking into consideration the factors perceived by the observer which, on the basis of the behaver's present inferred field, will affect his future field.[4]

3. From the inferred future field the future behavior is predicted.

4. Since the approach assumes a one to one relation between the phenomenal field and the concurrent behavior, the accuracy of the inferences can be checked. This gives the psychologist using the approach a method of successive approximation by which each reconstruction of the subject's field becomes more accurate, leading to equally accurate predictions of his behavior.

We do not feel that this approach, particularly as used in step 2, is just "common sense." It is certainly subjective and, because the inferences are made in terms of the behaver's perceptual field, we have called it phenomenological.

## THE PERCEIVER IN A PHENOMENOLOGICAL SYSTEM

This brings us to the perceiving ego which Dr. Smith has, somewhat to our surprise, found hidden in at least one of our remarks. We have used the term self to mean something else, at times, than the phenomenal self; and we will try to be more careful in the future. But we still have some reservations about Dr. Smith's formalization of the concept which we carelessly introduced.

It is quite logical to infer that if there is organization there

---

[4] Most of the theoretical constructs and principles presented in *Individual Behavior* describe the processes by which these potential causes of behavior are rejected or admitted and modified.

may be an organizer and that if there are perceptions there must be a perceiver. We have at times made such an inference, as Dr. Smith points out. But we do not need to make it. It is not a necessary or even helpful part of our system. But it is a necessary part of Dr. Smith's, which is why he has to be insistent about it. As a construct it has the grave (but not fatal) defect that inferences about it are very difficult to check and the fact that he has to resort to such a concept serves to illustrate the difficulties we can get into when we fail to define the time limits of our causal field. When events which were part of the field at time x are lumped together with events which were parts of the field at time x-y and x-z the organization of the field is lost. Objects and events in the phenomenal field derive their meaning from the field at that instant. Out of that context they will have different meanings, like food before and after a heavy dinner. An incident which would be traumatic in one phenomenal situation can be highly gratifying in another and be barely perceived in a third. If events and objects from different phases of the same developing field are treated as if they were independent, stable entities operating in a single field, an accurate reconstruction of their true field relations becomes impossible. The task of a psychologist attempting to predict behavior from such data is as difficult as would be the task of a person who was given a thousand words cut individually from a book and scrambled and then asked to predict what would happen in the next chapter.

The common-sense way of explaining organized behavior which seems to emerge from such an unorganized field is to endow the unorganized field with a hidden organizer. The six-year-old daughter of one of the writers did it the other day.

"Why did you do that, Frances?" she was asked.

"Oh, my brain told me to do it."

"Well, why did your brain tell you to do it?"

"Oh, (with a giggle) I guess its brain told it to do it."

Such explanatory constructs are fairly common in psychology, but they have never been very fruitful. Dr. Smith's ego is a much more sophisticated construct than the "brain's brain" but they are both second order constructs set up to explain the first order constructs which are set up to explain the observed behavior. In effect they are attempts to explain a mystery by a greater mystery.

In our own approach this assumption of a hidden organizer is, as we have said, neither necessary nor helpful. When organization is found it does not need to be explained in order to be used in prediction. It only needs to be described. The essential characteristic of any organized field is its tendency to maintain its organization in the face of intruding forces. Since the phenomenal field, at any given instant, is organized the behavior of its parts can be predicted from knowledge of the field itself, without knowing why the field is organized. Our procedure is analogous to that of a meteorologist predicting the weather over a given area. Considering his map as the representation of a dynamic field he predicts the future states of the field, taking into account the probable transformation and effect of forces coming up over the edge of the map from the outside. It is not necessary to postulate a non-observable selective agency to determine the effect of these forces on the meteorological field. The meteorologist's analysis of the field itself, at the time of their entrance, provides all the information that is necessary.

It is quite reasonable for Dr. Smith to explain the individual organization of a behavioral field by postulating an hypothetical construct to do the organizing. But since our causal field is already organized we do not need to use such a concept. At the present time it seems much safer to make as few constructs as possible and base our predictions on the dynamics of the phenomenal field itself.

In these terms our definition of the basic human need as "the maintenance and enhancement of the phenomenal self" (5) is a little too limited and we may have to return to the earlier position that "the fundamental need . . . (is) the preservation of the organization and integrity of the (phenomenal) field and especially of that part of the field which is the phenomenal self"[5] (6, p. 412). This is wordier and harder to apply at once but somewhat more accurate.

In returning to the earlier formulation, which states more explicitly the function of the whole phenomenal field, we are accepting Dr. Smith's point that regression cannot, without forcing, be considered a mechanism for defense of the phenomenal self. Some of the devices that are sometimes called regression can, for example the bed-wetting of the three-year-old in a home where there is a new baby. But others cannot. As we see it, "regression," like all of the Freudian devices, is a manifestation of the organized nature of the phenomenal field. Since it is not a closed field its organization is always in a state of fluidity, moving toward adjustment. In some cases the attack from the outside is so violent that organization can be maintained only by consolidation at a lower (but not necessarily earlier) level, i.e., by "regression," or by abandoning part of the field, i.e., by "dissociation." The so-called "self"-protective mechanisms like rationalization and identification may occur where the attack on the field is less severe. In these cases the reorganization required is less and can take place without much effect on the phenomenal self, which acts as a point of reference

[5] Our reasons for believing that, in a phenomenal field which includes a phenomenal future, maintenance of the self also requires its enhancement are given in *Individual Behavior*. We wish we could find a better term than self-enhancement. It does not carry the full weight of meaning since to many people it carries the connotation of purely selfish behavior. It can also imply a growing extension of the self into the rest of the phenomenal field and a decrease in the feeling of conflict with it. Consequently the greater the self-enhancement the less will be the chances that another person will interpret the individual's behavior as selfish. The maximum degree of self-enhancement, as we see it, would be achieved by the individual who feels at one with the universe, so completely a part of the universe that he does not need to defend himself against any other part.

for the rest of the field and is consequently very resistant to change.

As a matter of fact, all objects and events in the phenomenal field have such a high degree of relation to the self that the statement that the basic need is for the maintenance and enhancement of the phenomenal self is a very close approximation of the actual situation and conveys much more to the reader than the longer and more careful statement. Certainly, if we are to see the behaver's field as he does himself we must stress the central position and active behavior of the phenomenal self.

Taking up some of the minor points made by Prof. Smith, we used "phenomenal field" and "perceptual field" instead of "consciousness" not as a "bow to current prejudice," (4) but in an attempt to make clear the fact that our concept took cognizance of the organized nature of the field and of the ground characteristics which have to be derived by inference rather than by direct report.

We have never been under the illusion that a subject could give an accurate report of his phenomenal field. Our reasons are to be found on pages 35–36 of *Individual Behavior* and in a symposium paper (1).

In general we think that Dr. Smith's position is well thought out and very similar to the one we would have to take if we started from the same premises. He will be neither disappointed nor surprised at our failure to agree with him at all points. Whether we look at it in terms of his need for ego-enhancement or in terms of our general concept of persisting organization of the perceptual field or our specific concept of maintenance of the phenomenal self, it would have been predicted by all of us that our point of view would change just enough to maintain our concepts of ourselves as responsible scientists, and no more. We shall accordingly not hold it against Dr. Smith if, after reading this, he still fails to agree with us.

We are grateful for the stimulation to our own thinking his presentation has afforded us.

## REFERENCES

1. Combs, A. W., & Snygg, D. Implications of the phenomenological approach for the evaluation of psychotherapy. (To be published.)
2. Lewin, K. Defining the "field at a given time." *Psychol. Rev.,* 1943, **50**, 292–310.
3. Maslow, A. H. The expressive component of behavior. *Psychol. Rev.,* 1949, **56**, 261–272.
4. Smith, M. B. The phenomenological approach in personality theory: some critical remarks. *J. abnorm. soc. Psychol.,* 1950, **45**, 516–522.
5. Snygg, D., & Combs, A. W. *Individual behavior.* New York: Harper, 1949.
6. Snygg, D. The need for a phenomenological system of psychology. *Psychol. Rev.,* 1941, **48**, 404–424.

# CHAPTER 14

■■■■■■■■■■■■■■■■■■■■■■■■■■■■■■■■■■■■■■■■■■■■■■■■■■■■■■■■■■■■■■■■■■■■■■■■■■■■■■■

# Phenomenological Personality Theories and the Data Language of Psychology

## BY RICHARD JESSOR

It is clear that an increasing number of theories of personality find it useful, if not necessary, to employ some construct referring to the *psychological* situation—e.g., life space (10), phenomenal field (13, 15), or meaningful environment (14). Such theories do not attempt to relate behavior to the physical or geographic environment. Instead, they attempt to make predictions by reference to the environment as it is perceptually, cognitively, or functionally responded to by an organism or class of organisms. In view of the generally recognized importance of such theoretical efforts, on the one hand, and in view of certain questions that have been raised about the methodological status of these efforts, on the other, it would seem opportune to examine the issues involved in some detail.

---

From *Psychological Review*, 1956, **63**, 173–180. Reprinted by permission of the author and the publisher.

The most frequently cited challenges to phenomenological[1] orientations in personality theory have questioned the degree to which such orientations may be considered to be truly physicalistic, and the degree to which they may be considered to be predictive rather than postdictive systems. These issues are, of course, not unrelated to each other. Lewin's system, perhaps because of the explicitness with which it is presented, has served most often as the protoype of phenomenological theories when these issues have been discussed. Brunswik (4), for example, describes Lewin's life space as postperceptual and prebehavioral, and doubts whether Lewin's predictions can, in a strict sense of the word, be tested. Spence (16) has stressed the failure of such field theories as Lewin's to provide us with laws that will enable control and manipulation of the behavior-determining psychological field. His analysis has gone further to emphasize the distinction between the types of laws that are achieved by phenomenological theories versus those attained by systems which do refer behavior to the physico-geographic environment. The former laws are called R-R laws, and are considered to relate one set of responses to another set of responses obtained earlier from the subject or the experimenter. The latter laws are referred to as S-R laws, and are considered to relate responses to independently measured physical and social environmental variables.

The aims of this paper are three-fold: to support the position that phenomenological theories of personality are compatible with the general scientific requirements of physicalism and predictiveness, to demonstrate that a fundamental distinction between these theories and nonphenomenological theories is difficult to maintain, and, finally, to suggest that a crucial issue

---

[1] The term *phenomenological* and its variants are used in this paper to refer to theories which employ some construct referring to the psychological situation, e.g., life space, behavioral environment, etc. The present usage divests the term of certain historical connotations, such as holism or introspectionism, which have accrued to it.

intrinsic to a discussion of the problems mentioned above—and one rarely raised in that connection—is the nature of the psychological data language traditionaly favored by S-R and by R-R theories.

## THE PROBLEM OF THE PSYCHOLOGICAL ENVIRONMENT

The essential characteristic of all constructs which refer to a psychological environment is that their nature and properties are response-inferred. It is unfortunate that some usages of such response inferences have been of the sort as to couple them closely in time to the behavior that is being predicted. This has given the impression of a very limited kind of predictiveness, if not, in actuality, a kind of postdiction. It has also raised the related question of the *independence* of the two sets of responses. Since the problem of prediction and the problem of independence of variables are both closely bound up with the problem of the definition of the stimulus, the latter will be reviewed at some length. In this way a clearer picture of the methodological status of the psychological-environment construct should emerge. It may be noted, parenthetically, that Lewin's theory, as an example of phenomenological theories, *is* considered by Spence (16) to achieve laws between independent variables; the emphasis of his remarks is on the point that the variables are all response variables.

The term *stimulus* in psychology implies, by definition, a relatedness to responses rather than independence of them. It is impossible to isolate, point to, or describe aspects of the environment as stimuli except insofar as they have some determinable relationship to the responses of some organism. To conceive, therefore, of stimulus variables as independent of response variables in general appears to be unwarranted. This point has been raised in connection with other problems by both Brown (2) and Bakan (1). Bakan has noted that variables are simply sets of categories, and *"categories are the result of someone's delineation, abstraction, and identification"* (1, p. 47). In this sense there are no stimulus variables which are not response-inferred or defined, *including the variables of physics and sociology.* The organism which is the reference point for the process of definition in physics is, of course, the experimenter. It follows from these considerations that all stimuli are response-defined at some time by some organism. The issue becomes that of *whose* response definitions, under what conditions.

There are two other ways in which the meaning of the term *independence* may be considered.

1. A distinction may be attempted between the responses of the subjects and those of the experimenter, that is to say, the stimulus definition by the experimenter may be considered independent of the responses of his subjects. Davis (8) has presented this position in its extreme in his recent call for a more physical psychology. Davis states: "For a 'stimulus' (external event) to qualify under the proposed canon, it would have to be something which an experimenter could ascertain without there being any organism for it to work on" (8, p. 10). This statement is worth examining closely. In view of our previous discussion, it may be noted that Davis concedes, at least, that the stimulus is defined by the response of the experimenter, i.e., "something which the experimenter could ascertain." More appropriate to the present point, however, is the fact that the word "stimulus" is placed in quotes by Davis. Obviously, this evidences recognition that external events may be considered stimuli *only* when some relationship is demonstrable between the presence or occurrence of the event and some behavior or response of an organism.

If this view were not held, in actuality, by psychologists, the result would be the investigation and manipulation of an infinite array of physically discriminable variables (discriminated by the experimenter), some of which may have effects on the

organism—e.g., a loud noise—and some of which may not—
e.g., a sound of a frequency too high to be directly perceived
by human subjects. Even the traditional S-R theorists manipulate
variables which are defined by the responses of their rats rather
than by themselves alone. The empirical law of effect is a
concept which illustrates how classes of noxious stimuli and
incentives are defined by the approach or avoidance behavior of
populations of rats. To summarize this point, it is possible for
experimenters to discriminate or identify variables independently of the responses of their subjects, but these variables may
be considered *as stimuli* only when they are functionally related
to, i.e., defined by, the responses of their subjects.

2. The second sense in which the independence of the stimulus may be considered is in terms of its independence from a
given or particular response. Stated otherwise, the issue is
whether the stimulus may be identified *before* the particular
response occurs. This is a crucial issue, since it involves the entire process of prediction and control. Most of the phenomenological systems have often been content to identify the stimulus
only *after* the given response has occurred and, more seriously,
have not adequately provided or described techniques or procedures for enabling the experimenter to *predict* behavior by
knowledge of the nature of the stimulus in advance of the occurrence of the particular response. Spence (16) is correct in
his criticism of such phenomenological approaches for not telling us what to do to an individual in order to manipulate,
change, or control his behavior.

This criticism, however, applies to phenomenological systems
such as those of Lewin, Snygg and Combs, and Rogers, *not*
because they utilize response-inferred constructs but rather *because they have traditionally and uniformly rejected a historical
approach to the problem of prediction*. It is only an ahistorical
phenomenology which has limited predictiveness, or is essentially postdictive. A historically oriented phenomenology (e.g.,

14) enables the experimenter to predict behavior by providing a basis for advance knowledge of the stimulus.

Let us examine this latter point in greater detail. The phenomenologists have maintained that behavior is a function of the psychological situation (10), the stimulus functions (9), or the meanings of stimuli (14), etc. The problem for them is to know, in advance of the given response, how the subject will constitute the stimulus situation, i.e., what meaning it will have for him. Since the meaning of a stimulus, or the precise way in which a variable functions as a stimulus, is inferred from the responses of the subject, it follows that, for the prediction of a given response in a particular situation, *the stimuli must be inferred from previous responses of the subject,* or similar subjects, in similar or systematically related situations.

This is precisely the way in which S-R behavior theorists proceed to define their stimuli in advance of the behavior of their rats. The way in which it is predicted that a pellet of food in a T maze will be an incentive stimulus for a hungry rat, and will result in approach and eating behavior, is simply by having observed that this rat, or other similarly hungry rats, *previously* approached and ate the food pellet.

For a similar approach to the problems of prediction in personality, it is possible to mention several well-known procedures which enable specification of the stimulus situation independent of and prior to a given response.

1. *Verbal report, by either the subject or the experimenter.* Spence has pointed out that ". . . the phenomenological approach has its advantages, particularly in the complex field of social behavior of the human adult. It is obviously much easier to gain some notion as to the relevant variables determining such complex behavior by asking the individual to verbalize than it is to employ the procedure of trying to hypothesize them from knowledge of past history" (16, p. 57). Unique to human beings is their ability to verbalize their perceptions of situations

or the meanings that they have for them. This information, in spite of its well-known limitations, is exceedingly valuable to the personality theorist interested in predicting the subject's subsequent behavior in those situations. And as Brunswik (5) has pointed out, it is possible to utilize verbal reports without falling back upon introspectionism.

Psychological tests may be considered as a specific example of this general procedure. Test data are essentially self reports or verbalized perceptions of stimulus situations. They are highly useful in attaining knowledge of the meaning or perception of future or subsequent real-life situations by the subject, to the extent that the test situation is similar to or systematically co-ordinated to the criterion or predicted situation.

2. *Observation of the responses of the general culture group to which a given subject belongs.* It is possible to define a stimulus situation for a given subject on the basis of previous responses by the culture group to which the subject belongs. Obviously, the accuracy or the applicability of such a culture-group definition for a given subject depends upon his related-ness to that group, or the similarity of his past experiences to those of the group members. Snygg and Combs (15), for ex-ample, point out that people who share common roles in a com-mon culture develop common characters in their phenomenal fields and consequently in their behavior. In short, similar social learning will result in similar perceptions of environments.

It will be seen that the broader the reference group, the less will be the likelihood that its definition of the situation will be useful or accurate for a *given* individual. If one were interested in the meaning of a classroom quiz situation for a particular college sophomore who is also a fraternity member, the re-sponses of the reference group of college sophomore fraternity members might be more applicable than those of college stu-dents as a whole, which in turn might be more accurate (that is, predictive) than those of the middle class as a whole, etc.

3. *The clinical method.* This leads to the third procedure, which assists us in coordinating idiographic and nomothetic approaches. In the preceding paragraph the use of culture-group definitions of situations was advocated. Since such definitions will apply only *more or less* to given subjects, they are useful for predictions about differences between *groups* of individuals, but will be unsatisfactory where specific individual prediction of behavior is desired. In the latter case it becomes necessary to reduce the reference points to the unique past experiences of the particular subject. By intensive study of the subject's previous responses in various situations, the personality theorist is able to establish the meaning or potential perception of a situation for a specific subject, and hence to predict subsequent behavior. This procedure, of course, is the clinical method, and the present description of it emphasizes its continuity with nomothetic procedures. More concrete elaboration of the implication of these three general procedures for defining situations will be made shortly.

The preceding discussion has stressed the point that all stimuli are response-defined at some time by either the subject or the experimenter. In view of this homogeneity, it seems unwarranted to establish a fundamental logical or methodological distinction between S-R and R-R theories. Viewed in this light, the use of constructs referring to a psychological environment would seem to require no special justification. The discussion to this point has also delineated at least the potential compatibility of phenomenological theories with the necessary demand for predictive adequacy.

## THE NEED FOR A PSYCHOLOGICAL DATA LANGUAGE

Granting the argument to this point does not at all lead to the conclusion that S-R and R-R theories do not differ in some significant way. The question to be asked is, Wherein is there a difference between these types of theories? The answer seems to lie in the data language that is favored to describe the situation or environment in which behavior takes place.

There is common agreement among various theorists that psychology thus far has neglected the development of an adequate descriptive terminology for the environment. While personality theorists have been interested for a long time in categorizing the behavioral or internal states of human subjects, they have paid far less heed to developing categories for describing different kinds of situations. Such attempts as have been made are suggestive, but remain limited in usage to particular theoretical orientations, and no widely accepted or universal descriptive terminology for the environment exists at present. It seems to the present author that one difference between the S-R theories and the phenomenological or R-R theories is that the former have heavily employed the data language of physics (despite the reliance on such terms as *cue* and *goal*), whereas the latter have tended toward a more psychological data language. The reliance by the former on physical terms seems to be one of the factors which has contributed importantly to the *appearance* of independent stimulus definition that was discussed above.

Undeniably effective use has been made by S-R theory of the language of physics. Such a data language has the tremendous advantage of being one in which, for historical reasons, maximum reliability or interobserver agreement can be attained, and which involves concepts for which accurate measures have been developed. Nevertheless, reliability alone is insufficient qualification for any language system. What is required is that it be adequate for the purposes and problems of a given science or level of description. Since the real world is neutral with respect to language systems, there is no a priori reason, beyond degree of reliability, for the use of the data language of physics by another science such as psychology. The remainder of this paper will attempt to point out possible reasons why the language of physics has proved unsatisfactory for personality theory, or for psychologists dealing with complex human social behavior, and proposes the development of a psychological data language.

It may forestall misunderstanding to state at this point that our quarrel is not with methodological physicalism, i.e., the insistence on objectivity via denotative reduction or observational reliability. Rather, the critique is aimed at the incorporation into psychology of the *language* of physics. The latter procedure is part of what Brunswick has designated as thematic physicalism, ". . . . the uncritical emulation of the . . . aims and problem content of physics by other disciplines" (5, p. 14).

Methodological physicalism in no way implies that the various branches of science must use the same language of description, more specifically the language of physics. Carnap (6) indicates recognition of the necessity for terms other than physical ones in his distinction between physics and biology. He notes, with respect to the latter science, that "The terms which are used in this field in addition to logico-mathematical and physical terms may be called . . . *biological terms*" (6, p. 412). Such terms, as well as psychological terms to describe situations, must, of course, be reducible to observable thing-predicates, i.e., to terms which designate properties which can be determined by direct observation. It is in this sense that Carnap discusses the unity of the language of science, while recognizing the absence of unity of scientific laws. It is congruent with such a position to call for laws which are clearly psychological, i.e., statements of relations between *psychological* terms.

The problem of a data language other than a purely physical one is much more acute for the phenomenological theories dealing with humans than for the S-R theories which have dealt largely with lower organisms. (a) The situations in which human social behavior takes place are far more complex than the typical rat-learning situation. For the latter it has been adequate thus far to employ the language of physics, since the manipulated stimulus variables are often simple physical dimensions such as amount of illumination, intensity of electric shock, etc., and since highly restricted and controlled situations are characteristically employed in such research. We do not imply that S-R approaches have utilized only the language of physics; we are maintaining that a large number of terms from that discipline are employed, and that when extension to complex human social situations is undertaken, such terms will prove inadequate, and more appropriate language will have to be invented. How to describe the situation where a college student is asking a coed for a date is an example; description in terms of the amount of illumination, atmospheric pressure, etc., will contribute little to a predictive analysis of such a complex situation. The Hawthorne studies (12) provide an excellent example of how a physical description of the stimulus situation in terms of changes in illumination was inadequate to account for the direction of changes in worker productivity. (b) Relatively greater variability of the human response repertoire would seem to be another reason for failure of the language of physics in personality theory. A wide variety of potential responses implies a multiplicity of potential definitions of the same situation by different subjects. (c) The presence in humans of language and memory, which allow for the symbolization of variables not physically present in the situation though instigated by the present situation, would seem to be a further complicating factor.

It is proposed that one of the immediately pressing tasks for psychology to undertake is the development of an adequate psychological data language to describe the environment. This is a language whose terms have reference to the nature (behavior) of some organism or class of organisms, since the existence and nature of stimuli depend upon the characteristics, needs, habits, expectancies, intelligence, etc. of organisms. It represents a different abstraction from and organization of the basic referential level, or level of observable thing-predicates, than does the data language of physics. A simple example is the term *goal,* which presupposes a directed or striving organism. The same situation, as described physically, would be described differently in psychological terms for different organisms or classes of organisms. Some tentative beginnings in this direction are referred to below.

Rotter (14) has proposed that situations be described by their cultural meanings in terms of the characteristic reinforcements or goals which are likely to occur in those situations. Since no situation always provides just one kind of a goal, situations may be characterized as mixed, or may be described in terms of the dominant or usual or most frequent goals likely to occur. Situations may also be described as ambiguous or unfamiliar where the expectancies for the occurrence of any particular goal are low. Thus, for prediction at the level of personality, situations may be described as love and affection situations, the college quiz may be characterized as an academic recognition situation, etc. Rotter goes on to state:

> In this sense people, too, may be thought of as situations; it makes good sense to speak of authority figure situations, heterosexual situations, and so forth when these terms imply that a particular kind of reinforcement is likely to occur (14, p. 202).

Murray (11) has presented a set of terms belonging to the category of Press, which describes the environment or stimulus situation according to the kind of effect—facilitating or obstructing—that it is exerting or could exert upon the organism. Lewin's (10) terms, such as valence, barrier, etc., are also of this sort.

Chein (7), too, has suggested a geo-behavioral language,

i.e., a set of concepts to describe the real world looked at from a point of view that is concerned with understanding behavior.

With these examples in mind, the question arises as to the reliability or intercommunicability of such descriptions. But this would seem to be the *only* question which legitimately may be raised, despite any feelings of discomfort over these psychological terms. That intersubjectivity of such descriptions can be achieved may be illustrated from a host of psychological research. Mention here may be made of a series of researches (14) carried out in relation to Rotter's social learning theory, in which characterizations of experimental situations in terms of the potential goals they involve for college students have led to predictions of behavior which have consistently received empirical support.

The development of a psychological language of description might well be enhanced by following the suggestion of McClelland (3, p. 145) that a phenomenological census be carried out to discover what things and attributes in the environment people look for and attend to in guiding their behavior. Fruitful concepts may also be derived from sociology and anthropology, which disciplines have concentrated heavily upon descriptions, with respect to human behavior, of social or cultural situations. Such descriptive terms will, of course, vary in their relevance for different culture groups and especially for different individuals.

It is the increased and explicit utilization of a psychological data language which enables a *rapprochement* between S-R and R-R or phenomenological theories of personality. Although it may be maintained that all psychological laws are fundamentally R-R laws, nevertheless it does make better sense to speak of S-R laws as the goal of psychology when the definition of S is made in *psychological* terms, and the issue of independence of S is restricted to independence from a particular response in a given situation.

## REFERENCES

1. Bakan, D. Learning and the scientific enterprise. *Psychol. Rev.,* 1953, **60,** 45–49.

2. Brown, D. R. Stimulus-similarity and the anchoring of subjective scales. *Amer. J. Psychol.,* 1953, **66,** 199–214.

3. Bruner, J. S. Personality dynamics and the process of perceiving. In R. R. Blake & G. V. Ramsey (Eds.), *Perception, an approach to personality.* New York: Ronald, 1951. Pp. 121–147.

4. Brunswik, E. Organismic achievement and environmental probability. *Psychol. Rev.,* 1943, **50,** 255–272.

5. Brunswik, E. The conceptual framework of psychology. Chicago: Univ. Chicago Press, 1952. (*Int. Encycl. unified Sci.,* v. 1, no. 10.)

6. Carnap, R. Logical foundations of the unity of science. In H. Feigl & W. Sellars (Eds.), *Readings in philosophical analysis.* New York: Appleton-Century-Crofts, 1949. Pp. 408–423.

7. Chein, I. The environment as a determinant of behavior. *J. soc. Psychol.,* 1954, **39,** 115–127.

8. Davis, R. C. Physical psychology. *Psychol. Rev.,* 1953, **60,** 7–14.

9. Kantor, J. R. *Principles of psychology.* Vol. 1. New York: Knopf, 1924.

10. Lewin, K. *Dynamic theory of personality.* New York: McGraw-Hill, 1935.

11. Murray, H. A., *et al. Explorations in personality.* New York: Oxford Univ. Press, 1938.

12. Roethlisberger, F. J. *Management and morale.* Cambridge: Harvard Univ. Press, 1944.

13. Rogers, C. R. *Client-centered therapy.* Boston: Houghton Mifflin, 1951.

14. Rotter, J. B. *Social learning and clinical psychology.* New York: Prentice-Hall, 1954.

15. Snygg, D., & Combs, A. W. *Individual behavior.* New York: Harper, 1949.

16. Spence, K. W. The nature of theory construction in contemporary psychology. *Psychol. Rev.,* 1944, **51,** 47–68.

# SELECTED BIBLIOGRAPHY

Allport, G. W. *Personality: a psychological interpretation.* New York: Holt, 1937.

Allport, G. W. The ego in contemporary psychology. *Psychol. Rev.,* 1943, **50,** 451–478.

Allport, G. W. *The nature of prejudice.* Cambridge: Addison-Wesley, 1954.

Allport, G. W. *Becoming.* New Haven: Yale Univ. Press, 1955.

Anikeeff, A. M. Reciprocal empathy: mutual understanding among conflict groups. *Stud. higher Educ., Purdue Univ.,* 1951, **77,** 1–48.

Ansbacher, H. L., & Ansbacher, R. R. (Eds.) *The individual psychology of Alfred Adler.* New York: Basic Books, 1956.

Asch, S. E. *Social psychology.* New York: Prentice-Hall, 1952.

Baldwin, A. L. Personal structure analysis: a statistical method for investigating the single personality. *J. abnorm. soc. Psychol.,* 1942, **37,** 163–183.

Bartlett, F. C. *Remembering.* Cambridge, Eng.: Cambridge Univ. Press, 1932.

Berger, E. M. The relation between expressed acceptance of self and expressed acceptance of others. *J. abnorm. soc. Psychol.,* 1952, **47,** 778–782.

Blake, R. R., & Ramsey, G. V. (Eds.) *Perception, an approach to personality.* New York: Ronald, 1951.

Boulding, K. E. *The image: knowledge in life and society.* Ann Arbor: Univ. Michigan Press, 1956.

Brown, W., & Alers, J. O. Attitudes of whites and non-whites toward each other. *Sociol. soc. Res.,* 1956, **40,** 312–319.

Bruner, J. S. Perceptual theory and the Rorschach test. *J. Pers.,* 1948, **17,** 157–168.

Bruner, J. S. One kind of perception: a reply to Professor Luchins. *Psychol. Rev.,* 1951, **58,** 306–312.

Bruner, J. S., & Goodman, C. C. Value and need as organizing factors in perception. *J. abnorm. soc. Psychol.,* 1947, **42,** 33–44.

Bruner, J. S., Goodnow, J. J., & Austin, G. A. *A study of thinking.* New York: Wiley, 1956.

Bruner, J. S., & Krech, D. (Eds.) *Perception and personality: a symposium.* Durham, N. C.: Duke Univ. Press, 1950.

Bruner, J. S., *et al. Contemporary approaches to cognition.* Cambridge: Harvard Univ. Press, 1957.

Cantril, H. *The "why" of man's experience.* New York: Macmillan, 1950.

Cantril, H. *The politics of despair.* New York: Basic Books, 1958.

Cartwright, D. Decision-time in relation to the differentiation of the phenomenal field. *Psychol. Rev.,* 1941, **48,** 425–442.

Cartwright, D., & Harary, F. Structural balance: a generalization of Heider's theory. *Psychol. Rev.,* 1956, **63,** 277–292.

Chein, I. The awareness of self and the structure of the ego. *Psychol. Rev.,* 1944, **51,** 304–314.

Chodorkoff, B. Self-perception, perceptual defense, and adjustment. *J. abnorm. soc. Psychol.,* 1954, **49,** 508–512.

Combs, A. W. Phenomenological concepts in non-directive therapy. *J. consult. Psychol.,* 1948, **12,** 197–208.

Combs, A. W. A phenomenological approach to adjustment theory. *J. abnorm. soc. Psychol.,* 1949, **44,** 29–35.

Combs, A. W. Intelligence from a perceptual point of view. *J. abnorm. soc. Psychol.,* 1952, **47,** 662–673.

Combs, A. W., & Snygg, D. *Individual behavior,* rev. ed. New York: Harper, 1959.

Combs, A. W., & Taylor, C. The effect of the perception of mild degrees of threat on performance. *J. abnorm. soc. Psychol.,* 1952, **47,** 420–424.

Corsini, R. J. Understanding and similarity in marriage. *J. abnorm. soc. Psychol.,* 1956, **52,** 327–332.

Creegan, R. F. The phenomenological analysis of personal documents. *J. abnorm. soc. Psychol.*, 1944, **39**, 244–266.

Dennis, W. Animism and related tendencies in Hopi children. *J. abnorm. soc. Psychol.*, 1943, **38**, 21–36.

Dennis, W., & Russell, R. W. Piaget's questions applied to Zuñi children. *Child Develpm.*, 1940, **11**, 181–187.

Frank, L. K. *Projective methods.* Springfield, Ill.: Charles C. Thomas, 1948.

Frenkel-Brunswik, E. A study of prejudice in children. *Hum. Relat.*, 1948, **1**, 295–306.

Gaffron, M. Some new dimensions in the phenomenal analysis of visual experience. *J. Pers.*, 1956, **24**, 285–307.

Gibson, J. J. *The perception of the visual world.* Boston: Houghton Mifflin, 1950.

Gilbert, G. M. Stereotype persistence and change among college students. *J. abnorm. soc. Psychol.*, 1951, **46**, 245–254.

Haigh, G. V. Defensive behavior in client-centered therapy. *J. consult. Psychol.*, 1949, **13**, 181–189.

Haigh, G. V., & Fiske, D. W. Corroboration of personal values as selective factors in perception. *J. abnorm. soc. Psychol.*, 1952, **47**, 394–398.

Heider, F. Social perception and phenomenal causality. *Psychol. Rev.*, 1944, **51**, 358–374.

Heider, F. Attitudes and cognitive organization. *J. Psychol.*, 1946, **21**, 107–112.

Heider, F. *The psychology of interpersonal relations.* New York: Wiley, 1958.

Ichheiser, G. *Misunderstandings in human relations.* Chicago: Univ. Chicago Press, 1949.

Ittelson, W. H. The constancies in perceptual theory. *Psychol. Rev.*, 1951, **58**, 285–294.

Kauffman, P. E., & Raimy, V. C. Two methods of assessing therapeutic progress. *J. abnorm. soc. Psychol.*, 1949, **44**, 379–385.

Kelley, E. C. *Education for what is real.* New York: Harper, 1947.

Klüver, H. The study of personality and the method of equivalent and non-equivalent stimuli. *Charact. & Pers.,* 1936, **5,** 91–112.

Koffka, K. *Principles of Gestalt psychology.* New York: Harcourt, Brace, 1935.

Köhler, W. *The place of value in a world of facts.* New York: Liveright, 1938.

Köhler, W. *Gestalt psychology.* New York: Liveright, 1947.

Krech, D., & Crutchfield, R. S. *Theory and problems of social psychology.* New York: McGraw-Hill, 1948.

Landsman, T. Four phenomenologies. *J. indiv. Psychol.,* 1958, **14,** 29–37.

Lecky, P. *Self-consistency: a theory of personality.* New York: Island Press, 1945.

Leeper, R. W. Cognitive processes. In S. S. Stevens (Ed.), *Handbook of experimental psychology.* New York: Wiley, 1951. Pp. 730–757.

Lewin, K. *A dynamic theory of personality.* New York: McGraw-Hill, 1935.

Lewin, K. *Principles of topological psychology.* New York: McGraw-Hill, 1936.

Lewin, K. *Resolving social conflicts.* New York: Harper, 1948.

Lewin, K. *Field theory in social science.* New York: Harper, 1951.

Luchins, A. S. On an approach to social perception. *J. Pers.,* 1950, **19,** 64–84.

Luchins, A. S. Personality and prejudice: a critique. *J. soc. Psychol.,* 1950, **32,** 79–94.

Luchins, A. S. An evaluation of some current criticisms of Gestalt psychological work on perception. *Psychol. Rev.,* 1951, **58,** 69–95.

Luchins, A. S. Towards an experimental clinical psychology. *J. Pers.,* 1952, **20,** 440–456.

MacLeod, R. B. Perceptual constancy and the problem of motivation. *Canad. J. Psychol.,* 1949, **3,** 57–66.

MacLeod, R. B. The place of phenomenological analysis in social psychological theory. In J. H. Rohrer & M. Sherif (Eds.), *Social psychology at the crossroads.* New York: Harper, 1951. Pp. 215–241.

Maslow, A. H. Dynamics of personality organization. *Psychol. Rev.,* 1943, **50,** 514–539, 541–558.

Maslow, A. H. The authoritarian character structure. *J. soc. Psychol.,* 1943, **18,** 401–411.

McGill, V. J. Some issues in current psychological literature. *Phil. phenomenol. Res.,* 1956, **17,** 89–104.

Moustakas, C. E. (Ed.) *The self: explorations in personal growth.* New York: Harper, 1956.

Murphy, G. *Personality: a biosocial approach to origins and structure.* New York: Harper, 1947.

Murphy, G., & Solley, C. M. Learning to perceive as we wish to perceive. *Bull. Menninger Clin.,* 1957, **21,** 225–237.

Murray, H. A., et al. *Explorations in personality.* New York: Oxford Univ. Press, 1938.

Newcomb, T. M. An approach to the study of communicative acts. *Psychol. Rev.,* 1953, **60,** 393–404.

Piaget, J. *The child's conception of the world.* New York: Harcourt, Brace, 1929.

Postman, L., & Schneider, B. H. Personal values, visual recognition, and recall. *Psychol. Rev.,* 1951, **58,** 271–284.

Raskin, N. J. The development of nondirective therapy. *J. consult. Psychol.,* 1948, **12,** 92–110.

Reymert, M. L. (Ed.) *Feelings and emotions: the Mooseheart symposium.* New York: McGraw-Hill, 1950.

Rogers, C. R. *Counseling and psychotherapy.* Boston: Houghton Mifflin, 1942.

Rogers, C. R. Significant aspects of client-centered therapy. *Amer. Psychologist,* 1946, **1,** 415–422.

Rogers, C. R. *Client-centered therapy.* Boston: Houghton Mifflin, 1951.

Rogers, C. R., & Dymond, R. F. (Eds.) *Psychotherapy and personality change.* Chicago: Univ. Chicago Press, 1954.

Rosenzweig, S. The place of the individual and of idiodynamics in psychology: a dialogue. *J. indiv. Psychol.,* 1958, **14,** 3–21.

Rotter, J. B. *Social learning and clinical psychology.* New York: Prentice-Hall, 1954.

Russell, D. H. *Children's thinking.* Boston: Ginn, 1956.

Sartre, J. P. Portrait of the antisemite. *Partisan Rev.,* 1946, **13,** 163–178.

Sartre, J. P. *The emotions: outline of a theory.* New York: Philosophical Library, 1948.

Sheerer, E. T. An analysis of the relationship between acceptance of and respect for self and acceptance of and respect for others in ten counseling cases. *J. consult. Psychol.,* 1949, **13,** 169–175.

Sherif, M., & Cantril, H. *The psychology of ego-involvements.* New York: Wiley, 1947.

Sherif, M., & Sherif, C. W. *Groups in harmony and tension.* New York: Harper, 1953.

Smith, M. B. The personal setting of public opinions: a study of attitudes toward Russia. *Pub. Opin. Quart.,* 1947, **11,** 507–523.

Smith, M. B., Bruner, J. S., & White, R. W. *Opinions and personality.* New York: Wiley, 1956.

Snygg, D. The psychological basis of human values. In A. D. Ward (Ed.), *Goals of economic life.* New York: Harper, 1953.

Snygg, D. Learning: an aspect of personality development. In D. K. Adams, *et al., Learning theory, personality theory, and clinical research.* New York: Wiley, 1954. Pp. 129–137.

Snygg, D. Scientific method in psychology. *J. gen. Psychol.,* 1955, **52,** 189–196.

Stock, D. An investigation into the interrelations between the self-concept and feelings directed toward other persons and groups. *J. consult. Psychol.,* 1949, **13,** 176–180.

Tagiuri, R., & Petrullo, L. (Eds.) *Person perception and interpersonal behavior.* Stanford: Stanford Univ. Press, 1958.

Taylor, C., & Combs, A. W. Self-acceptance and adjustment. *J. consult. Psychol.*, 1952, **16**, 89–91.

Tolman, E. C. Cognitive maps in rats and men. *Psychol. Rev.*, 1948, **55**, 189–208.

Vernon, M. D. *A further study of visual perception.* Cambridge, Eng.: Cambridge Univ. Press, 1952.

Vernon, M. D. The functions of schemata in perceiving. *Psychol. Rev.*, 1955, **62**, 180–192.

Weiner, M. L. Perceptual development in a distorted room: a phenomenological study. *Psychol. Monogr.*, 1956, **70**, No. 423.

# INDEXES

# INDEX OF NAMES

# INDEX OF SUBJECTS

# Notes on the Contributors

HADLEY CANTRIL is Chairman of the Institute for International Social Research and Director of the Office of Public Opinion Research at Princeton University.

ARTHUR W. COMBS is Professor of Education at the University of Florida.

LAWRENCE K. FRANK is retired and resides in Belmont, Massachusetts. Formerly he was director of the Caroline Zachry Institute of Human Development in New York City.

RICHARD JESSOR is Associate Professor of Psychology and Director of the Clinical Training Program at the University of Colorado.

ALFRED E. KUENZLI (editor) is Associate Professor of Psychology on the Alton campus of Southern Illinois University.

ABRAHAM S. LUCHINS is Professor of Psychology at the University of Miami.

ROBERT B. MACLEOD is Professor of Psychology at Cornell University.

THEODORE M. NEWCOMB is Chairman of the Doctoral Program in Social Psychology at the University of Michigan.

VICTOR RAIMY is Professor of Psychology at the University of Colorado.

CARL R. ROGERS is Professor of Psychology in the Departments of Psychology and Psychiatry at the University of Wisconsin.

SAUL ROSENZWEIG is Professor of Psychology in the Departments of Psychology and Neuropsychiatry at Washington University.

M. BREWSTER SMITH is Professor of Psychology at the University of California, Berkeley.

DONALD SNYGG is Professor of Psychology at the State University of New York, Oswego.

DANIEL W. SOPER is Associate Professor of Education and Psychologist in the P. K. Yonge Laboratory School at the University of Florida.

*Set in Intertype Garamond*
*Format by James T. Parker*
*Manufactured by The Haddon Craftsmen, Inc.*
*Published by* Harper & Brothers, *New York*